TAMPA

In Civil War and Reconstruction

TAMPA

In Civil War and Reconstruction

CANTER BROWN, JR.

Tampa Bay History Center
Reference Library Series No. 10

University of Tampa Press
Tampa, Florida
2019

Manufactured in the United States of America
Printed on acid-free paper

The University of Tampa Press
401 West Kennedy Boulevard
Tampa, Florida 33606

ISBN 1-978-1-879852-68-6 (hbk.)
ISBN 1-978-1-879852-48-8 (pbk.)

On the cover: "Tampa Bay from the Mouth of the River" engraving by P. O. Mueller, circa 1860s, from an 1890 photograph in the Burgert Brothers collection of the Tampa-Hillsborough County Public Library; adapted and tinted by Ana Montalvo.

Unless otherwise specified, illustrations in this book are from the collection of the author. For a key to abbreviations used to credit other sources, see page 200.

First paperback edition, 2019
The Library of Congress catalogued the first edition of this book as follows:

Library of Congress Cataloging-in-Publication Data

Brown, Canter.
Tampa in Civil War and Reconstruction / Canter Brown, Jr.— 1st ed.
p. cm. — (Tampa Bay History Center reference library series ; no. 10)
Includes bibliographical references (p.) and index.
ISBN 1-879852-68-3 (alk. paper)
1. Tampa (Fla.)—History-19th century. 2. Hillsborough County (Fla.)—History-19th century. 3. Florida—History—Civil War, 1861-1865.
4. Florida—History—Civil War, 1861-1865—Social aspects. 5. United States—History—Civil War, 1861-1865—Social aspects. 6. Reconstruction—Florida—Tampa. 7. Reconstruction—Florida—Hillsborough County. I. Title. II. Series.
F319.T2 B765 2000
975.9'65—dc21 00-011156

This book is dedicated to the
Lykes and McKay Families,
pioneers, leaders, visionaries,
and extraordinary supporters of the
Tampa Bay History Center

Contents

Introduction

The eras of Civil War and Reconstruction at Tampa and in Hillsborough County have received little attention from historians. Especially, the tumultuous years following the peace at Appomattox Court House appear to us as a hazy memory at best. The principal published general work on Tampa's past, Karl Grismer's *Tampa: A History of the City of Tampa and the Tampa Bay Region of Florida*, covered the period in a single chapter entitled, "When Tampa Slipped Backward." Contrary to Grismer's thesis that nothing much happened in the town and county from 1865 to 1877, records actually reveal a multi-layered, richly textured experience that included remarkable men and women, black and white heroes and villains, carpetbaggers and unreconstructed Rebels, and more complications than the mind can factor, all helping to lay the foundations for our modern city. It truly is a story needing to be told.

As is true of the Civil War and Reconstruction periods, much of Tampa's intriguing story has remained unavailable to readers. Grismer's *Tampa* reached publication almost one-half century ago and has been out of print for decades. Subsequent work by James W. Covington, Julius J. Gordon, Tony Pizzo, Leland Hawes, Donald L. Chamberlin, Robert P. Ingalls, Susan Greenbaum, Brent R. Weisman, Geoffrey Mohlman, Kyle S. VanLandingham, Rowena Ferrell Brady, Robert W. Saunders, Spessard Stone, and many others dramatically has altered our understanding of times and personalities; yet, the need for synthesis grows more evident with the passage of time.

In light of these circumstances, in 1999 the Tampa Bay History Center launched with publication of *Tampa Before the Civil War* a series of books offering in narrative form a critical re-examination of Tampa's past. The present volume concentrates, as the title suggests, on the city's experiences from the secession crisis of 1860 to the moment of Democratic "redemption" of the South and Florida in early 1877, with emphasis on the dynamics, personalities, and events central to Tampa's evolution in the wartime and post-bellum world. It is not intended to replace works such as Grismer's. Rather, this book supplements and updates previously published material, while offering new information and perspectives informed by the fine research of recent years.

The Tampa Bay History Center—a not-for-profit organization sponsored by Hillsborough County, the City of Tampa, and private donors—offers *Tampa In Civil War and Reconstruction* to recognize the importance of serious inquiries into the history of the greater Tampa Bay region. The History Center also presents this publication as an example of how rich area history has been for those who lived it and can be for those interested in reading it today. Our trustees, members, and staff hope that readers young and old will find it interesting, helpful, and relevant to their lives in the modern world. Further, we hope that this book and future publications, exhibitions, and related activities will spark new and expanded efforts at researching, writing, and appreciating the Tampa Bay region's fascinating, diverse, and meaningful history.

Acknowledgments

The Tampa Bay History Center gratefully acknowledges the support of Leland M. Hawes and Julius J. Gordon, whose generosity assisted in the publication and distribution of this work. Thanks are extended to Mr. Hawes, historical writer for the *Tampa Tribune*, and to former Tampa Historical Society president George B. Howell III of the Holland and Knight law firm for reading the manuscript and improving it with helpful criticisms. Additional thanks are given for assistance and encouragement to: the Honorable Richard Ake, clerk of the circuit court of Hillsborough County; the Honorable Pam Iorio, supervisor of elections of Hillsborough County; Sam Rastin and Kathy Regan, Hillsborough County Records Center, Office of the Clerk of the Circuit Court, Tampa; Curtis Welch, City of Tampa Archives; Yetive Olson, Julius J. Gordon, and Frank North, Tampa; Paul Camp, University of South Florida Library Special Collections, Tampa; Emily Briggs, Hillsborough County school board, Tampa; J. Allison DeFoor, II, Tallahassee; Dr. James M. Denham, Florida Southern College, Lakeland; Dr. Larry E. Rivers, Florida A&M University, Tallahassee; Dr. William W. Rogers, Florida State University Emeritus, Tallahassee; Dr. David J. Coles, Longwood College, Farmville, Virginia; Dr. Roger Landers, Brooksville; Dr. Joe Knetsch, Florida Department of Environmental Protection, Tallahassee; Cynthia C. Wise, State Library of Florida, Tallahassee; Vernon Peeples, Punta Gorda; Gert H. W. Schmidt, Jacksonville; Kyle S. VanLandingham, Kerrville, Texas; J. Harvey Littrell, Manhattan, Kansas; Rodney Dillon, Fort Lauderdale; Zack Waters, Rome, Georgia; Lewis G. Schmidt, Allentown, Pennsylvania; and, certainly not least, Barbara Gray Brown, Tallahassee. As always, many thanks, as well, to Richard Mathews, Ellen White, and Ana Montalvo of the University of Tampa Press for producing such a beautiful book.

TAMPA

In Civil War and Reconstruction

1. By 1860 the tiny village of Tampa was the main trading center for settlers on the Florida Gulf Coast frontier, but the town itself was not growing at the pace that the early businessmen had expected. This rendering of a general store and one of Captain James McKay's sailing ships at the dock is a detail from "Old Tampa Bay 1862" by artist Jed Dyer, a mural that once graced a wall of Morrison's Cafeteria in Tampa. (*Sunland Tribune*)

"like the stormwhipped billows of an enraged sea"

The Breaking of the Nation, 1860-1861

Beginning in 1860 and for two decades thereafter, the town of Tampa, Florida, and its residents endured trials almost beyond the understanding of those who call the city home at the start of the twenty-first century. Repeatedly during those years, the violent face of nature and of man shone savagely, leaving local people struggling to understand why, as one man expressed near the era's end, "We . . . encounter more ills and inconveniences than are incidental to human life ordinarily." The tales of those times encompassed bloody civil war, terrifying plague, and brutal vigilante reprisals, but they involved golden dreams, as well, ones punctuated by the sharp ring of cattle hooves on deckboard planking and the shrill sounds of irresistable steam-driven turbines. Villains abounded. So, also, did men and women intent upon building a better world. Too often, the distinction came down to a question of whose world would it be and, more importantly, who would decide?[1]

In 1860, Tampa sat isolated from the United States, a tiny village hanging onto its existence as the principal trading town on the frontier of Florida's lower Gulf coast. Where local expectations had run high in the not-too-distant past, the town's prospects had dimmed considerably within the previous few years. That it existed at all could be attributed in great part to the largess of the United States government. Pursuant to treaties entered into with Florida's Indians a few

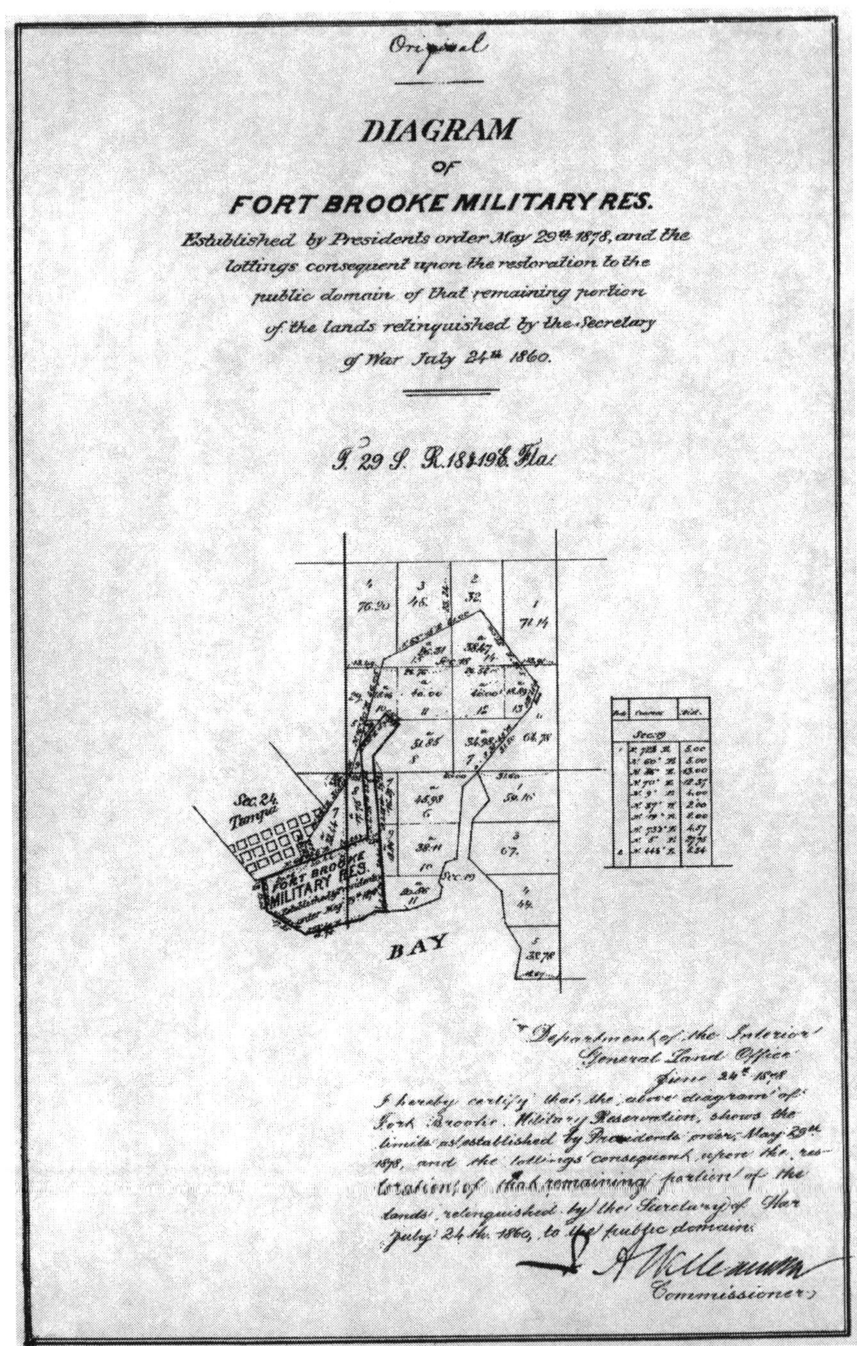

2. This document shows the division into lots of the Fort Brooke property returned "to the public domain" in 1860. (Florida Department of Environmental Protection)

months earlier, the army in January 1824 had opened Fort Brooke (named for its founder Colonel George Mercer Brooke) on land lying on the eastern side of the Hillsborough River's junction with Hillsborough Bay. For thirty-five years thereafter, the military had poured untold resources into the local economy. The government's generosity abruptly had ended in late 1858 and early 1859, though. At that time the last of the garrison's men had withdrawn with the close of the area's final Indian war, the Billy Bowlegs or Third Seminole War. When Ordinance Sergeant John Flynn auctioned off the post quartermaster stores on March 22, 1859, the act signaled the end of an era.[2]

Fort Brooke's closure dealt a dramatic blow to a Tampa economy that already was reeling from social conflict, epidemic catastrophe, and dashed hopes. The conflict had arisen out of the Bowlegs War's last months when discharged volunteers had spawned a local crime wave, resulting in the organization of a "regulator" group aimed at ridding the town of "undesirable" elements. Before anyone really understood what was happening, the Regulator violence had translated itself into lynchings. When some local leaders opposed the "secret sworn band," the Regulators turned their ire upon their political opponents. Associated most closely with the Regulators were Mayor Madison Post, Deputy Mayor William Brinton Hooker, law student John A. Henderson, newspaper editor Henry A. Crane, and physician Franklin Branch. Attorney and former legislator James T. Magbee stood as their principal foe and political target.[3]

By summer 1858 Tampa's struggle with Regulator justice had reached its peak, not so much because the movement had attained its logical conclusion as that nature intervened. In September, the "terrible plague" of yellow fever beset the community. During the following five months, perhaps 25 percent of the population contracted the dreaded "yellow jack." Those who could abandoned the town. "In almost every family were the dead and dying!" lamented Baptist minister Jeremiah M. Hayman, whose mother-in-law and daughter succumbed but whose wife survived. Of the dozens who did not recover, most were children and women. Grief lay like a heavy pall on the living.[4]

Memories of the yellow fever epidemic and the victims it claimed lingered painfully. Even when the mind of man dimmed on the event, a pair of monuments stood to remind Tampans of this almost-Biblical plague. In a frontier town where organized religion had found little fertile ground in which to flourish, two new churches had joined the solitary existing one. Now, residents not only could take comfort from Methodist services, they could attend Baptist and Roman Catholic rites, as well. Dr. Joseph S. Baker joined the Reverend Hayman and others to organize the Baptist congregation with proper formality in 1859. The Hillsborough County board of commissioners managed to execute the proper deed for the church, located on the southeast corner of Tampa and Twiggs Streets, only on March 1, 1860. One month earlier, Father C. S. Mailley had arrived to constitute St. Louis Parish and to celebrate mass in the new church at Twiggs and Monroe (later Florida Avenue). The region's Roman Catholic families delighted in their first regular pastor, although, as Bishop Augustin Verot acknowledged, the Frenchman could "only stutter and murder their language."[5]

A Stirring of Passions

Dashed hopes resulted from the military's departure, the social conflict, and the toll taken by disease, but they also derived from what many Tampans saw as the perfidy of outsiders. For most of the previous decade, the local people had looked for their ultimate salvation to the construction of a railroad that would link their town with the outside world. Florida, after all, was a state where roads consisted mostly of sandy trails that turned into muddy quagmires in wet weather. Bridges, where they existed, tended to be rude constructions that floated away on seasonal storm waters. Stage coaches served as the only common carrier overland. One victim of the level of service then available recorded his impressions of the trip down from Ocala, the nearest town of any consequence. "I reached my post after a disagreeable ride, (the most disagreeable I believe I ever had), of about ninety miles, on an old barouche, which was filled inside with trunks, boxes, etc., and careened all to one side," he noted. "After one breakdown, and many stoppages to mend up, I arrived in Tampa, after having travelled on and in that old barouche for thirty-two hours through the most dreary country I ever saw." In such a situation, the steel ribbons promised the only surefire method for lifting the barrier of Tampa's isolation, while tying it to markets elsewhere and offering desperately needed settlers a method of easy access.[6]

The man whom Tampans believed more than any other would lift their isolation through delivery of a railroad was United States Senator David Levy Yulee. His Florida Rail Road, intended to link

Fernandina on the Atlantic coast with the Gulf of Mexico, had received public support and, in 1855, Tampa's backers had succeeded, as least they believed that they had succeeded, in tying state subsidies to Yulee's commitment to build "to the waters of Tampa Bay." Before the Bowlegs War flared in December of that year, it seemed only a matter of time before the promise was kept. When the conflict ended, though, it turned out that Yulee had used the interval to reorient his plans to his own benefit. When word arrived at Tampa in the fall of 1858 that the senator now favored a Gulf terminus at Cedar Keys, infuriated townsmen burned him in effigy on the courthouse square. After the new year opened, they joined with like-minded Floridians, including Governor Madison Starke Perry of Alachua County, to organize a competitor for Yulee's road, to be known as the Florida Peninsular Railroad. This act launched Tampans and their ally Perry into open conflict with the senator's political power. The fight persisted into 1860 when the contest stalled as the issue of which line deserved the state subsidies wound its way through the court system. Meanwhile, the Florida Rail Road reached Cedar Keys in June 1860.[7]

Little wonder then that Tampans' passions stirred hot as the 1850s neared their close; yet, additional tragic events were to add complications and place upon them greater burdens. On the larger scale, the nation reeled toward disintegration. The new Republican party had committed itself to barring the extension of slavery into new areas, and many southerners feared that abolitionist elements were intent upon mandating total emancipation. Republican electoral victories in 1856 and 1858 threatened to place the party in power nationally in 1860, fuelling calls by southern "fire eaters" for secession of the South from the Union. Fears raised by these calls found resonance in the botched October 1859 attack of abolitionist John Brown and his followers on the United States Arsenal at Harper's Ferry, Virginia. Many enraged southerners cried out for Brown's blood while dreading the implications of his actions. As one historian observed, "'The public mind' rolled and tossed 'like the stormwhipped billows of an enraged sea.'"[8]

The national tragedy sounded echoes in events occurring at Tampa during December 1859, the month in which John Brown went to his martyrdom at the hands of a Virginia hangman. Previously, the town's race relations, at least those between black and white, had proceeded in a fairly secure and relatively easy manner. Although no free blacks lived there, likely one-quarter of its population consisted of slaves. They pursued a myriad of domestic and other responsibilities, usually performing the most difficult labor and least desirable chores but also working often alongside whites. In the small community it was difficult for most whites not to see slaves as human beings and to treat them accordingly. "Slavery here is a very mild form," army officer Oliver O. Howard, later head of the Freedmen's Bureau, wrote in March 1857. "You wouldn't know the negroes were slaves unless you were told."[9]

Tampa's bubble of complacency about local race relations burst just after news of John Brown's execution reached town. A slave named Adam had been tried for the murder of a man to whom he had been leased. Local attorney Ossian B. Hart joined with Brooksville lawyer Joseph M. Taylor to defend the accused. State Attorney Henry L. Mitchell prosecuted. In the supercharged atmosphere that followed Brown's Harper's Ferry raid, a jury convicted Adam and sentenced him to hang. Hart appealed to the state supreme court for a reversal and won a new trial. On December 16, 1859, the sheriff legally executed a white murderer by hanging. Memories of regulator-inspired vigilante justice fresh in their memories from the previous year, some of the crowd rushed the jail, grabbed Adam, and lynched him next to the white man. The action would influence the course of Tampa's future and that of Florida as a whole.[10]

Diminished Circumstances

At first, though, it seemed that the lynching merely added a new weight to the burdensome problems under which Tampans already were laboring. Indicative of them, Mayor James McKay alerted townsmen in January 1860 that their municipal corporation—not yet five years of age—teetered on the brink of bankruptcy. Numerous claims upon city funds, especially from ex-officials Madison Post and William B. Hooker, strained the budget. Post was suing for his money. McKay had cut back on municipal expenses and proudly asserted that his economies had permitted the town "nearly" to pay off its debt. Still, insufficient funds remained in the treasury to erect a fence around the "City Burial Ground," which subsequent generations would know as Oaklawn Cemetery. Perhaps indirectly telegraphing his own estimate of the town corporation's future, McKay chose not to seek reelection.[11]

The town's appearance reflected the sag in its fortunes. "As to the buildings, the majority of them were rough, small houses, and in the country the houses nearly all [were] built of logs," recalled one longtime resident. "There were some plastered houses, but only a few, and these were looked upon almost as mansions," she continued. "There were few streets and nearly all bore the name of a president or a noted general," the woman related. "But we never used the names of the streets enough to remember what they were." The description added more detail. "Washington Street was the only business district until a venturesome man named Hall built on Franklin St., a small structure with a store below and a couple of rooms upstairs which he occupied with his wife and baby," the reminiscence noted. "The town at that time did not extend further [north] than Zack street, and Oaklawn cemetery was way out of town," the woman declared. "Cows roamed all over town," she concluded, "and their favorite camping ground at night was on the south side of the courthouse." Josiah Ferris remembered that lawyers "in going to and from the courthouse," completed in 1855 and facing Franklin Street between Madison and Lafayette (now Kennedy), "followed a trail" to reach their goal.[12]

3. The Stringer family home, built in the 1840s, was something of a mansion at the time. Constructed of milled lumber, it was a fine example of the more substantial early wooden housing in Tampa. (TBHC)

Even had Tampa contained the energy to expand to its legal limits, the municipality would have remained tiny. It consisted of a 160-acre tract ceded by the federal government in 1848 out of the Fort Brooke military reservation. To the south lay the abandoned fort, which remained in government hands. Whiting Street served as the demarcation line. Eastward (of East Street) could be found marshlands that remained inside the post's reservation. They overlapped a distinct natural boundary zone evident to one and all. "On the north and east of the city," a visitor recorded, "is a small growth of oaks called the 'scrub,' and is almost impenetrable and serves to remind one of a walled city." Everywhere within the "walled city," sand intruded upon daily life. As the visitor observed, "The town . . . lay at the mouth of the Hillsborough River on a high, dry sand beach." He added, "The streets are very sandy and one takes good exercise in walking over them."[13]

Westward of Tampa the land remained mostly unsettled. No bridge yet spanned the Hillsborough River so close to its mouth. Rather, a ferry landed at Jackson Street's foot to connect Tampans with the primitive trail northward to Brooksville or else northwesterly to Old Tampa (Safety Harbor) and the few settlements at Clear Water Harbor on the coast. "The ferry consisted of a rowboat for foot passengers and a big flat barge for accommodation of teams, cattle and horses," explained a local woman. "It was operated by a heavy cable which lay on the bottom of the river when not in use." She added: "When a team was to cross, a hinged platform was let down so that the end rested in the mud, and the horses had to drag their load up the steep incline onto the barge, the cable was laboriously pulled up and hand-over-hand the hardworked ferryman pulled at it, the barge sometimes swinging out into the stream in spite of the efforts of the ferryman. When the other shore was gained, the hinged platform was let down on the other side and with much protest on the part of the horses and much urging from the driver the plunge would be made down the incline into the mud if the tide was low but onto hard sand if the tide was high."[14]

A handful of families resided on the river's western bank or else nearby. Importantly among them, Jesse Carter maintained a home where the University of Tampa now stands and Indian war veteran Robert Jackson and his wife Nancy kept house not far to the south near the river. Several Spanish or Cuban natives lived "in a cluster of little shanties" around the mouth of Spanishtown Creek, which emptied into Hillsborough Bay from today's Hyde Park neighborhood near the southern end of Magnolia Avenue. Since these individuals evidenced a culture far different from that of most Tampans, the townspeople tended to look upon them as "odd characters," although they were quick to purchase fresh fish and oysters from them. Also, a Frenchman who lived a bit down the bayshore intrigued the locals. Named Augustus Santhorant, he possessed "among other odd things, a baby's coffin in which he kept coarse salt to salt the fish on which he chiefly subsisted." One onlooker reported that Santhorans "used to eat young alligators, which he said was very good, but he was not partial to buzzard meat, as it did not taste much like turkey."[15]

Just as the townspeople were well acquainted with the Spanishtown Creek settlers, so too did they know virtually everyone else around. There were not that many people to know. When census takers toured the community in 1860, they discovered only 445 whites living within town limits (with less than 3,000 residents each, Pensacola and Key West vied for status as the state's largest city). Thomas E. Jackson estimated that another 100 lived nearby. Four or five years earlier, Tampa's total might have approached 700 or more. Now, the diminished number of white Tampans divided fairly equally between male and female, but only 185 persons had attained the age of twenty-one. The exact number of slaves who lived within town limits remains open to question. Hillsborough County's population in 1860 totalled only 2,981 individuals, and the county then included what is now Pinellas and Polk Counties. Of that figure, 564 persons were held in slavery (about 15 percent). Given the nature of rural life in the region, it seems likely that a greater percentage would have lived in town than in the countryside. So, a figure of 100 to 125 black residents would not appear unreasonable.[16]

Local Wealth and Influence

The relatively low number of slaves living within the county did not mean that slavery comprised an unimportant part of the local economic structure. All real estate located within the county as late as 1861 amounted in assessed value to $108,402. Slave value almost doubled that figure at $200,035. When cattle, horses, and other farm animals, plus personal property, are added to these figures, a total of slightly more than $800,000 is reached as the value of all of Hillsborough's taxable property that year. Given that about one-quarter of all wealth within the county thus consisted of slaves,

4. William Brinton Hooker.

many local residents would feel an immediate concern when national politics began to threaten their financial well-being.[17]

Who were the Tampans so closely linked to slaveholding? Physician John P. Crichton led the 1860 list with seventeen bondservants. His colleague Dr. Franklin Branch possessed four. Next in line came lawyer James T. Magbee, who held thirteen persons. Magbee's fellow attorney Ossian B. Hart owned five, while law student John A. Henderson kept one slave. Methodist minister and farmer Leroy G. Lesley's holdings totalled ten individuals. His son John T. Lesley's added to three. Local merchants also joined the list, with Christopher L. Friebele holding ten slaves; Louis G. Covacevich, nine; James McKay, Sr., seven; and John Darling, five. Port Warden William Cooley owned nine men, women, and children; cattleman William B. Hooker, eight; and Jesse Carter, five. It is not without interest then that, when Tampans chose their city officials on February 1, 1860, they opted for leadership at the hands of the town's largest slaveholder by choosing Dr. Crichton as their new mayor.[18]

That is not to say that the wealthiest local men were the largest slaveholders. To the contrary, William B. Hooker with vast holdings in land and cattle may have stood at the pinnacle of the town's financial elite. As if to emphasize the point, in 1859 he had constructed a new home on the northeast corner of Madison and East Streets that contained "33 or 34 rooms, with passages, piazzas, etc." Surrounded by an orange grove, the structure comprised Tampa's only true residential showpiece. "What a glorious place for 4th of July festivities! a camp meeting! or, a Dance!" proclaimed the *Florida Peninsular*, the town's only newspaper.[19]

Hooker's one true rival for the title of wealthiest local man was merchant John Darling. An 1860 report listed his assets at $62,795,

5. John Darling. (TBHC)

placing him among the state's wealthiest men. A Vermont native, he had come to Florida as a soldier during the Second Seminole War of 1835-1842. He and a friend, Thomas P. Kennedy, utilized contacts with army officials to build a substantial business catering to the Indian trade as well as to the needs of frontier settlers. Kennedy & Darling stood as one of Tampa's premier business establishments, and, after his partner's 1858 death, Darling continued with a new associate, ship captain Henry Proseus, to push expansion of area settlement and railroad construction. Darling represented the county in the legislature in 1855 and would be remembered for his Masonic ties and as a strong friend of the Tampa Baptist Church.[20]

While Hooker and Darling led local men in wealth, they took second place to another businessman in terms of entrepreneurial dynamism and, likely, community respect. A Scotsman by birth, James "Mac" McKay had arrived at Tampa in 1846. In association with his mother-in-law Sarah Cail, he had helped to tie the town to the outside world through acquisition of several small ships and the erection of Tampa's first civilian-controlled wharf. Further, McKay and Cail had sought to enhance their considerable local real estate investments through publicizing the potential they saw in town and area development. The investments included a store and Tampa's principal hotel, the Florida House. Located at the corner of Marion and Lafayette (Kennedy) Streets, this public accommodation was operated by McKay's son-in-law, onetime army lieutenant Robert B. Thomas. Sarah Hanes Brown, a slave, assisted him as chambermaid.[21]

Another of McKay's investments held great significance for the community. In the early 1850s he had pioneered what became Tampa's first dependable local industry. This business, a sawmill, stood on the Hillsborough River where Henderson Avenue later

6. Alfonso DeLaunay was an influential pro-slavery advocate as postmaster and journalist. (TBHC)

would touch the stream, a place that came to be known as Waterworks Park. McKay entrusted its operation to his friend William J. Campbell. Not far away from the site, at a location on the western edge of modern Seminole Heights, McKay developed a five or six acre tract as, in the words of his grandson Donald B. McKay, a "slave stockade." There lived workers McKay either purchased or leased for mill purposes. Available sources suggest that among those who lived at the stockade and worked in the mill at various times were Wade Smith, Cyrus Charles, and, perhaps, Isaac Howard. One unintended consequence of mill operations was that they sometimes brought McKay into conflict with John Darling, who served locally as the state's eyes and ears for spotting timbering depredations on public lands.[22]

Several individuals wielded greater local influence through control of the local newspaper than their personal wealth otherwise would have suggested. In late 1858 William James Spencer, then nineteen, purchased the *Florida Peninsular* from retiring editor Simon Turman, Jr. By October 1859 editorial authority rested in the hands of Tampa's Virginia-born postmaster Alfonso DeLaunay. A man of strong pro-slavery convictions, DeLaunay boasted early in his tenure that the *Peninsular* would be edited as a "State Rights Democratic Journal as WE understand it." When the slave Adam suffered lynching in December, DeLaunay justified the action, in the words of one historian, as "just an example of good old local law and order." The editor also minimized local news coverage to highlight and sensationalize regional and national political matters.[23]

An additional group of men joined Tampa's leadership core through their control of the town's commercial houses. Nine large general stores served the region. Their market extended beyond

Tampa northward toward Hernando County (which then encompassed Pasco and Citrus) and southward to the Manatee River, where sugar plantations generated considerable desire for goods. More recently, the houses increasingly had looked to the east, where an agricultural and cattle grazing frontier had begun to prosper. Farming especially had taken hold in what is now eastern Hillsborough County and in the vicinity of modern Bartow in Polk County. The only settlement to the east of Tampa that even approached the status of a village, though, stood at Fort Meade, where the larger cattle owners had begun to concentrate. Below there, the frontier of settlement had pushed since the Bowlegs War's 1858 close down the Peace River into the northern reaches of today's DeSoto County. In April and May 1860 a Tampa-based expedition would explore the river south from Fort Meade, attempting to assess the region's potential. Not surprisingly, its members included a Tampa merchant, Edward A. Clarke. The *Peninsular*'s editor considered the survey so important that he ran the expedition's journal in full, to the expense of some political coverage, from late June to early August.[24]

While claiming distinct attributes, Tampa's commercial houses evidenced common elements. Each store naturally reflected the personality and business skills of its operator. New York-born Edward A. Clarke, though of modest means, captured the public's imagination through something akin to modern advertising techniques when he christened his place at Washington and Marion with a catchy name. He called it "the Blue Store." A sharp businessman, Clarke declined extending a courtesy that most other local concerns quickly embraced. "Credit is dead," he declared, "and bad debts killed him." As mentioned, James McKay's store and Kennedy & Darling appealed to wide clienteles. This fact permitted John Darling in early 1860 to erect a large new two-story building at Tampa and Whiting Streets, with room enough left over for use as a hall for the Royal Arch Masons. State Grand Scribe Charles Slager of Jacksonville installed the chapter there in March 1861. Six other establishments also catered to the region's trade. W. G. Ferris & Son and Christopher L. Friebele's store ranked high among competitors, with their owners each possessing assets of around $25,000. L. G. Covacevich claimed a little over $10,000, with Michael Wall, Robert F. Nunez, and Jose Vigil trailing. Each business operated on a wholesale and a retail basis, primarily bartering cotton, corn, hides, and such for finished goods, groceries, liquors, and similar commodities.[25]

Cattle Schemes and Other Diversions

Though Tampa's merchants could boast of long experience and enduring relationships with customers, they faced the uncertainties of changing times and conditions as the decade of the 1850s ended and that of the 1860s began. With frontier expansion in the years immediately following the Bowlegs War's conclusion, interior markets created by new settlements had aided them to weather Fort Brooke's closing and other recent calamities. If their customers were to continue to enjoy the delights of a consumer economy, though, they required a solution to a considerable problem. The people of the frontier possessed extensive cattle herds, but—in that era before refrigeration—they could find no market for their beeves in a state with few roads and no cities of consequence. The owners—and just about everyone in the interior owned at least a few head of cattle—approached their leader Jacob Summerlin, Jr., in search of an answer. Summerlin then put his head together with James McKay, and the two men determined to transport beeves on board McKay's vessels to the highly desirable market at Havana, Cuba. Test runs in late 1858 and 1859 proved the scheme practical, and the entrepreneurs looked forward to 1860 when they would launch the trade on a large scale.[26]

Tampans, otherwise depressed by recent events, viewed McKay's initiative as the answer to their economic prayers and were pleased to add support for the venture. With town backing, the captain sought during 1860, as he explained it, "to obtain the privilege of occupying Fort Brook Fla for the use of my cattle prior to their shipment for Havana market," but bureaucratic wheels turned slowly and not until January 1861 was he able to arrange a lease. In the meantime, the captain headquartered operations on the mostly uninhabited Interbay Peninsula. "In January, 1860, there was constructed a pasture fence, beginning on Hillsborough bay just near the [1921] site of the Spanish sanitarium," explained James McKay, Jr., "extending across the peninsula about two miles north of Port Tampa, to old Tampa bay, for the purpose of concentrating cattle." Docks at Ballast Point were readied for the loading of ships once cattle arrived.[27]

At that point, a disaster occurred that properly might have served as an omen of difficult times ahead for McKay and for Tampa. On the night of March 2, the town fire bell rang out to alert citizens that the McKay sawmill was being consumed by flames. In the absence of any effective firefighting system, the mill proved a total loss. Damages, including burned lumber, amounted to $5,000-$6,000. Although sawmills possessed a notorious reputation as fire traps, given the tumultuous times rumors spread of arson. Without apparent justification, Editor DeLaunay suggested abolitionists as the culprits and called for vigilante action. "As this fire may be but the 'beginning of the end,'" he proclaimed somewhat cryptically, "would it not be prudent to look after such characters who 'toil not, neither do they spin,' and yet are decked out so gay in fine apparel!"[28]

With the town's principal industrial enterprise now leveled to ashes, the cattle shipping plans took on enhanced importance. McKay hurried to New York and Chicago to find a suitable steam-powered vessel for the trade. During his absence 8,000 head of cattle were ranged below the Interbay Peninsula fence. The captain found his ship and had steamed it to the Tampa docks by late July. The passage of the *Salvor*, as McKay dubbed his cattle boat, came under the umbra of yet another omen. During early July a comet surprisingly had sliced the skies over Florida, foretelling by its appearance who knew what dark fate. Despite the specter, Tampans rejoiced. "A New Era in the History of Tampa," shouted the *Peninsular*. "Verily, our little city is 'coming out of the woods.'" The excitement only intensified with public announcement that W. G. Ferris & Son also had entered the cattle shipping business with their own vessel, the *Scottish Chief*.[29]

Would that it had been so. The problem was water. In McKay's absence, expected summer rains had failed to arrive, as a result of which drought parched the landscape. "Having a very dry spell," remembered James McKay, Jr., "every pond and alligator hole went dry." Although the *Salvor* and the *Scottish Chief* labored mightily to transport the herds awaiting shipment on the Interbay Peninsula, their small carrying capacities proved woefully inadequate. "Before those cattle could be shipped out some 2,000 head of them died," McKay continued. "A large number of them being poor [but alive], they were turned loosed in Manatee county." The elder McKay and his associate Summerlin responded to the tragedy forcefully. They quickly relocated the focus of their shipping efforts to a site southward of the limits of frontier settlement on the Peace River but near dependable fresh water supplies and easy Gulf access. In the wilderness that today is Punta Gorda, they constructed an 800-foot dock at the river's mouth. From that point they commenced shipping cattle in the first week of November 1860.[30]

The loss to Tampa of the cattle shipping business hit most townspeople as something they would just rather not have to ponder.

MILITARY BALL.

The Compliments of the "Perry Guards" for Wednesday Ev'g,

JULY 4TH, 1860,

at 8 o'clock, at the "Palmer House."

Com. of Arrangements:

Lt. McKay, 1st Serg't Leonardy, Pr't Snell,
H. M., A. DeLaunay, H. M., M. L. Shannahan.

Com. of Invitation:

L'ce Serg't Nunez, Sec'y Crane, Pr't Turman.

Com. of Reception:

L'ce Serg't Nunez, C'l'r B'r Wells, Sec'y Crane.

FLOOR-MANAGER—Capt. R. B. THOMAS.

7. The "Perry Guards" was a volunteer militia formed in Tampa in the heat of pre-secession tension, but this invitation offers evidence that it was in part a diversion from the summer heat.

Already during 1860, they had sought diversion from their woes in numerous ways, attempting, it seems, to think about anything other than their mounting problems. Partly, they had manifested this through the intense excitement they exuded at thoughts of their forthcoming delivery thanks to McKay's shipping scheme. As the nation's crisis intensified, they also invested a great deal of energy in partying, albeit after their own fashion. Under the tutelage of the young Englishman James Butterfield, they formed a glee club and a cornet band. Butterfield spurred the young onto greater heights with a "music academy," sponsoring community concerts and performances on special occasions such as the *Salvor*'s Tampa arrival. Sunny excursions on the bay vied for attention with the call of the literary club. The restless locals danced when they could, as well. They turned out 200 strong, for example, when Mayor Crichton's "inaugural ball" was held in February. This was happening in a town that could not afford to fence its own cemetery.[31]

One diversion generated pure elation. Local people could not stop talking about ice. By 1860 they had been denied the frigid treat for half a decade or more. Now, things definitely had changed for the better. W. G. Ferris and O. B. Hart had joined with others to build and operate an icehouse. Robert Jackson managed the concern after it debuted in the spring.[32] William Ferris described in an April 26 letter the delivery of the first load of ice by a Boston schooner, not to mention the delicious dreams stirred by that momentous occurrence:

> it is the first load of Ice that has been landed here in six years and it is quite a treat to see it we expect to keep cool this summer if Ice can do it as we have one hundred and thirty tons the first snow I ever saw was when the schooner opened her hatches it was frozen on the Ice that was a curiosity also we have also a Soda Fountain and an Ice Cream Saloon just fixed up so that this summer we can enjoy ourselves better than we ever did in this place.[33]

Secession

Try as they might to party away their problems, Tampans discovered in the fall of 1860 that the world would not go away. Thanks to drought and the cattle fiasco, they were not able "to keep cool this summer," nor in the months that followed did they "enjoy ourselves better than we ever did in this place." Instead, they discovered themselves on the edge of a precipice, feeling at the time and for a while, most of them, that they had very little left to lose.

The situation did not really begin to hit home until the late summer and early fall, just as the meaning of the relocation of McKay's and Summerlin's cattle shipping business sank into the local consciousness. Of course, early in the year editor DeLaunay of the *Peninsular* already had been striking out at the evil designs of "black Republicans" and their abolitionist cohorts, doing his best to politicize a town that often chose not to listen. So strident did he become that the Spencer family grew concerned at his extremism. By mid-March they had ousted their editor in favor of Simon Turman, Jr., considered a more moderate man. Undaunted, DeLaunay resurrected his pulpit through a new organ, the *Sunny South*. One journalistic historian described its tenor as "rabid indeed." From its editorial desk, DeLaunay kept up a drum beat for southern independence.[34]

Despite the community's lack of enthusiasm for extreme politics, DeLaunay's words touched Tampans in a way that set the stage for other events to drive home his message. To some extent the change came about because of timing. Just as various regional and national happenings heated up the political atmosphere in the late summer and early fall, local people found themselves seeking subjects of interest other than the depressing meaning of the McKay departure or the waning away of the desperate gaiety upon which they had depended for much of the year. One such occasion arose in early September when the "fire eating" Jackson County planter John Milton came through in support of his soon-to-be-successful campaign for governor. Suitably radical in his declamations, Milton stirred fears, anxieties, and passions. Only a few days afterward, echoes of the talk carried local reverberations when the town council established a night watch "to guard the city against fire and any disorder by white men or slaves." Every white male between the ages of eighteen and forty-five years was compelled to serve, unless otherwise exempted.[35]

Other aspects of the election campaign added fuel to the fire. James T. Magbee, whom William Brinton Hooker and James McKay had helped to oust from his federal position of collector of the port in the midst of the 1858 Regulator tumult, took on Hooker's son-in-law Samuel Hope in a bitterly fought state senate contest. When ballots were counted following the October 1 polling, Hope had carried Tampa but Magbee had taken the district. A tie in a race for the state house then prolonged the fevered electioneering as the desire of Peace River area residents to withdraw from Hillsborough threatened to deal another blow to Tampa's fortunes. Planter Joseph Howell favored creation of Polk County while planter William I. Turner opposed it. On October 20, Howell and Polk County scored a win, leaving bitter feelings among the majority of Tampa voters who would have preferred otherwise.[36]

By the time national elections took center stage the first week of November, most Tampans' emotions hovered near a frantic point. Fears of the meaning of a Republican triumph and an Abraham Lincoln presidency ran wide. Many believed that a general slave uprising might ensue. When a Hernando County bondsman named Hamp murdered his owner in October, his subsequent lynching helped to calm no troubled waters. Condemnations especially poured out on those who would threaten slavery. "I do so much wish those *Snarling bull dog* Abolitionist[s] Horace Greeley and Tom Bennet could be shut," complained Catharine Hart, "they have done more and are doing more every day to exasperate the South than any thing else." Meanwhile, everyone waited and watched.[37]

The news of the Republican triumph landed in Tampa with all the force of a cannon ball, as it did in other parts of the South. Months earlier the *Peninsular* had warned local residents that a Lincoln victory meant disunion. For many it now seemed proper and timely to stand up and be counted among one's fellows as being right on the issue. A woman calling herself "A Lady Secessionist" struck the chord. "Is there nothing for us to do?" she demanded. "Can we not come out boldly and show Mr. Abe Lincoln that the 'irrepressible conflict' has begun!"[38]

Public meetings held in late November allowed emotions to flow. The first convened at Fort Alafia on November 24. There, several dozen men—organized by defeated legislative candidate William I. Turner, publisher William J. Spencer, and law student John A. Henderson—drafted a petition requesting the governor to call a convention to consider whether "to sever our connection with the present Government." They declared, "We will not submit to the administration of this Government by said Lincoln [and] we will maintain the rights, liberties and honor of the Sovereign State of Florida at any and all hazards." Also taking instrumental roles in the session were state attorney Henry L. Mitchell, editor Simon Turman, and John A. Henderson's brother William B. Henderson.[39]

Their petition drafted, the organizers thereupon called a public meeting to be held at Tampa on November 26. Reportedly, 400 persons attended. "They are calling public meetings in our portion of Country, we had a very spirited one here last monday night, to which the Ladies were invited; and attended to[o] in large numbers," reported Catharine Hart. Alfonso DeLaunay and Methodist minister Oscar A. Myers warmed up the crowd with "logical and earnest speeches, which carried conviction of the necessity of such resolves, on the part of the South, to the heart of every auditor." Available documentation suggests that Myers proved the more persuasive of the two. "[He was] one of the eloquent ones [who] in 1860 came out of the pulpit to the political arena and made public speeches to the people in favor of secession and most bitterly denouncing and even

8. and 9. Simon Turman, Jr., (left) and James Gettis went to Tallahassee as the pro-secessionist delegates from Hillsborough County. (TBHC)

ridiculing the Union," O. B. Hart recalled. In the end, seventy-six men appended their names to the Alafia petition. Included were the principal members of the 1858 Regulator leadership, the owners and editors of the local newspapers, and almost all county slaveholders and Tampa merchants. As would have been expected, music was "called for" during signing ceremonies. The cornet band "promptly responded with one of their unique and soul stirring performances."[40]

Most white Tampans clearly accepted or embraced the sentiment of the times as expressed in the Alafia petition, but it should be noted that not all did so. While the point will receive attention at greater length in subsequent chapters, numerous area men opposed talk of secession. Two of them were O. B. Hart and James McKay. "When the rebellion broke out in 1860 and Florida undertook to secede, Judge Hart . . . remained true to his principles and firm in his attachment to the Union," one report noted, "believing that to be worth more than slavery or party, and proclaimed from the stump his devotion to the Union and his opposition to all its enemies, in defiance of the secessionists around him." McKay described his sentiments and those of many area cattlemen. "The people from whom I was obtaining cattle, numbering about 150 persons, or families, never could see any benefit they could derive by breaking up the Govt., but to the contrary," he declared. "I stood in the front rank in my section of country, resisting with all my might the pestiferous progress of disunion sentiment."[41]

In the excitement of December 1860 demands for secession easily drowned out loyalist pleas by men such as Hart and McKay. When Governor Perry called a convention to consider the issue, Hillsborough County sent as delegates pro-secessionists James Gettis, a lawyer-mentor of Henry L. Mitchell and John A. Henderson, and editor Simon Turman, Jr. Interestingly, the latter man boasted Pennsylvania as his native state, while the former hailed from Indiana. In any event, Gettis and Turman joined with others of similar disposition at Tallahassee on January 10, 1861, to declare Florida's independence, following only South Carolina and Mississippi. The two Tampans then walked with their colleagues from the Capitol to former Governor Richard Keith Call's mansion, the Grove, to announce their action. The outspoken Unionist and friend of Tampa's O. B. Hart thereafter spoke to the delegates from the steps of his home. "Well gentlemen," he declared, "you have just unlocked the gates of Hell, from which shall flow the curses of the damned." And so it was to be at Tampa.[42]

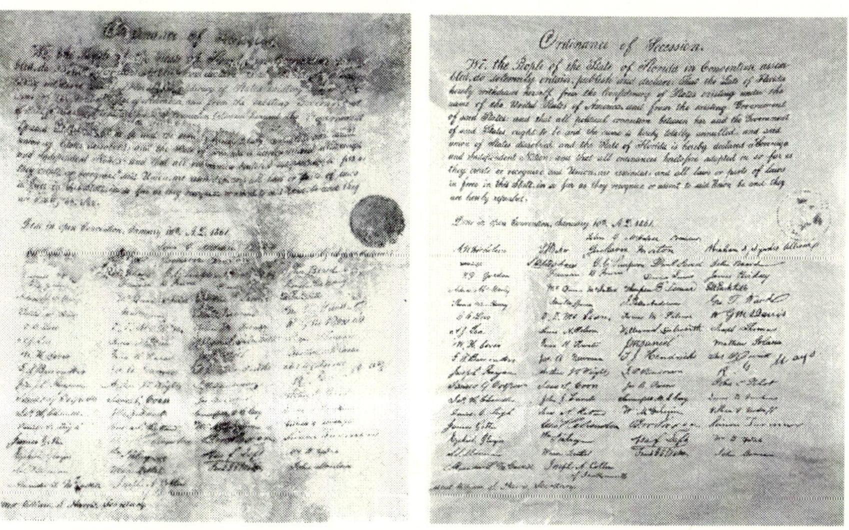

Ordinance of Secession.

We the People of the State of Florida in Convention assembled, do solemnly ordain, publish and declare: That the State of Florida hereby withdraws herself from the Confederacy of States existing under the name of the United States of America and from the existing Government of said States; and that all political connection between her and the Government of said States ought to be and the same is hereby totally annulled, and said union of States dissolved; and the State of Florida is hereby declared a Sovereign and Independent Nation; and that all ordinances heretofore adopted in so far as they create or recognize said Union are rescinded; and all laws or parts of laws in force in this State, in so far as they recognize or assent to said Union, be and they are hereby repealed.

Done in Open Convention, January 10th, A.D. 1861.

10. The document declaring Florida's secession was signed by both of the delegates from Hillsborough County. The signature of James Gettis is fourth from the bottom of the first column; Simon Turman's signature is third from last in the fourth column. (FSA)

II. This map of Florida, circa 1860, from United States Navy files shows not only how much the state was filled with unsettled wilderness, but also how the shape and development of the long peninsula defined the nature of military operations and indicated the importance of naval skirmishes to achieve superiority. (*ORN*)

*"The state of things—
Tampa is fearful"*

The Pains of Anticipation, 1861-1862

Florida's secession from the Union in 1861's early hours unleashed passions at Tampa that the passage of time has tended to obscure but that resounded with a deafening clamor during the ensuing year and one half. Forces little understood and beyond local control seized upon existing tensions to turn neighbor against neighbor in a scene chillingly familiar to townspeople who had lived through the Regulator terror of three years past. Old grudges bore new fruit against the backdrop of an external war that remained distant militarily but which loomed with frightening intensity as each day passed into the next. So many must have pondered a truly fatal question, how long before we begin killing ourselves this time?

Word that Florida had separated from the other states arrived locally on Sunday, January 13, 1861, courtesy of a stage coach driver who had hurried himself from Gainesville. The news set off rounds of noisy celebration. The town's brass band marched joyously through the streets, while other young men repeatedly discharged Fort Brooke's remaining few cannons. At the courthouse citizens gathered to gossip excitedly about what it all meant. That evening local pastors intoned a Methodist, Baptist, or Roman Catholic prayer, while placing their stamp of approval on the act of disunion.[1]

The excitement persisted for days. On Monday, militia colonel William I. Turner stoked the martial fires by occupying Fort Brooke's grounds with a small force of followers. One historian of the action described the company as "undoubtedly ardent secessionists in civilian dress, armed (if at all) with the weapons used to fight Billy Bowleg's warriors." Still, the military had returned to Tampa, a condition with which local people were quite comfortable. On Thursday, they came together at the courthouse to vent their own enthusiasms and to hear the brass band's rousing airs once again as soon as the politicians had had their say. That night fireworks lit the sky to the delight of those assembled, doubtlessly expressing the common understanding that, just as was true of the fireworks, the secession excitement would not hurt anyone once the confusing dust of disunion had cleared.[2]

That is one important point to remember when casting back upon those heady days of secession. Most people did not believe there would be a war. Merchant John Darling, one of Hillsborough County's fervent Secessionists, later summed up the early 1861 sentiments of many of the locality's white people. "In giving this vote [for secession, I] was not influenced by any hostility towards the Govt. of the U.S.," he declared, "but it was given under the conviction that it was a rightful and proper remedy to break down the policy of Negroe emancipation believed to be intended by the Republican Administration then about to come to office." Darling added, "Nor had [I] any idea that war would be the result until [President Abraham Lincoln's] proclamation of 15th April 1861." The *Florida Peninsular* confirmed Darling's memories. On February 2 it reported, "The tenor of news from Washington this week is quite pacific." Temporary editor Erasmus M. Thompson (editor Simon Turman was away at the secession convention) then quoted the Charleston *Courier* as concluding, "The question of separate State secession is at rest."[3]

In those days before President Lincoln called for Union volunteers in the wake of the surrender of United States troops at Fort Sumter in South Carolina's Charleston Harbor, the whole idea of disunion could be seen as a lighter thing, an action without serious or, at least, lethal consequences. It allowed the politicians to bluster, while offering the young men a way to express loyalty to their state and region, an action which they would have defined as patriotism. Thus, when one-time Bowlegs War officer John T. Lesley announced the formation of "The Tampa Guards" in late January, local boys and young men flocked to its banner. Drills held at least weekly kept the guards (later called "The Sunny South Guards") eager for the cause. On the other hand, they suffered at first from little threat of discomfort, dislocation, or danger. As one student of the company has noted, they

12. John T. Lesley organized an impromptu local secessionist military unit called "The Tampa Guards," later known as "The Sunny South Guards." (TBHC)

avoided "orders [that] might have called them from the parties, parades, and parlors to the digging of earthworks." Eventually, though, frustration due to the lack of any real military responsibilities would lend itself to a desire for a greater show of commitment. And, that would cause problems for Tampa.[4]

Local loyalists likely were the first to bear the burden of ardent young Rebels with time on their hands. At first, a climate of tolerance for differing opinions graced the town. On January 26, for instance, the *Peninsular* boasted that "No 'Reign of Terror' has marked the overthrow of a great government; no Cromwell or Robespierre has been needed to kindle the flames of popular disaffection; no crowns have fallen; no blood has flowed." In such an atmosphere Unionists proclaimed their convictions. Among them stood lawyer Ossian B. Hart, merchant James McKay, army veteran Robert Jackson and his wife Nancy Collar Jackson, undertaker John T. Givens, storekeeper Louis G. Covacevich, farmers Samuel and Jesse Knight, the brothers Vincent and Bartholomew C. Leonardy, and numerous others. "I always opposed those wicked heresies," Hart recollected, "and could not agree nor act with them, simply because they precipitated us into secession, rebellion, and war against our country, as too many others did."[5]

As the weeks passed, though, the young men of the Sunny South Guards could not restrain their passions and began efforts to intimidate their opponents, a circumstance common in Florida at the time. This increasingly became the case after the organization of the southern confederacy in February, Abraham Lincoln's inauguration in March, and, in April, Fort Sumter's surrender and the eruption of fighting at Pensacola. A Jacksonville man explained the general state of affairs. "The Union men . . . for two or three months [after secession] continued to utter their sentiments of opposition to the movement," he recorded, "but gradually the reign of terror gained full swing and the time came when for a northern man to utter openly his love for the Union would be almost suicide." The man added, "Men who were born and reared in the south could speak against secession long after it was unsafe for northern men to do so." Details of the anti-Unionist campaign at Tampa are lacking, but O. B. Hart described the consequences. "By the events of war the protections of the National Government could not reach him," a newspaperman noted, "and common prudence compelled silence."[6]

Trial for Treason

The hardening of the times and of relations between Tampans already could be seen clearly by late March. By then the Confederate States flag floated on a staff above James McKay's store. Not far away, at the establishment of New York-born W. G. Ferris the United States banner yet waved, except that its owner had turned it upside down. The pull toward greater conflict then accelerated with ensuing events. Not later than mid-April Colonel William I. Turner had conscripted "every available man" to build earthworks at Fort Brooke and was placing a set of five cannons along the waterfront. After the Peninsular cried "To Arms! To Arms!" on April 20, it took only a few days before many of Tampa's older men desired to prove their allegiance to the new Confederate States by organizing a volunteer company of their own. Labelled "The Silver Grays," the unit contained almost all the town's leading secessionists and major slaveholders, as well as a few Unionists. William Cooley headed the company as its captain,

13. William I. Turner. (*Sunland Tribune*)

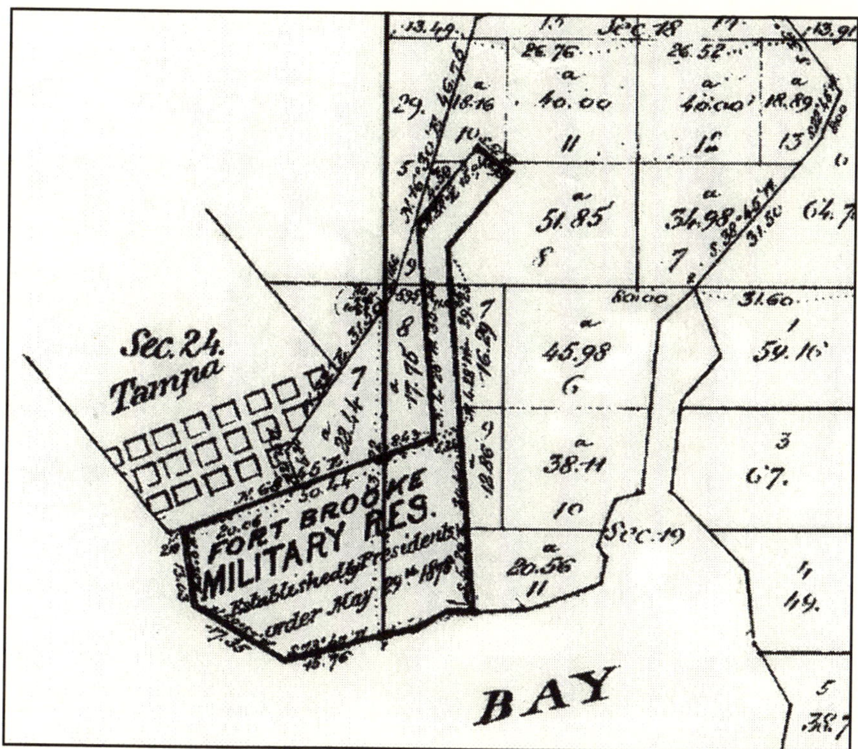

14. Secession allowed local entrepreneurs the hope of profit from subdividing and selling the property of the Fort Brooke military reservation. (Fla. Dept. of Environmental Protection)

with John Darling and John Jackson assisting as officers. Louis G. Covacevich and John T. Givens now stood in the ranks shoulder to shoulder with Alfonso DeLaunay, John P. Crichton, Jesse Carter, William B. Hooker, and Franklin Branch.[7]

Meanwhile, the secession convention and the legislature were attempting to rule the state as it careened toward war. In doing so both bodies tackled several high-voltage issues that further stirred public excitement. Before the legislature adjourned in early March, it approved a military bill that called for raising troops and the organization of a more-effective militia system. The convention delegates thereafter carried on without the legislature and upon their own authority. Particularly, they moved to take control of all United States lands located in Florida. Tampans delighted in the action because it gifted them with a boon. Tucked away in the law's details was a special provision that authorized the Hillsborough County commission to survey, subdivide, sell, and otherwise administer the Fort Brooke military reservation. Profits loomed rich for the taking thanks to secession.[8]

Lastly and with local repercussions not far distant, the convention defined and penalized treason. It specified, in part, that the crime was committed "If any person shall, by speech or writing, strive to stir up a rebellion in this State against the authority of the State or the Confederate States, or shall by word or deed endeavor to create sedition or be engaged in any seditious or rebellious meeting, assembled to incite resistance to the authority of this State or of the Confederate States, or shall endeavor to seduce any one in the military or naval services of this State or of the Confederate States to desert or betray a trust reposed in him or them." The *Peninsular* published the ordinance in full in its May 18 issue.[9]

Coincidentally, public anger had been building at, of all people, James McKay. Since November 1860 the captain and his partner Jacob Summerlin had been shipping one boatload of cattle after another to Havana, Cuba. The venture's success had pleased area cattlemen enormously, but many of Tampa's businessmen still chafed at McKay's temerity in relocating the enterprise from their town to Charlotte Harbor. That act had deprived the merchants of a slice of a potentially lucrative pie, particularly since McKay was importing Cuban goods into Florida for direct sale to frontier families. Among the irate merchants stood John Darling, whose conflicts with the captain could be traced back at least one decade. In the circumstances, Darling took action by organizing a public meeting on May 4 to protest cattle shipments to Union-occupied Key West. The principal shipper, of course, was McKay. Now, tempers seethed at the man who, until recently, had been lionized as Tampa's hero.[10]

15. A cattle drive to Tampa. (FSA)

McKay took several precautionary steps in light of the changed circumstances, but soon events took a turn for the worse. Especially, he protected his large cattle holdings from possible seizure under the treason law by transferring them to his partner Summerlin on May 31. Then, the captain's position deteriorated with the coming of June. Emotions flowed early in the month when, at the Southern Baptist Convention's request, the local Baptist church conducted a day of fasting and prayer for the Confederacy. Less than two weeks afterward the Confederacy's own "day of humiliation and prayer on account of `national sins, etc.," as proclaimed by President Jefferson Davis, heightened sensitivities further. These acts combined with the strains of the recent past to send tempers flying. At the Baptist Church members summarily dropped longtime supporter Jesse Carter from their rolls for "unchristian conduct" in the wake of an argument with a fellow Baptist. Down at the Masonic lodge, the spirit of fellowship fared no better. The same week, one-time county sheriff Edward T. Kendrick suffered expulsion as a result of accusing lawyer James Gettis of accepting a bribe from Darling's late business partner. Darling joined with Gettis, William B. Hooker, and Henry L. Mitchell to eject Kendrick as a blasphemer and "habitual liar."[11]

As these scenes and circumstances unfolded, attention shifted back to McKay. Word trickled from Key West to Tampa's Confederates that the captain had been cooperating with old friends of his who now commanded United States forces at the island city. He had brought them supplies, helped them to deport secessionists to the mainland, and leased them his steamer. For the young men who made up the Sunny South Guards this was all too much. They prepared to act.[12]

McKay discovered his change of fortune when he landed in a fishing smack at his wharf on June 26. "Within half an hour after our arrival at Tampa," he related, "an armed possy of men went down & took possession of the smack, stating that she belonged to *Unionists*, and must be seized; they being reckless, ignorant people." The guards' action in seizing private property proved too much for many of Tampa's merchant leaders, even for John Darling. He—along with McKay, C. L. Friebele, L. G. Covacevich, Edward A. Clarke, and Franklin Branch—sought to interpose the authority of their friend Colonel William I. Turner over that of guards captain John T. Lesley. The businessmen long had associated closely with Governor Madison Starke Perry, and he acceded to their wishes, giving McKay an order for return of his vessel.[13]

The Sunny South Guards refused to bow. The gubernatorial appeal took some time, during which the local unit was mustered into the regular service of the Confederate States as Company K, Fourth Florida Infantry. This removed them from state jurisdiction. Two days later, on July 3, 1861, a United States gunboat, the *R. R. Cuyler*, took up station in Tampa Bay, initiating the Union blockade of the port. Within twenty-four hours, after the guardsmen celebrated the Fourth of July "in a manner clearly indicating their appreciation of the Liberty bequeathed to them by the Revolutionary Sires," they prepared to act once again. "The night previous to which the Smack was to be turned over to me," McKay explained, "the persons who held her in charge *set fire* to her, and burned her up."[14]

The crisis was building to a crescendo. When McKay headed north to discuss affairs with the governor, word circulated that he was "a general agent of the Government and a traitor and should be hung." Many of the rumors derived from a *Peninsular* letter penned by the captain's old nemesis State Senator James T. Magbee, who was more than ready to avenge McKay's role in the senator's 1858 removal from federal office. Then, word arrived of the South's victory (or so it was seen) at the First Battle of Bull Run. Amid the swirl of excitement, Magbee found his opportunity to strike. State Attorney Henry L. Mitchell had resigned to enter Confederate service with the Sunny South Guards. The senator volunteered to act in Mitchell's stead and filed petty treason charges against McKay. When the accused returned to town, Magbee ordered him arrested.[15]

Strange turns of events were about to become the rule. The trial convened on August 10 at the county courthouse. Three justices of the peace weighed evidence presented by Magbee, who sought a sentence of death by hanging. Rebuttal came from McKay's lead attorney O. B. Hart, who was assisted by secessionist James Gettis. Brigadier General Joseph M. Taylor of the Florida Militia, an old associate of the defendant who temporarily had relieved Colonel Turner of Fort Brooke's command in late July, "sat himself on the trial." Cattlemen threatened to break up the "long and acrimonious" proceedings before the justices agreed to set McKay free on $10,000 bond pending a new trial during the circuit court's October term. Taylor then arranged for the captain to pass the R. R. Cuyler's blockade in a schooner bound for Key West. There, McKay retrieved his steamer, the Salvor, and headed for Havana. He picked up a cargo that may have included supplies for the Fort Brooke garrison (guns and ammunition reportedly were found aboard). Unfortunately, while steaming through the keys toward Tampa on October 14, a

16. Tampa Bay was sufficiently important to Confederate trade that it attracted a Union naval blockade beginning in July 1861. (*ORN*)

17. Private John Lowe in his militia shirt in Tampa, 1862. (*Tampa Bay History*)

18. Ships blockading Tampa Bay. The *James L. Davis* is at center. (Chapin, *By-Gone Days*)

United States warship intercepted the Salvor. Finding contraband on board, the warship's commanding officer seized the vessel and held its captain as a prisoner of war. James McKay would not see Tampa for seven months.[16]

Troubled Times

As the tumult of the McKay trial subsided, the military presence at Fort Brooke came before long to resemble an occupying force more than the band of patriotic neighbors that had taken up the abandoned post in January 1861. Colonel Turner resigned his militia position to accept a captaincy in the Confederate States army. This act placed Captain John T. Lesley in charge by August 21. His tenure proved shortlived. With Confederate army orders in hand, Major Wylde Lyde Latham Bowen of Lake City took up the reins of authority in early September, bringing with him two companies of the Fourth Florida Infantry and an intention to wring order out of chaos. Bowen quickly stationed Lesley and the remaining Sunny South Guards away from Tampa at Shaw's Point near the Manatee River's mouth. As the major sought to institute regular drill and discipline among the post's remaining garrison, Lesley battled for redress, refusing to recognize Bowen's authority. That status quo held for the time being.[17]

Just as Major Bowen and Captain Lesley began to lock horns at Fort Brooke, Key West's Union authorities acted to introduce another factor into the Tampa equation. On September 6 Major William H. French had ordered all residents of Key West to take an oath of allegiance or else be removed from the island. He also directed the families of local men who had joined Confederate forces to leave. The act, according to a report dated September 8, "caused a vast amount of commotion among the secessionists here, and they are about to commence their flight Northward or towards secessia." The correspondent added: "A large number leave with their families and household goods and gods next week. All go to the first rebel port, Tampa—a poor and unimportant town in the bay—already filled to repletion with half starved rebels from Key West, and unable to support any considerable increase to her population."[18]

The Key West refugees arrived at a difficult time, although Major Bowen sensed a bright lining to the cloud. Rains had pelted Tampa through September, complicating attempts to supply the 250-man garrison (including the Sunny South Guards). With little food available and fevers sending many of his men to sick quarters, Bowen recognized the need to put the newcomers to work. He directed the construction of an artillery battery on a small, marshy island three-quarters of a mile out in Hillsborough Bay. "Both Soldiers and Citizens have done considerable work on the Battery &[,] to continue the work[,] there will be [a need] to secure the aid of the Citizens," he recorded on November 24.[19]

Fortunately, newly installed governor John Milton helped to regularize the refugees' labor contribution requirements in late November. In implementing the legislature's military act, the governor called into Confederate service the Florida Volunteer Coast Guard. It was to be made up, in good part, of one-time Key West residents. He placed one company in the charge of ship captain Henry Mulrennan, reportedly "the first man [at Key West] to hoist the rebel flag and salute it with seven guns." Mulrennan, in turn, sent a detachment to Tampa under Lieutenant Walter C. Maloney. They called themselves "The Key West Avengers."[20]

If Major Bowen believed that he would be around to supervise the Key West Avengers, events proved him incorrect to the detriment of Tampa's civilian population. In early December 1861 he and the Sunny South Guards received orders, just as the Avengers were taking up their posts at Tampa, to report immediately to Fernandina.

Essentially, this left the Avengers, who tended to be rough-hewn seamen or else hard-bitten frontier characters, to set the tone for community affairs. As Methodist minister R. L. Wiggins noted in January 1862, "I sincerely hoped that many of them would seek and obtain religion; but alas!"[21]

The problems with the Avengers did not evidence themselves clearly until the new year had gotten fairly underway. Although rumored attacks constantly aroused the fears of Tampans, they remained safe for the time being from assault. Nearby areas fared less fortunately. On January 16 United States military personnel raided Cedar Keys and destroyed the Gulf terminus of Senator David L. Yulee's Florida Rail Road. Ten days later elements of the Tampa Bay blockading force captured Captain Archibald McNeill's sloop *Mary Nevis*. Tampa had depended upon the vessel to haul mail and supplies to and from to the small settlement at Manatee (now Bradenton). In early February the raiders returned to the Gulf coast, attacking Manatee directly and also occupying for a time Abel Miranda's settlement at Big Bayou on Point Pinellas. The incursions naturally added to Tampa's refugee population.[22]

All of these events took place as news of greater Confederate disasters rained on Tampa. Among other things, General Ulysses S. Grant took control of the Tennessee River by capturing Forts Henry and Donelson on February 6 and 16. On the eighth federal troops scored another victory at the Battle of Roanoke Island, leaving Pamlico Sound and much of the North Carolina coast under Union authority. Even before Donelson fell, Confederate General Braxton Bragg had called for Florida's abandonment so that Confederate assets could be concentrated elsewhere. Meanwhile, a United States fleet was assembling at Key West aimed at an advance upon the South's largest and richest city, New Orleans. The war for southern independence had turned sour.[23]

Through January the Avengers had responded to events with restraint. Chasing around the bay area kept many of them busy much of the time. Then, threats of attack upon Tampa prompted them, despite poor winter weather, to construct artillery positions at the mouth of Spanishtown Creek in today's Hyde Park section. "All hands at work on the batteries today," recorded one member of the company on January 22. "Had to knock off several times in consequence of rain but finished the one that was began yesterday and nearly finished another." He added, "Rained very heavy all night with a plenty

19. Abel Miranda and his wife, who had settled at Point Pinellas, were among pioneers forced out of their homes by the naval blockade. (Pizzo, *Tampa Town*)

20. Major Robert Brenham Thomas. (TBHC)

of thunder and lightning." Fearful Tampans, grateful for whatever protection they could receive in increasingly difficult circumstances, embraced the coast guardsmen despite their less-than-sophisticated demeanor. "I received an invitation from some ladies in Tampa to call over and spend the evening," noted Robert Watson on February first. "I accepted the invitation and went over after supper." Of the occasion, Watson commented, "Was introduced to several of the fair sex and passed a very pleasant evening."[24]

February's disasters altered conditions markedly, and not for the better. Food supplies had dwindled, miserable weather had fostered illness and bad tempers, and threats of wartime violence had erected a pall of fear over the community and garrison. By March 1 refugees were informing authorities at Key West that "the Confederates [at Tampa have] grown desperate since the loss of Fort Donelson, proclaiming death to all Union men who dare express their sentiments." Further, the refugees reported that "the Confederate soldiers plunder the gardens in the neighborhood of Tampa as fast as any edibles are produced." As these events unfolded, the local people discovered that they no longer possessed the authority to protect themselves. On February 22, Fort Brooke's commander declared martial law in the town and suspended civilian government. For some Tampans, the hunters had just become the hunted.[25]

An important change in the Fort Brooke military command had taken place prior to the declaration of martial law, but it took some time for the development to make itself truly felt. It occurred on February 10 when Major Robert Brenham Thomas took command upon the orders of General James H. Trapier, then heading Confederate forces in Florida. Thomas was a well-regarded Tampan. A West Point graduate of the Class of 1852, he had served until resigning his commission in 1856, when he went into business with his father-in-law W. G. Ferris. Sadly, his wife and daughter soon died. In 1858 Thomas remarried, this time to Sallie McKay, daughter of Captain James McKay. He taught at the Kentucky Military Institute for one year before returning to Tampa to run the Florida House Hotel. He had helped to organize what became the Sunny South Guards in January 1861 but yearned for service closer to the front. "When the rebellion was raised, I, like others, deemed it my duty to go with the state," he explained. "I entered State Service, was transfered from that to what was called Confederate States Army and was commissioned First Lieut." Thomas distinguished himself in Virginia and Kentucky, but by the late winter of 1862 he suffered from serious illness. The Tampa assignment was intended to allow him to recuperate.[26]

The situation faced by Thomas upon his arrival at Fort Brooke would have taxed an officer in perfect health, much less a man who needed rest and family care. His forces consisted principally of Co. E, Fourth Florida Infantry ("Lafayette Rangers") and the Key West Avengers. Both units presented problems. "The military conditions which greeted Thomas at Fort Brooke were appalling," observed one historian. Thomas sought to enforce discipline as best he could, but his efforts availed little. This stayed the case even after Thomas swore the Avengers into Confederate, as opposed to state, service in March as Co. K, Seventh Florida Infantry.[27]

The unmilitary demeanor of the Rangers may have exceeded that of the Avengers, although the condition differed only by degree. One Avenger expressed shock in a diary entry about the condition of the Rangers' barracks in mid-May. "Went over and had a look at the quarters and of all the dirty houses that I ever saw they beat all," he wrote, "hog pens are cleaner." Reports continued to flow into Key West about depredations visited upon local residents by the soldiers and guardsmen, and northern newspaper correspondents were all too happy to share the tidings with their readers. In early April, it was said that "the rebels [are] growing more and more desperate, refusing rations to their prisoners who were unwilling to enlist in the rebel cause, and threaten[ing] them with violence." Deserters confirmed several weeks later "reports of want and desperation previously received from that quarter."[28]

One shining moment of heroism was allowed to Major Thomas. On April 14 a United States schooner, the *Beauregard*, drew to within one and one-half miles of the fort. Under a flag of truce, Lieutenant

William B. Eaton demanded Fort Brooke's surrender, threatening "to bombard the town" after twenty-four hours if appropriate action were not taken and suggesting that noncombatants depart. Thomas forthrightly responded, "I cannot accept the proposition to surrender, though for the sake of humanity, I accept your terms in regard to the removal of the women and children." For once his troops backed their commander. "Our men gave three cheers at the prospect of having a fight," recorded Robert Watson, "which made the men in the Yankee boat look down in the mouth as they expected to see us all look frightened and ready to surrender." Most civilians did depart, but the threat proved an empty one. Maria Louisa Daegenhardt remembered that her father took the family to a farm nine miles from town. "We took all we could carry with us not knowing what we would find when we came back," she related. "We staid 5 days but when we came back the gun boat was gone & they had not thrown a shell."[29]

When the *Beauregard* pulled away from Tampa, the time in town of the Rangers and the Avengers was growing short. Fernandina, Jacksonville, and St. Augustine had been occupied by the Union in March. That month, the state abolished all of its militia organizations and the Confederacy decided essentially to abandon coastal defense in Florida. On April 7 General Grant, however narrowly, bested the Confederates at Shiloh. By month's end New Orleans had surrendered. About the same time, Pensacola came under the United States flag. Orders arrived at Tampa in May for the departure of the Lafayette Rangers, an act accomplished on the twentieth. The Avengers moved from Spanishtown Creek into the Rangers abandoned quarters, but only temporarily. They simply awaited the arrival of replacements before themselves departing on June 27. With individual exceptions, they would not be missed.[30]

Civilian Decline

Through the months as Fort Brooke's garrison changed and circumstances altered its relationship to the community, Tampans endeavored to adjust their lives to swings of fortune and, eventually, to survive increasingly trying times. Interestingly, they had begun the period by attempting to do away with their municipal government. Amid the hoopla of secession in January 1861, unnamed "TAXPAYERS" proposed a "PUBLIC MEETING!" in order "to devise means for relieving this place from the encumbrance of a Corporation." Their call argued: "The one which now exists is beneficial to none, save a few Officers; it is a source of needless expenses to the people, and, as troubles are likely to come upon us soon and the State may be levying additional taxes, it will be well to retrench superficially."[31]

It turned out that Dr. Franklin Branch and *Peninsular* publisher William J. Spencer lay behind the scheme to abolish local government. When the citizens met, though, Henry L. Mitchell on behalf of the town council convinced the men to support continuation of the corporation but agreed to a suspension of tax collections for the ensuing year. The gathering then nominated a "no taxation" ticket. Headed by Hamlin V. Snell as mayoral candidate, it carried Spencer as its choice for town marshal. Tampa's larger merchants, with John Darling's leadership, attempted to forestall the attempt to curtail town services. They failed. On February 2 the "no taxation" ticket prevailed, although it appears that the results pleased few. When the town's second newspaper—Alfonso DeLaunay's staunchly pro-secessionist *Sunny South*—carried on February 19 a report of the mayor's inaugural ball, it noted, "There was but slim attendance, considering the general invitation to the citizens of Tampa—and visitors."[32]

By the time of the February election, some Tampans already were voting on the town's future with their feet. As early as December 1860, Leroy G. Lesley had advertised that he was selling out preparatory to a move to Hernando County. With the passage of time, numerous others followed. Candymaker Jose Vigil departed for New Orleans in early 1861, for example, while Lesley made good on his earlier declaration. By the next year the trickle had mounted to a slow stream, especially after Fort Donelson's fall in February. William B. Hooker removed his family to a Hernando County plantation. Christopher L. Friebele closed his Tampa store and reopened at Brooksville. John Jackson carried his loved ones "some 10 or 15 miles from town." Others trod similar paths.[33]

Some Tampans likely followed another stream, that of area Unionists seeking United States military protection. By mid-summer 1861 Union troops had landed on Egmont Key in Tampa Bay's mouth, and thereafter the tiny island and the ships that called there served as beacons for refugees. The key's status became official in the winter of 1862. "I mentioned in one of my late letters that Capt. Eaton of the barque Ethan Allen was about to take possession of a light house in the neighborhood of Tampa Bay, and make it a refuge for the Union men of Florida, who come off to seek protection on board his ship," reported a correspondent of the *Boston Daily Journal* on March 7. He added, "I learn that his plan is working successfully, and that he has a colony of several families within range of his guns." The refugee camp remained on the island through the war, a thorn in the side of local Confederates.[34]

Perhaps even more Tampans would have departed the vicinity in 1861 and early 1862 had it not been for the opportunity to share in the potential prize of Fort Brooke. Secession meant that the United States government no longer controlled its large military reservation at Tampa. As seen, the Florida secession convention acted in April 1861 to assume authority over it. The delegates, in doing so, handed control to the Hillsborough County board of commissioners. Three months later the commissioners advertised for proposals to survey the property. W. T. Coons won the bid. The Confederate military's presence slowed down his work, though. Coons managed to deliver a preliminary map in February 1862 (he named the principal new east-west avenue as "Jeff Davis Street"), but the surveyor proved unable to deliver a completed plat satisfactory to the board. Meanwhile, the county lawmakers champed at the bit to obtain desperately need funds from land sales, while Tampa speculators' expectations of profit soared high. Conditions thereafter slipped so low that in May 1862 the commission suspended the survey attempt and removed all documents connected with it, together with the rest of the county's records, to Cork, a rural community four or five miles west of today's Plant City.[35]

The disappointment of the speculators could not possibly have matched the heartbreak by then suffered in many Tampa households. It began with some mothers' tears as their sons prepared to go to war. Later, news of casualties stirred even more widespread grief.[36] Nancy Jackson believed that her "sorest trial" during the war came with "the enlistment of two of their sons in the Confederate army." She related her experience to an interviewer:

> When my John enlisted with the Confederates I though I could not have it so. His father was sick then and I knew they were to be sworn in that day [April 25, 1862]. I slipped out just from my own impulse, with my sunbonnet on my head, and went over, or started to go over to where Captain Robert Thomas had the boys in camp. John was under age, only a schoolboy, and I was his mother and was

> going to forbid their taking him away. When I got near enough I saw them all in line with their hands raised to be sworn in. I knew I was too late. I nearly fainted. I stopped where I was under a tree, and finally got back home. Father saw something was the matter with me as there were tears in my eyes, and he said, "Mama—that is what he always called me—what is the matter?" I managed to tell him. He tried to comfort me, telling me he did not believe Thomas would have paid any attention to me if I had got there before they were sworn in.[37]

While many of Tampa's women stood loyally and enthusiastically behind the Confederate cause and the service of their men in support of it, complications necessarily arose that divided families and loved ones. A number of couples married in order to enjoy intimacy and the strength of commitment before the young husband departed to an uncertain future. Not unusually they did so without parental consent or, at least, the consent of both parents. Maria Louisa Daegenhardt recalled such a situation and the loneliness of a bride who could not acknowledge her marriage publicly. Her story stemmed from the June 1862 nuptials of her sister to blacksmith John Henry Krause, a private in Company B, Seventh Florida Infantry, and from the young couple's concerns about father John Daegenhardt, a "true Christian" who "did not believe in slavery." As Maria remembered:

> They wanted their marriage to be very secret as he was to leave right away to join his company in Charlston. Sister Mary gave me .50 cents to keep quiet about it, but I just had to tell my Teacher [Louisa B. Porter]. I knew she loved sister Mary. She sent her a large bunch of Roses & sister wondered how she knew, but I never told of it and afterward bought a prettie brown Pitcher for my 50 cents & thought I made a big bargan. I kept it so long.[38]

John Henry Krause's departure from Tampa for service in the Confederate States army highlighted yet another drain on the town's population during 1861 and 1862. Some young men—such as Robert B. Thomas, James McKay, Jr., *Peninsular* publisher William J. Spencer, its editor Simon Turman, Jr., Drew Givens, and T. W. Givens—could not wait to serve the cause. They left Tampa in 1861 searching for a unit in which to enlist. As time passed, local companies such as the Sunny South Guards entered Confederate service and were called northward. A second spurt of enlistments came in February and March 1862,

21. John A. Henderson in his Civil War uniform.

after the Confederate Congress passed a conscription act covering white males eighteen to thirty-five years of age. Rather than await the draft, dozens of the area's remaining eligible men signed up with what became Company B, Seventh Florida Infantry. Krause served in its ranks. Captain James Gettis, and Lieutenants William B. Henderson, John A. Henderson, and Robert F. Nunez led its men.[39]

The departures, from whatever cause, left Tampa a place populated mostly by white women, children, and older men, plus a declining number slaves (some left when owners moved away) and whatever troops made up the garrison. This particularly was so after Company B, Seventh Florida Infantry, filed from town in the summer of 1862. For the civilians, conditions deteriorated with the local economy's collapse and pressures on available food and supplies brought about by the influx of Key West refugees. Already in the spring of 1861, times had turned hard. "Business is quite dull," reported William Ferris on May 3, "we are scarcely doing anything in the line of selling goods." Less than one year later, rumors reaching Key West insisted, "The state of things—Tampa is fearful." The account continued: "They are literally starving. They have no coffee, no tea, no flour, no cloth of any kind, except their common homespun, for which they pay $1.25 per yard. They all say they cannot hold out much longer if the blockade is not broken by England."[40]

If ever a situation cried out for leadership, this one was it. By late spring 1862 Tampans yearned for better days and for a guide to take them there. As events proceeded, the assistance of the United States government permitted them to turn once again to the man upon whom they repeatedly had relied in the past for answers to difficult problems. A hint that such a possibility existed came in late spring. Key West Avenger Robert Watson, then stationed near Clear Water Harbor, noted the moment in his diary. "A horseman came from Clearwater with the information that Lt. Maloney had arrived at that place," he recorded on May 16, "and that Mr. Jas. McKay & sons had arrived at Tampa."[41]

22. The Leroy G. Lesley home in Tampa. Even as late as 1862, many settlers held out hope that their village might retain its simple charms and survive the larger conflict with its way of life and its natural beauty largely unscathed. (Lesley Family)

23. An artist's representation of Tampa Confederate Joseph Robles capturing a Union raiding party. (TBHC)

"O Lord, O Lord have mercy on me"

A Question of Survival, 1862-1864

The Civil War's middle years found Tampa a town without purpose, a small gathering of bewildered souls bent on finding a way out from under the specter of violent destruction but who often stood at odds with one another in making the attempt. Forces centered far beyond the community exerted almost unbearable pressures that, if successful, would have rendered their efforts a tragic failure. It seemed to townspeople at times, especially when war visited them firsthand, as if all hope were lost. Had it not been for the vision of a man once accused of treason, the events of those years might have proved the fears far more appropriate than any fanciful sense of hope.

In some respects, the tale involved the struggle of two intelligent and determined men to achieve mutually inconsistent goals, the first of whom was James McKay. By way of background, the captain's experiences had taken him after his fall 1861 incarceration as a Union prisoner of war first to Key West and then to Washington, D.C., before returning him to Tampa. During that period, the captain had exploited his pre-war friendships with United States military and government officials to gain the attention of key figures at the Lincoln Administration's highest levels, a process that, ultimately, resulted in his release from custody.[1]

But, and this should be remembered, McKay acted from motivations far greater than his simple self interest. He believed that the

24. and 25. Captain James McKay, Sr., and Matilda Cail McKay. (McKay, *Pioneer Florida*)

economic future of the Tampa Bay region and, for that matter, all of southwest Florida depended upon the cattle industry, particularly the ability of local owners to sell their beeves for an advantageous price paid in hard cash. Undoubtedly, most area residents agreed with him. Even those Tampa merchants who begrudged McKay's 1860 relocation of his shipping operation to Charlotte Harbor understood the industry's key significance. The immediate problem arose from the fact that neither the Union nor the Confederacy desired to pay owners other than in paper money or bonds, assuming that they wanted to pay for the beef at all. At Havana, on the other hand, buyers willingly parted with a gold doubloon (worth about $15) for each head of cattle cleared through customs. The answer for McKay, then, was to find a way to protect the herds until he and the other owners safely could ship their cattle to Cuba.[2]

A second part of McKay's dilemma concerned the flagging confidence that he and other prominent cattlemen held in the Confederate nation's ultimate victory. The captain and many of his associates had been Unionists at the time of secession. While events had muted their public opposition to withdrawal from the Union, it had not turned them into Rebels. This fact permitted McKay, during his imprisonment, quietly to approach United States officials with certain propositions. "I would prefer my property in the Hands of the Federal Govt which is known to those in authority here," he wrote from Key West in October 1861, "but I can not have it so expressed to go home, my family and all I possess after many years hard work is in Florida." His overtures eventually attracted the attention of Secretary of State William Seward who, in January 1862, ordered authorities to deliver McKay to the senior cabinet officer's Washington office.[3]

McKay's stay in the nation's capital came during heady times and resulted in the sealing of a bargain that he hoped would ensure his own survival and that of the Tampa Bay region's other settlers. He got to the city during the week when Fort Henry fell into Union hands. He remained there when Fort Donelson surrendered and soldiers raised the United States flag over the Tennessee capitol at Nashville. The captain witnessed firsthand preparations for General George B. McClellan's massive Peninsula campaign and likely overheard talk of the imminent assault upon New Orleans. In such an atmosphere it must have seemed as if the Confederacy's days clearly were numbered and that the men who would decide southwest Florida's future wore blue uniforms, not gray. McKay understood that, under the circumstances, it would take a tempting proposition to interest the United States government. The one that he worked out with Seward fit the bill. The captain agreed, on behalf of his associates, to turn over 30,000 head of cattle to the Union military in return for the early occupation of Tampa and protection of the cattle trade. Presumably placing his personal approval on the project, Abraham Lincoln intervened to allow McKay's release from prisoner of war status on March 20.[4]

The captain took one month to reach Key West following his release from custody and almost another before he landed at Tampa. McKay must have used a good portion of that time pondering the challenges ahead. To the good, he probably knew that his son-in-law Major Robert B. Thomas commanded Fort Brooke's Confederate contingent. At Key West, he likely learned of Tampans' dissatisfaction with the post's garrison and also of the United States Navy's plans for the town's occupation. He would have been encouraged to find that Pensacola soon would be taken, an act that occurred on May 12. All in all, things appeared to be going well. "You may rest assured," he informed the army's adjutant general on April 24, "of everything in my power being done for the restoration of the Union."[5]

The exact date in mid-May on which McKay returned to Tampa is uncertain. News of his coming and the reasons therefore may have preceded him, though, thus explaining why the county commission hurriedly transferred the county's records to the countryside on the seventh. It is known that, from Tampa on May 14, Presbyterian minister Edmond Lee informed his wife at Manatee, "I am still in hopes we shall soon have peace." Within days thereafter the Confederacy's Lafayette Rangers departed Fort Brooke and the Key West Avengers began preparing to do the same. The days passed away as McKay and knowledgeable townspeople awaited the coming of the Union warships, an event perhaps already scheduled for June 30.[6]

John W. Pearson and the Oklawaha Rangers

The carefully laid plans almost worked and likely would have had not chance (or, at least, unfortunate timing) decided the matter otherwise, thus introducing to Tampa and James McKay the man who would become the captain's nemesis. His name was John W. Pearson. A South Carolina native who had helped to develop Putnam County's Orange Springs as a resort prior to secession, Pearson had embraced the Confederacy wholeheartedly, raising his own company of volunteers—the Oklawaha Rangers—to fight for its cause. The very idea of Floridians cooperating with the Union outraged Pearson. When—sometime in the week or two prior to June 30—he and his men arrived at Fort Brooke to relieve the Key West Avengers, they long had been spoiling for a fight. As his biographer noted of the captain, "He brought [to Tampa] a pugnacious attitude that had been lacking in previous [Fort Brooke] commanders."[7]

Major Thomas's leave-taking and his replacement by Captain Pearson occurred so soon before the anticipated Union movement that McKay could not alert Key West authorities in time. So, the long-awaited warships steamed into Hillsborough Bay, as planned, to be met with a surprise. "On Monday morning, June 30, the gunboat [*U.S.S. Sagamore*] hove into sight in the bay," Pearson reported, "and after sounding and maneuvering to get a favorable position came to anchor, turned her broadside to us and opened her ports, and then started a launch, with a lieutenant and 20 men, bearing a flag of truce, toward the shore."[8] As would have been expected given his fervor, Fort Brooke's commander decided to confront the sailors before they touched land. A naval officer described what then occurred:

> Men to be seen occasionally at the town. Returning the 2d cutter threw up one oar as a signal the rebels would not surrender—Lieut.

26. The *Ethan Allen* was one of the Union vessels that called upon Tampa to surrender. (*Tampa Bay History*)

> Bigelow raising his hat, "Good day sir" to officer in rebel boat . . . no reply by the rebels—Lieut. Bigelow "I am sent by the Commander of the 'Sagamore' and 'Ethan Allen' to demand surrender of town unconditionally and all the ammunition"—Rebel replied "Have you any written communication—We have no such thing in the book as surrender," and turned away for the shore. They were given time to leave the town until 6 P M when the 'Sagamore' opened on the town with the 11 inch and the rifle. After the third shot from us they replied from one of their three batteries firing solid shot which fell short two hundred yards or more.[9]

Thus, on June 30, 1862, Tampa suffered its first real taste of war at a moment when a good number of local people expected peace to blossom. Sad to say, the trials had some time left to run. The United States naval officer in charge likely assumed, since he expected the town's quick surrender, that he needed only to evidence a face-saving show of force. "The Yankees being refused the unconditional surrender of Tampa, and giving but three hours to remove the women and children, began to shell the place, ceasing with night," explained Methodist minister W. L. Murphy. Unsure now of his next step, the officer withdrew his ships overnight, perhaps anticipating word from town. When it did not arrive, he returned the following morning for a second attempt at carrying out his orders. "After two and a half hours shooting next day, they went away," Murphy continued, "by a gracious providence having done no damage to either man or beast, house or fence."[10]

Thanks to Captain Pearson's intransigence, the affair of June 30-July 1 left Tampa firmly in Rebel hands. Newspapers in the North and the South trumpeted his defiance, some insisting that his refusal to surrender had been buttressed by "three or four terrific yells" from his men. Others noted that he had duped the navy men by positioning pine logs in gun batteries in the place of missing cannon. A *New York Herald* correspondent offered a different slant on events, though, by claiming slackening courage on the defenders' parts when an artillery shell destroyed one of their positions. "The second shot [fired on the morning of July 1] was a direct line shot, and struck directly in the battery and silenced it," he wrote, "the rebels taking refuge behind the large oak trees that stood near, and most of them fled to the woods for a more secure place of refuge soon after."[11]

The incident also gave birth to numerous war tales that survived through the years, some of which were anchored in real happenings. To cite one example that would carry tremendous importance to the town, storytellers later would recount how lawyer James Gettis emerged as the town's Confederate hero. Designated captain of Company E, Seventh Florida Infantry, the forty-six year old Pennsylvanian had found himself too ill to leave with his company three days earlier. Now, he heartily grasped the opportunity to fight the Yankees. "He took command of one of

27. The modest frame house that was the law office of James Gettis. (*Sunland Tribune*)

the batteries manned by a green squad of my men who never fired a cannon before," Pearson reported. "Captain Gettis acted with that cool firmness which characterizes the man in all his various spheres at the bar and legislative councils."[12]

The Crumbling of Slavery and Other Echoes

Aside from stirring a few colorful tales and wreaking a little property damage, the bombardments of June 30-July 1, 1862, initiated processes that changed Tampa's future in significant ways. For one thing, with the explosions likely came the local beginnings of what the great African American sociologist W. E. B. Du Bois called the "slow, stubborn mutiny of the Negro slave."[13] Just as was true of local whites, slaves endured the terror of violence in a world gone mad, an experience that would change anyone. Although written regarding an attack in 1863, Maria Louisa Daegenhardt left her impressions of the war's intense emotional impact on black and white:

> While we were at dinner one large shell came whizzing ove[r] our home knocking the shingles off the roof of the dining room. We were all so frightened. Mothers said, "O children pray." I ran quick to the corner where the old Franklin stove was, knelt down,& quickly said my prayer[—]now I lay me down to sleep. O can I ever for get those day[s]. Mother quick told [us] to come & go out of the town. We hurried up along the river bank. There was an old negro woman living there. We went to her house, shells flying. Then we saw a bright flame of fire up the river. We ran down to the bank to look . . . While we were all there looking, a shell came near us & bursted and O such screaming. The negro woman fell down on her hands & knees hollowing, ["]O Lord, O Lord have mercy on me."[14]

Just as the bombardments terrorized, they also inspired slaves to consider the war's implications. President Abraham Lincoln had not forgotten Tampa. Time and war had not passed the town by. For those slaves not in the direct line of fire, the sounds of artillery blasts and the whistle of cannon balls began to play like the music of freedom. When they could, black men and women would strain to better see and hear these evidences of the war for emancipation. Sarah Hanes Brown, a Lesley family slave, recalled laboring with others at salt works on the Alafia River. "Sarah would tell how the slaves would wade out into the mouth of the river when they heard the cannons firing," recorded Theodore Lesley," and they could see the Union gunboats, across the bay, bombarding Tampa."[15]

Wait, you say, the Civil War in 1862 was not yet the titanic struggle over emancipation that it was to become. Remember, though, that the Battle of Antietam was fought only two and one-half months after Tampa's initial shelling. It took President Lincoln less than one week thereafter to announce his intention to issue the Emancipation Proclamation, effective January 1, 1863. No documentary evidence exists to indicate when Tampa slaves learned of the action, but it appears likely that the news got to many of them within several weeks. The community's white Unionists would have received the word relatively quickly from blockading ships and refugees coming and going. A few of them already believed that the institution was doomed. As O. B. Hart declared, "I foresaw at the beginning of the rebellion that the ordinance of secession was the death knell of slavery." One overheard conversation within the informality of a small town household would have sufficed to convey the message of the war's new purpose.[16]

Slowly, the changing order of things manifested itself in town. Some slaves doubtlessly joined their fellow bondsmen from the countryside to escape to Egmont Key and the blockading squadron. "By the year 1863 the blockading boats on the Florida Coast were exerting every effort possible in lending aid to the runaway negro slave," remembered Dick Robles. "At Tampa and Bay Port, where war-ships guarded and patrolled the coast, many negroes had stealth[il]y stolen away to the beaches, signaled the boats and been carried away by them to Key West, and other centers then in the hands of the Federals."[17]

Those slaves who remained in town tended over time to begin exercising more independence of thought and action. Theodore Lesley illustrated the point with a reminiscence about Sarah Hanes Brown:

> One day during the war Sarah went into the house and found grandmother [Indiana Livingston Lesley] rocking Aunt India and both of them crying. She asked them why they were crying, and grandmother replied that her husband and father of her child was away in the war and that he might be killed and they never would see him again, etc. Sarah then asked her if she remembered when she was first brought to Tampa she would cry for her mother and they would spank her. And for her not to cry as it would not do her any good.[18]

Despite laws to the contrary, some slaves began to meet together far from the prying eyes and ears of their owners. We know, for example, that religious gatherings often took place. The Reverend H. H. Hunter preserved Tampa slaves' memories concerning "places where they could listen to itinerant ministers who brought them messages of hope and comfort from the Bible." Hunter wrote, "Several old citizens recall one of them, located about three miles west of the city, where services were held in a discarded wooden shack." He then described the slaves' creative solution to a most-difficult problem. "Due to the long hours that the slaves had to work, many of the services, if not most of them, were held after dark," Hunter observed. "Their method of lighting the church for those services was ingenious. Platforms were built outside of each window and in front of the door, and on these raised surfaces fires of pine knots were lighted, giving enough illumination inside for the minister to hold services."[19]

It would not be long before the clandestine meetings evolved into a more public demonstration of growing independence. The traditions of Mt. Sinai African Methodist Episcopal Zion Church indicate that, by 1863, several slave members of Tampa's Methodist Episcopal Church South sought and received tacit, if not official, permission to withdraw in order to form their own fellowship. The names passed down include those of Dorcas Bryant and her son Samuel, Samuel's future wife Sarah Hanes Brown, and others. Reportedly, these individuals began to hold informal services not in the Methodist Church but in the county courthouse.[20]

Just as the bombardments eventually helped to alter the institution of slavery at Tampa, they affected, as well, the strength of Confederate resistance to the Union military threat. This happened because Captain John W. Pearson realized from his ineffectual attempts to strike United States warships on June 30-July 1, 1862, that he needed to improve the quality of his artillery. Dick Robles recalled that Fort Brooke's two remaining guns—they were called "Hornet" and "Target"—"were not over 3 feet in length" and that one of them "shot a shot about the size of a stick of dynamite." Pearson's superiors declined to provide modern weapons, so the captain set out to make his own. He, with J. J. Lovingston and Wesley Mansell, traveled to Orange Springs where Pearson owned a foundry. There, they rifled both cannons, thereby extending their range, accuracy, and firepower.[21]

It was thought that Pearson's reworked artillery now could dominate Hillsborough Bay down to Ballast Point, if not further. An Ocala newspaper suggested that the Union navy, after learning of the new development, tried stealth to overcome the captain's firepower. According to the report, on October 26, 1862, a vessel appeared in Hillsborough Bay, "with patched sails and without any colors flying, having the general appearance of a merchant vessel running the blockade." Pearson declined to allow local pilots to attend the ship, and the following morning "the innocent looking craft commenced shelling the town." Only slight damage resulted to two houses, the report continued, because "the vessel did not get within range of our guns."[22]

The October 1862 test of Fort Brooke's guns kept the United States Navy away from Tampa for five months until Captain Pearson blundered in a manner that compelled the warships to return as a matter of honor. The set of incidents began when Pearson grew short-tempered at the steady drain of area slaves to the blockading squadron. In late March 1863 he ordered Lieutenant Robert D. Harrison to take an eighteen-man detachment to Gadsden's Point to disrupt the traffic. On the twenty-seventh Harrison dressed three of the men as slaves, complete with blackened faces, and, in the case of two, dresses. When Union ships appeared, the three signaled with smoke and by waving a flag that they wanted to be picked up. A boat with sailors pulled toward shore under a flag of truce, as the disguised Confederates shouted "Thank God! Thank God! I am free!" As soon as the boat hit the beach, one of the Pearson men grabbed his musket and demanded the sailors' surrender. Met with a refusal, the rest of the Confederate detachment fired, wounding four men. The blockading vessel then shelled the beach, while the sailors made their escape.[23]

The Confederate treachery infuriated Union naval commanders who determined to inflict punishment upon Tampa in revenge. Subsequently, the steamer *Tahoma* and the schooner *Beauregard* entered Hillsborough Bay on April 2 and approached Ballast Point. The *Tahoma*'s captain then set out in a gig to survey the situation and to test Fort Brooke's guns. When the boat neared within one-quarter mile of the shoreline, Captain Pearson sent three shells screaming toward the tiny vessel. Having tricked the Confederates into revealing the locations of their artillery positions, the Union captain returned to his steamer, rearranged his small flotilla "so as to give them a raking fire," and blasted away at Fort Brooke and Tampa. One *Tahoma* officer estimated that 150 "shot and shell" struck "square into the town driving the Rebels from their Battery." Even more importantly for the future, when Pearson shot back he got off only

28. William S. Spencer. (Hillsborough County Sheriff's Office)

one round and his fire then fell short "about three hundred yards." The vaunted rifled cannon had failed. The United States Navy no longer feared their power, and the warships would return.[24]

Life Amid the Ruins

The tremendous pounding endured by Tampans on April 2, 1863, created panic and resulted in substantial harm to property. The *Tahoma* officer declared that "with the glass I could see that many of the houses were knocked higher than a burnt boot." John Darling concurred. "We have been damaged more on this occasion than previously," he informed a friend. Damage that some historical accounts have attributed to the June 30-July 1, 1862, bombardments, almost certainly happened at this time. W. G. Ferris's house on the north side of Washington Street between Florida and Morgan Avenues took a hit, for instance. The shots found the courthouse, as well. The building was struck "in the gable end and the shell went clear through the wooden structure." One account noted that, when the impact occurred, county tax assessor William S. Spencer was shaving in his assigned room, whereupon "he took quick flight, leaving his office open." Clerk of the Circuit Court W. C. Brown soon passed the open door and saw the tax records lying unattended. He grabbed them up "and took the books to his home on Morgan Street near Washington for safekeeping." Having done so, Brown stored the tax books in his attic and forgot about them. They remained there unremembered for more than fifty years.[25]

The April 1863 incident capped off nine months that had seen conditions deteriorate in Tampa, along with the regard local people held for Captain Pearson. For one thing, the number of the town's inhabitants had continued to slide, a fact that helps to explain the lack of human casualties from bombardment. "Great numbers of the population who were financially able moved away," Theodore Lesley concluded. They relocated, he found, mainly to Cork, Alafia, and Lake Keystone. As early as March 1862 the Baptist church had offered letters of dismission to all of its members. The Roman Catholic priest departed in January 1863. With the "hard times," reported a church historian, many of Father Mailley's parishioners left, as well. Some viewed Tampa merely as a "dead town."[26]

There was more. Also in January 1863, smallpox beset interior settlers, cutting Tampa off from its hinterlands. In that same month, the Emancipation Proclamation theoretically freed local slaves while townspeople reeled from news that their own Company K, Fourth Florida Infantry, had been mauled at the Battle of Murfreesboro, Tennessee. Simeon Moody and Thomas Cothran died there. Among area men wounded were B. P. Haskins, James H. Johnson, Hiram A. McLeod, Jasper Sloan, John W. Weeks, and Thomas Willis, while names of the captured (several of whom also were wounded) included Robert F. Fletcher, George W. D. Handcock, John M. Hendry, William W. Lemacks, Samuel A. Miley, and Elbert White. Reports of the heroism displayed by many of the company's men did little to assuage the pain felt in local households.[27]

At the same time, Tampa's men in service agonized over word received of conditions at home. Within weeks following the Battle of Murfreesboro, to cite one example, Captain John T. Lesley, the commander of the Fourth Florida's Company K, resigned his commission to return home. "I have several negros now uncontrolled and a large stock of Cattle roaming at large which will necessarily go to distruction unless some attention is given to them," he informed superiors. "[B]esides My effects are in that portion of the State of Florida where it is almost impossible to obtain provision at any price." He concluded, "My private affairs have been neglected and are fast going to ruin."[28]

As Tampans looked around them to try to understand why matters had gone "to ruin," they increasingly blamed John W. Pearson. In good part, their sentiments had arisen from the captain's enthusiastic enforcement of the Confederate Conscription Act. This law, passed in April 1862, had subjected all white males aged 18 to 35 to the military draft. Five months later the Confederate Congress had extended the upper age limit to 45. The statutes created dilemmas, as would be expected, for area residents who did not support secession or else simply did not want to serve in the Confederate army. Additionally, it placed tremendous burdens on family members and friends who backed the Confederacy but whose loved ones desired to avoid military service for whatever reason. In a sparsely inhabited frontier region, the law eventually would touch just about everyone in a unwelcome fashion.[29]

The Oklawaha Rangers, to the contrary, held no reservations about the conscription act and, at Pearson's orders, set out looking for eligible men. By August 1862 reports of their excessive zeal were reaching Union authorities. "These guerrillas are scouring the woods, looking after deserters and conscripts," noted the *Tahoma*'s captain, "they rob, murder, and steal indiscriminately, if the reports of the refugees are to be credited; Union men they threaten to hang, and do shoot, as we have lamentable proof." He added, "It is said that every man capable of bearing arms has been forced to join the rebels in this part of Florida." Onetime Hillsborough County school teacher Francis C. M. Boggess, then working in the cattle business at Fort Meade, endured the experience. "The woods were full of conscript officers," he recorded. "They allowed a man no time to prepare to move his family," Boggess continued. "He was arrested and carried off at once. He had no choice; he had no rights." Tales of acts of cruelty soon circulated in Tampa and elsewhere in the region. O. B. Hart later recounted such a story, that of "a good old gentleman acquaintance of mine." This individual, according to Hart, "had been hanged, not quite to death, to make him tell where his sons in the swamps were."[30]

Resistance to the conscription act in south Florida and other cattle regions helped to convince the Confederate Congress that its troops needed beef more than it needed soldiers, but their action failed to stem the Rangers' excesses. In October 1862 the legislators approved an amendment to exempt one man from the draft for every 500 head of cattle. James McKay's partner Jacob Summerlin received authority to decide upon exemptions for south Florida. With uncounted herds roaming the prairies, virtually anyone who desired such could be exempted. Still, the Oklawaha Rangers pressed their cause, searching for individuals who chose not to apply for exception. "While I was at the farm, Lt. [David] Hall, Capt. Pearson's conscription officer was through the country after deserters and men subject to the war with orders to take me dead or alive and one evening he passed 400 yards from me," William McCullough recalled of events occurring at Fort Meade in June 1863. "Lt. Hall was gathering every man in the country, that he had special orders to take my humble self and carry me to Tampa where they would handle your humble servant in a public manner—for what—for making free use of his tongue against their most unholy cause, and for what the seceders claim to be fighting for."[31]

By the summer of 1863, the seeds of trouble planted by their excesses ripened for Captain Pearson and the Rangers. Perhaps partially from objections to the actions of some of their comrades, a number of men "took leg bail" as they used to say and desertion emerged as a major problem within the company. It grew to such an extent that Pearson discontinued sending reports of troop strength and desertions to his superiors. Tampans, too, made their feelings known. They forwarded their complaints directly to Pearson's commanding officer Brigadier General Joseph Finegan, charging the Rangers with "bad discipline and interference with private property." Taken with Pearson's blunder that resulted in the bombardment of April 2, these circumstances compelled most Tampans to look forward to the captain's departure from the town. Their patience received its reward in October 1863 when the Rangers left Fort Brooke for other duties.[32]

Up to that time townspeople had received little news to cheer them. They maintained no municipal government (marital law had seen to that), most local stores had closed, and communications with the rest of the South had deteriorated. The stage coach still ran between Tampa and Ocala, but it came and went irregularly. Besides, "the stage was not very comfortable" and "the trip was certainly tiresome." By the summer of 1863 a letter typically required a minimum of one week to ten days to arrive from Tallahassee. Both newspapers long had suspended. Finally, the shelling of April 2 had closed the last available school. Luckily, O. B. Hart stepped in to keep the cause of education alive. "In consequence of the frequent bombardment of this place, and the unsettled state of the community, our school teacher Mrs. Louisa B. Porter, considering her school broken up, and being about to take steps looking to a removal from here," he informed the Duval County probate judge on April 3, "I Ossian B. Hart guardian of Mary E. Hart in order to secure to said Mary the advantages of continuous schooling including music and use of piano, have this day agreed to pay said teacher at the rate of four hundred

29. Members of the Baptist Church received letters of dismission in 1862. After that time, services were suspended for a year and one half. (Sherrill, *Call to Greatness*)

dollars a year, to remain and teach said Mary, said teacher reserving the privilege of making a school under such limitations and restrictions as she may chose."[33]

Who would be surprised, then, to learn that Tampans increasingly had turned to the comforts of religion? Father Mailley held Mass until January 1863 and occasionally visited his parish thereafter. For the Baptists, unfortunately, the picture shone not quite so brightly. After March 19, 1862, they enjoyed services only on rare occasions for the next year and one half. "The church has been in a languishing condition up to [August 12, 1863]," clerk J. D. Haygood recorded, "when we succeeded in obtaining the services of our Brother Edgar Hames, who has preached to us every Sunday when other appointments did not conflict." Hames's availability seemingly extended only to December, after which Baptist services, apparently, ceased for the war's duration.[34]

That left the Methodist church as the white community's center for religious celebration and comfort, much of which was expressed in song and the act of singing. As seen earlier in this chapter, the congregation's African American members in 1862 and 1863 chose to begin gathering separately at the courthouse. Likely, white Roman Catholics, Baptists, and nonbelievers filled the empty places. One of Louisa Porter's students, Emma Miller, left her memories of the church, as articulated by a descendant:

> Emma joined the Methodist Church.
>
> It was an austere church then. It was also heroic, yet without bigotry—a combination rare in any group banded together to follow a cause. . . . It was stripped of vain pomp and glory, but the words used in administering its sacraments had worn a rich panoply of tradition long before King James was born; these words marched like an army with banners.
>
> The church was bare. Out of this bareness arose new splendors. For one, the congregation sang without organ or choir. Perhaps because hymnbooks were scarce, perhaps because some people present could not read, the minister read the hymn aloud, two lines at a time, so that singing and reading alternated. Emma would listen, caught in the very vortex of beauty, for over her head voices of the slaves in the gallery [before their withdrawal from the church] poured down to join the voices around her. When the hymn had been sung through, the congregation sang the last two lines again, turning, to be ready to kneel. That surging change in the direction of the voices was beauty almost too great to be borne. She was engulfed in majesty—winged soprano voices, interlacing tenors and altos, voices that came between these in untaught harmonies colorful as tapestry, basses like drums of eternity. She turned with the others. She knelt and prayed.[35]

One minister above all others could be credited for creating in the Methodist church a place of community gathering and sanctuary. A native of Ireland, William L. Murphy had been preaching since 1846. He first had come to Tampa in 1856, departed for other assignments, and returned during the war as the district presiding elder. He was, it was noted of him, "a devout Christian, an able minister, and a gentleman in all the relations of life." He devoted himself to Tampa. "It is my impression that these are noble people," he declared on one occasion in 1862, "good Methodists." His labors through the difficult period would have exhausted anyone, and so they did Murphy. He would die not long after the peace in 1865, mourned as "a man of prayer, of faith and of zeal [and] a good and useful preacher."[36]

Slim Rays of Hope

Despite the community's seemingly irredeemable predicament, a few rays of hope from sources other than the churches spread a measure of warmth to offer comfort to townspeople. As time passed, several leading citizens returned from the army, whether from exhaustion, illness, or wounds. John T. Lesley's February 1863 resignation already has been mentioned. William B. Henderson's leave-taking had come the month before, while James Gettis's followed in April. Pneumonia sent Robert F. Nunez south in August. To remain at home, these veterans often accepted local Confederate government positions. In this manner John Darling became receiver of moneys for the Land Office, John A. Henderson accepted the duties of war tax collector, and Erasmus M. Thompson served as receiver under the sequestration act.[37]

A number of individuals helped to prop up the local economy and to supply necessities through blockade running. Christopher L. Friebele and Edward A. Clarke, married to Wall family sisters, had partnered for that purpose by 1862. William G. Ferris with his steamer *Scottish Chief* made the dangerous run to Havana, as well. Jacob Mickler came to town from St. Augustine late in 1862 and made at least one trip. Samuel Mitchell likewise profited from his daring, as did William H. Kendrick. A number of others also braved the blockade from Tampa and nearby places.[38]

Naturally, James McKay led all the others when it came to slipping through the blockade. From summer 1862 until October 1863 he passed unharmed through six voyages to Cuba. McKay's steamer *Salvor* having been sold for prize money by its navy captors, the captain used the *Scottish Chief*. As was true of most of the other blockade runners, he carried cotton as his cargo (the legislature had outlawed cattle exportation). Bringing back medicines, rum, foodstuffs, and other supplies, McKay and his fellow runners relieved in at least a small measure the deprivation endured by the region's frontier settlers.[39]

That relief came at a cost to Tampans, a dynamic that they were beginning to take for granted. The navy rankled at the runners' success and decided to make an example of the *Scottish Chief*. On October 16 it was docked several miles above town on the Hillsborough River, along with a schooner, the *Kate Dale*. The Oklawaha Rangers had bid their farewell days before, to be replaced on the twelfth by Company A, Second Battalion, Florida Volunteers under the command of former United States senator John Westcott.[40] The attack commenced the next morning. O. B. Hart described it in some detail:

30. The burning of the *Scottish Chief* was a heartfelt loss to many Tampans. (*Tampa Tribune*)

> About 110 Yankee sailors after shelling us all day, landed at night near Ballast Point, . . . and dragging a whale boat on land towards this place several miles, hid the boat in a thicket and took a bee line for the river several miles below here, where the steamer *Scottish Chief* lay, preparing to run the blockade. They reached her about sun rise, drew her across to the South side of the river, burst her and with five of her crew, started back to the place of landing, where they were overtaken by about 31 soldiers and citizens, about 12 of whom were mounted, and after a sharp but short conflict were driven into the bay and to their boats in confusion, with two of our citizens prisoners, making several prisoners in all taken by them.
>
> Our troops and people brought home five Yankee prisoners, two of them wounded, and one, a very old man, who had become worn down by fatigue. Also some small arms, such as Enfield rifles, Colt's revolvers, swords, cartridge boxes, haversacks, hard biscuits, caps, pants, jackets, and some very fine jewelry and other spoils.[41]

The loss of the *Scottish Chief* and the *Kate Dale* struck Tampans a hard blow, but not as severe a one as the bombardment. The morning of the attack, the *Tahoma* and the *Adela* "ran in abreast of the [Fort Brooke] batteries and shelled them slowly during the day." Reports noted that "the firing was in an unusual degree accurate and precise."

One man insisted that 230 shells rained down. The ball that struck the Florida House "crashed through the front of the house, broke a mirror on the wall of the front room, plunged through the wall, and, its force spent, dropped on the kitchen floor in the midst of members of the [Reason Duke] family." Another blasted the roof off the Daegenhardt family dining room. Henry Krause's blacksmith shop suffered a hit, with the ball burying itself in sand under the forge. The courthouse took another blow, and the Masonic hall stopped a round. A shell that landed in the cemetery later singed off Addison Mansell's whiskers, eyebrows, and a good deal of his hair when he "poked a red hot wire into the opening" after pouring out the gunpowder. Henry A. Crane's daughter almost was killed when a shell "burst inside a house hurling a forty-pound fragment across the dinner table."[42]

Stunned by the barrage, Tampans attempted in its aftermath to assess what reason for optimism they yet possessed, and just about the only words they could conjure were James McKay. Since his May 1862 return, he more than anyone had kept the town going. Elected to the county commission late that year, the captain helped direct assistance to the needy and strove to maintain some government services. McKay's blockade running adventures had bolstered sagging morale, filled local cubbards, and permitted two drug stores to remain in business. Who knows what other boons McKay granted to the community and its residents?[43]

As he served the community, McKay also walked a tightrope, never forgetting his agreement with the United States nor his responsibilities to the region's cattle-owning families. His quandary grew in summer 1863, when Governor John Milton set up a commissary service to provide needed beef and other commodities to Confederate armies. Milton appointed a friend, Quincy's Pleasants W. White, to coordinate the effort. White, anxious to find someone who knew how to ship cattle, turned to McKay. Now, McKay served as a Confederate commissary official, while balancing his other obligations. It was no mean chore.[44]

With Jacob Summerlin and other leading owners, McKay devised a plan to supply a minimum number of beeves to the Confederacy while driving the remainder eastward across the Kissimmee River, far from the grasp of more-avid procurement officers. This would save the herds and the area's economic future, pending Union occupation of south Florida (or the war's end) when sales in Cuba could resume.

Heavy rains through the late summer caused flooding that permitted McKay to delay operations. The first drive left the cattle-gathering center at Fort Meade only on September 24, 1863. By then, the captain had managed to bring cheer to many an area family by arranging for forty local boys to be returned home from the regular army for cattle driving purposes. His son James McKay, Jr., numbered among them. A few additional drives ensued during the fall, but supply always fell far short of expectation.[45]

James McKay's efforts to maintain the precarious and constantly evolving balance that had permitted south Floridians to survive with some hope for future economic wellbeing appeared to be succeeding as the New Year arrived. The draft exemption for cattlemen had saved many from enforced departure from home, while Captain Pearson's reassignment had removed the principal local obstacle to McKay's plans. The captain even had managed to save dozens of other local boys from the dangers of the front. For the time being the cattle rested safely, fattening and reproducing. Then, the world interfered yet again to Tampa's detriment. The Confederacy had lost the Battle of Chattanooga in November 1863, followed by numerous setbacks elsewhere. Its armies demanded reinforcements, and the Confederate Congress agreed on February 17, 1864. The new law upped the draft age to 50 and repealed the cattlemen's exemption among others. The reverberations were not long in coming. Real civil war was about to upset McKay's delicate balance. In the process, it would lead to Tampa's occupation by the Union. The devastation of much of south Florida would follow.[46]

No. 2 Mayor's Office, City of Tampa
$299.58 June 28th 1861
To Ed't Clarke Esq
City Treasurer
At sight pay to the Order of Kennedy & Darling Two Hundred & Ninety nine 58/100 Dollars, being for repairs of Cannon Carriages & Implements, ammunition &c. for defence of the City, with Eight per cent interest per annum on said Amt. from this date until paid — See minutes of Tampa City Council this date —

Attest
J. Darling
Depy City Clerk

John Jackson
Acting Mayor

31. Not only did the conflict bring great personal sacrifice and uncertainty, it placed extraordinary demands upon a fragile local government with few financial or material resources. This 1861 memo authorized by acting mayor John Jackson pledges payment to Kennedy and Darling for repairs and ammunition used in defense of the city against Union attack. By 1864 it was clear that the town lacked the resources to successfully follow the seccesionist cause its leaders had chosen for it. (Joan Kennedy Biddle)

32. The major battle fought in Florida during the Civil War took place near a highway and a railroad that ran between Jacksonville and Lake City. This historic Battle of Olustee occurred on February 20, 1864. When it was over the Confederate troops had won the day, preventing the largest Union attack on the state's interior and preserving the supply lines from Florida that were essential to the operation of the Confederate troops. (*Harper's Weekly Magazine* from FSA)

"I am led to think God has forsaken us"

The War at Home, 1864-1865

The February 1864 action of the Confederate Congress in repealing the conscription exemption for cattlemen set the fuse for open warfare in the Tampa Bay region. The Civil War became for south Floridians, as one pioneer put it, "a war among ourselves." Ties and loyalties of long standing were rendered asunder as the dynamics of the larger war pressed local people to attack one another. Already exhausted by trials of almost a decade, Tampans staggered through the period. Sometimes, they compromised in ways that otherwise would have been unthinkable and later would need to be forgotten. By early 1865, the very idea of peace had become almost too precious to contemplate.[1]

It should be noted that, even before the exemption's repeal, some Tampans had taken up arms in United States service. Henry A. Crane, once a soldier in the regular army, became one of the first. The newspaperman, teacher, and photographer had fled the town in October 1862 just weeks after local Confederates led by Abel Miranda murdered refugees John and Scott Whitehurst, who had returned to gather food at their farms north of Clear Water Harbor. Along with the Tampan went two of the Whitehursts' neighbors, Henry Thompson and Levi S. Whitehurst. The party crossed the peninsula to Indian River Inlet where they boarded a blockade vessel. Crane thereafter joined the United States Navy as a master's mate.[2]

By late 1863 United States authorities had organized several dozen other south Florida refugees for military service in the region. In mid-December these "Florida Rangers" occupied Useppa Island in Charlotte Harbor. Their superiors then rethought the Rangers' placement, relocating them in early January 1864 to the abandoned military post at Fort Myers under a new name, the Second Florida Cavalry. The undisciplined volunteers required an experienced hand to guide them, and the Union command turned to Crane. Commissioned a captain, he began exploring the interior from Fort Myers for cattle and enlistees. At first, little success came Crane's way. A skirmish with cowhunters near Fort Denaud on the Caloosahatchee River taught him caution, although good fortune was about to come his way courtesy of the Confederate States of America.[3]

First, though, Fort Brooke's small garrison and the civilians at Tampa appear to have received a warning not to interfere with the Union outposts on the mainland. On Christmas Eve 1863 the United States warship *Tahoma* anchored off Fort Brooke preparatory to firing one shell just before midnight. After fine tuning its position the next morning, it resumed the bombardment. "About 9 o'clock the *Tahoma* opened fire upon the garrison and continued it for two hours at intervals," reported post commander John Westcott, "throwing 150 and 32 pounder shells into the town and garrison." Having endured the cannonade, the captain added with a certain bravado, "We were ready . . . to have received them properly if they had attempted a landing."[4]

If the Christmas Day 1863 bombardment was meant as a warning, it turned out to be little needed. In February the United States Army launched a major drive eastward from Jacksonville. Confederate officials quickly ordered all troops at their disposal to a rendezvous near Lake City, including those stationed at Tampa under Captain Westcott. While the Rebels could claim a victory at the ensuing February 20 Battle of Olustee, word of Fort Brooke's abandonment quickly spread to the ears of United States military officials. "Yesterday 5 deserters and refugees came down from Tampa, who report that the soldiers have all left Tampa," one general noted on February 19, "and that none remained in Western Florida south of Tampa." The news tantalized Captain Crane. "What a fine time for capturing [Tampa] and destroying their guns," he declared on the twenty-fourth. "The holding of Tampa is not a matter of importance," he acknowledged, "[but] the moral prestige of its capture would enable me to assume the offensive, which I earnestly desire."[5]

The realization of Crane's desire to take Tampa depended upon the strengthening of the Second Florida Cavalry, a process that already had begun thanks to the draft law change. One month following the statute's approval in Richmond, the head of Florida's Confederate commissary service summarized the results by labeling subsequent events as "the general stampede of the children of the wilderness." He explained his point. "Many of the stock owners in Florida were exempt under the Law which has been repealed as owners of 500 head of cattle," Pleasants W. White wrote on March 17. "Many of these men alarmed by reports that they would be conscripted have gone to the enemy & others have left their homes and taken refuge in the remote southern portion of the Peninsula," he continued, "and in many instances large stocks of cattle have been left unattended by the men employed by the owners to look after them."[6]

Just as White observed, a slow stream of southwest Florida men who objected to Confederate service began to make its way to Fort Myers. None of the men commanded greater influence or respect than former Manatee County sheriff James D. Green of today's Hardee County. Green's presence acted as a magnet to draw cowhunters and even a few owners to the federal lines. Commissioned an officer, he led raids into the grazing lands up the Peace River. A long-time friend and associate of cattle king Jacob Summerlin, Green also shared an initimate acquaintance with James McKay. "Since my last I regret to say, that the enemy including deserters and traitors from our Cattle Region, with one named *James Green* at their head, the very *person* who travelled with you from my House to Tampa [in August 1863], and who would not partake of Dinner with us if you Recollect, at my home," the captain alerted Pleasants W. White on March 25, "he has carried away and induced several to desert and join the enemy at Fort Myers, where over 100 of U. S. troops are stationed." McKay added, "On the 21st Inst they came about fifty strong to Fort Meade."[7]

McKay might have expressed himself to his Confederate superior as truly alarmed, but his concerns rested not so much with Jim Green and the Second Florida Cavalry's growth as with the plight of others of his associates who did not want to leave their homes and cattle to enlist at Fort Myers or to fight with Confederate armies in Virginia, Tennessee, and Georgia. As had been the case for years, the local people looked to McKay for leadership. Once again, he came through for them. The captain had suspended collection of cattle for Confederate armies in January after the Fort Myers outpost's establishment. Now, he informed White that he needed his own military force to defend the ranges and drive the beeves. "No Cattle may be expected from this District untill the enemy is got Rid off," he insisted. That force, McKay felt, essentially should be composed of two elements, the local boys who had been detailed from the army as cowhunters and area men made subject to the draft by repeal of the cattlemen's exemption. The proposal proved an excellent one and lightened heavy hearts in many of the region's homes. When approved by Confederate authorities in due course, McKay's idea had given birth to the "Cow Cavalry."[8]

The Drums of War

The effect, then, of the draft exemption's repeal had been to separate most of the remaining white, male residents of southwest Florida into armed camps. "The people, when abandoned by the military authorities, were about equally divided in sentiment and action," Theodore Lesley explained. "The one part declaring for the enemy—the other for the Confederacy," continued the grandson of Cow Cavalry company commander John T. Lesley. "The men of means, who could subsist their families elsewhere, were about moving," he added, "and things looked as though the abandonment of the country to its fate was inevitable."[9]

33. James McKay's Tampa home. (Susan L. Mueller)

While most men now had enlisted in a military unit belonging to one side or the other, the greater number of them still preferred not to fight. Literally, a classic civil war had come into being in southwest Florida, with brother pitted against brother, father against son, and uncle against nephew, not to mention friend against friend. For their part, the majority of Second Florida Cavalry men desired primarily to stay out of the Confederate army while protecting their families, disrupting cattle shipments to the North, and stripping Rebels of their wealth. A few intended to avenge personal wrongs. "This was a regiment not to be lumped," one United States officer observed. "Each man had a history of his own, sometimes more startling than fiction," he added. "In some the burning cottage, the destruction of home and household goods, the exposure of wife and children to cold, penury, and starvation, if not a worse fate, filled the background of a picture not colored by imagination." The officer concluded: "Nearly all had been hunted, many by dogs. It's not a pleasant thing for a man to be hunted as though human life was of no more value than that of a fox or a wolf, and it leaves bitter thought behind."[10]

The complications for men in the Cow Cavalry service were similar to those faced by Second Florida Cavalry enlistees. "Residents often joined more from a desire to defend themselves and their community than for any abstract loyalty to the Confederacy," commented historian Robert A. Taylor. The largest company served under cattleman Francis A. Hendry of Fort Meade, a Unionist closely associated with James McKay and Jacob Summerlin. In fact, Summerlin enlisted in Hendry's company as a private. Several of the other cow cavalry companies similarly evidenced mild, if any, disposition toward fighting.[11]

Important exceptions existed. The officers and men of several of the Cow Cavalry companies held strong Confederate sympathies. Tampa's John T. Lesley and his father Leroy G. Lesley, then of Hernando County, headed two such units. The younger Lesley's company, known as the Sandpipers, usually is credited with being the first of the outfits organized. Also known as Company B, First Florida Cow Cavalry, its roots may be traced to the gathering of local residents to man the Fort Brooke cannons after Captain Westcott's troops departed in February 1864. It has been said that the Sandpipers' company rolls "read like a who's who of Hillsborough County society." Headquartered either at Fort Brooke or else at Cork near today's Plant City, the men protected Tampa from Union incursions overland. They performed other functions, as well. "Their duty, besides gathering cattle," explained Theodore Lesley, "was the patroling of the coast around Tampa, and furnishing soldiers to guard the salt makers on old Tampa bay."[12]

Ardent Rebels such as the men in the Lesley companies likely assisted the Confederate cause even before their units formally coalesced. They did so, in part, by supporting conscription agents in "combing the woods" for potential draftees. As had occurred during 1862, the zeal with which such men went about their work infuriated many area residents and bolstered Union recruiting efforts. The story is told, for example, about how the agents changed the loyalties of Carlton family members. Family head Daniel W. Carlton, according to one report, "drove his sons in the Rebel Army, with shouts of exultation." Then, in May 1864 the conscription agents came looking for Daniel's son Albert, then aged nineteen and opposed to Confederate service. Confronted, the father refused to give away his son's hiding place, whereupon the conscription agents "carried him off in Irons northward." Son Reuben, then home on leave from the Confederate army and enraged by the treatment accorded his father, immediately took himself to Fort Myers and enlisted in the Second Florida Cavalry. "I have the pleasure to-day of seeing him bear arms under our *glorious* old *Banner*," reported Henry Crane. Albert followed Reuben in June.[13]

In the face of the common preference, tensions in Tampa and southwest Florida understandably mounted at a rapid pace, and, as a result, bloodshed and devastation of property resulted even before the Cow Cattle companies received authorization. The first engagement came on April 7, 1864, when Second Florida Cavalrymen under Henry A. Crane and James D. Green clashed with cowhunters and drovers led by James McKay, Jr., at Bowlegs Creek near Fort Meade. Only two Confederate casualties resulted, but Union torches soon kindled flames at nearby Rebel farms and storehouses. "They then . . . burned our home and all that we had," lamented one Confederate survivor.[14]

By then, the lure of Tampa as a prize loomed too great for the United States forces to resist for long. Still, preparations and coordination, plus a yearning to avoid unnecessary bloodshed, served to force patience. Available records are sketchy, but it seems that James

McKay, Sr., aided local Unionists to ensure that fighting was avoided when the time arrived for the town's capture. As he did so, he likely believed that higher-ups were about to order his men to assignments elsewhere, leaving the place defenseless. In any event, by early May the troops at Tampa consisted only of thirteen Confederate soldiers under John Darling's command and McKay's cowhunters and drovers. They numbered thirty-three men in all. That intelligence came into Union hands on May fourth when the commanding officer of the *U. S. S. Sunflower*, as he described it, "went up to Tampa . . . to communicate [and] to ascertain the strength of the place." The next day, McKay sent his command to Fort Meade under the leadership of James McKay, Jr. The senior McKay then absented himself from Tampa, headed for Gainesville. The local Unionists thereupon "tipped off" United States forces that Fort Brooke lay virtually unoccupied.[15]

A Brief Return to the Union

The assault on Tampa followed in less than twenty-four hours after McKay's cowhunters and drovers got under way.[16] Briefly, the plan of attack aimed at taking possession of the town at daybreak of May 6, 1864, requiring troop movements hours before. "We landed, one night about one o'clock, from our ship, in the small boats, some sixty men under the command of Ensign Cox, at Gadsden Point, in the woods . . . ," recalled a naval officer, "while the gunboats [the *U. S. S. Honduras*] landed about two hundred and fifty men some two miles below the town on the south side." The men involved in the Gadsden's Point landing made their way as quietly as they could to the Hillsborough River's western bank opposite town "to prevent escape by water." The larger force offloaded at some point north of the Alafia River's mouth. It contained 140 men of the Second Florida Cavalry, three dozen black soldiers of the Second United States Colored Troops, and 30 seamen from blockade vessels. They moved northward to the government road and turned west to Tampa. One mile outside town James D. Green learned from a local slave that no ambushers lay in wait. "When the party arrived at the neck of land between the river on the west and the marsh on the east, pickets were posted to intercept all who might attempt to escape or to enter the town," reported Colonel Stark Fellows. "Captain [Henry A.] Crane, Second Florida Cavalry, with a small party, proceeded to the hotel and arrested some of the leading citizens."[17]

The takeover did not proceed quite as peacefully as Fellows described. Darwin Branch Givens always insisted that he sounded the alarm, although, at the time, he was only five years of age. "I, with Jerry Perkins, was playing in the white sand road just above East Street where it intersects with [Kennedy Boulevard]," he recalled. "I saw them coming down the road with bayonets fixed and glistening in the noonday sun," he continued. "Knowing something out of the ordinary was happening, I took to my heels and ran home and told father that the 'devils' were taking the place." Givens's sister Anne Givens Harrison picked up the story from there. "We were all at breakfast and my younger brother, D. [B.], came running in and told my father the Yankees were coming," she told an interviewer, "marching into town, fifty thousand of them." She added, "Father told him to run over to a hotel on the northwest corner of what is now Franklin and [Kennedy] and tell Judge Gettis and the other gentlemen who were living in the hotel."[18]

Everything happened so quickly at that point that surviving accounts diverge. Darwin Givens believed that he reached the Florida House in time and hailed several men back to his father's home. Meanwhile, the Union troops were double timing up what is now Kennedy Boulevard. "My father just had time to call Mr. [Reason] Duke and Mr. [James] Gettis to come over to him," Givens related, "which they

34. A house on Marion at Twiggs, Tampa, circa 1864. (TBHC)

did just as the soldiers came around the block to father's back gate [off Morgan at Kennedy]." Givens continued: "I was holding his hand and Mr. Crane said to the captain, 'Do not take my friend Givens, I'll stand good for him.' But they took the other gentlemen."[19]

Henry Crane told a different version of the story. A *New York Herald* reporter expressed it in this manner:

> In the course of his peregrinations through the town [after its capture], Captain Crane entered a hotel where some twenty of the principal men of the place were just sitting down to breakfast. The Captain, who was alone, saluted the expectant breakfasters by politely saying, "Good morning, gentlemen." To which courtesy one of the company responded with considerable energy, "Jesus Christ, he is come at last; and I'll bet he has one thousand men at his back." Of course, the company were all taken considerably aback by such a sudden apparition; and they were incontinently made prisoners.[20]

There may be some truth in the Crane account. Local Unionists knew that the occupation was to occur, as possibly did some others. By pre-arrangement, the men may have gathered at the hotel to await Captains Crane and Green, although it seems likely that Darling, Gettis, and others had been kept in the dark. Maria Louisa Daegenhardt certainly believed that the United States forces already knew who was in town and where they could be found. She recalled them awaiting her brother-in-law Henry Krause, who was home on furlough but out hunting early that morning. "O how we did try to watch for him to warn him, but could do nothing," she recorded. "We saw him coming in from the wood with his gun, not knowing what was waiting for him," Maria added. "They walked up to him, took his gun, & led him down to the Garrison, a prisoner."[21]

It seems clear that the first stage of the occupation proceeded smoothly and without gunfire, but that situation did not last for long. The *Neptune*, a blockade running sloop loaded with cotton, rested at the wharf just below the Jackson Street ferry. The men assigned to it heard the commotion in town, grabbed their arms, and prepared to resist. A brief fire fight ensued as several men attempted to swim the river to escape. One or more of them may have been wounded. A number got away.[22]

Coincidentally, a few Rebel volunteers attempted to man one of Fort Brooke's artillery positions. "A brief skirmish at the battery left one Confederate dead and several others wounded," observed Civil War historian David J. Coles. To avoid the possibility of further such encounters, the Union officers called in the heavy guns. "One of our gunboats ran up the bay, a short distance," noted a naval officer, "and soon shelled out with their guns a small earthwork that was situated in the town at the mouth of a small river called Fort Brooke, and which was destroyed in a very short time." When the officer later toured Fort Brooke, he found it "completely 'knocked into pie.'"[23]

The small show of resistance may have stoked the anger of some of the Second Florida Cavalry's men. Already bearing hard grudges for treatment they had received at the hands of, or else upon the orders of, Confederate officials who resided in town (Darling, Gettis, John T. Lesley, and John A. Henderson among them), their tempers now boiled over. "My orders against pilfering were very stringent," observed General Daniel P. Woodbury, who headed the the Union forces. "The colored troops on shore behaved remarkably well," he insisted, "[but] the refugee troops having personal wrongs to redress were not so easily controlled."[24]

Two men, particularly, had incurred Unionist ire, and they faced the brunt of the soldiers' fury. "Colonel John Darling and Captain James Gettis were left with nothing but what they had on," local historian Tony Pizzo commented. Each man suffered the ravaging of their places of business, their homes, and their other properties. Stunned by events and before he realized that he was one of only a few victims, Darling at first believed that "our town was completely sacked except a few private houses." Once time had passed and he had calmed, the merchant scaled down his report. "The Town was partially plundered, and one of the principal sufferers from the raid was your Petitioner," he averred, "who lost on that occasion over $10,000 in money and valuable papers [and] was subjected to imprisonment for about thirty six hours."[25]

Likely because Darling and Gettis were associated so closely in the public mind with Tampa's masonic chapters, they too suffered intrusion. The Union men broke into the Masonic lodge. After destroying furniture located within, the soldiers, according to a lodge historian, "seized the regalia, jewels, and other equipment" of Hillsborough Lodge No. 25, F. & A. M. The Royal Arch Chapter's holdings met a similar fate. Regarding what he termed "the plunder of our Chapter rooms," Darling informed the state general secretary,

35. Ossian B. Hart.

"The furniture was as complete, I think, as any Chapter in this State, having cost us over $500.00, including a fine set of jewels, all of which was carried away, except a few articles; and with the books they also took the charter." Finally, the Odd Fellows Lodge received attention. Its minutes reflected the "carrying away or destroying [of] the current minutes and account books and set of the ritual including the Rebekah degree book, as well as a large portion of the implements and furniture of the lodge."[26]

Before the pillaging could range too far out of hand, the town's leading Unionist stepped forward to bring matters under control. "All public property belonging to the Confederate government was of course seized," future Hillsborough County judge Charles E. Harrison declared, "but private property was respected by special orders of General Woodbury at the intercession of Ossian B. Hart, a southern loyalist who then lived here."[27] Harrison's wife Anne Givens Harrison added:

> Judge Ossian B. Hart, a prominent citizen at that time . . . saw to it that Tampa did not suffer as many other places did. Only a few of the homes were searched for money or valuables. The looters did come to our home, but they only ripped open a feather bed and turned out drawers and such like. No, they didn't get either our money or our silver. Father had only a few days before put the buckskin bag, in which it had been stored, in a secret place in the chimney.[28]

Once the heat of the moment had passed, Hart with Woodbury's cooperation maintained order and a calm atmosphere as the hours ticked away. A careful search of the town and its vicinity disclosed about $6,000 in money belonging to the Confederacy, some interesting mail at the post office, a part of the hidden equipment of the Egmont Key light, a little ammunition, and a few muskets. The troops took time to locate slaves and inform them of their freedom. Likely, they were asked if they wanted to depart when the troops left and most said yes. A few southern newspaper correspondents happened to be visiting and were detained, along with a batch of notorious Rebels including Henry Mulrennan, late of the volunteer coast guard. All told, the Union forces arrested thirty-nine persons for various reasons. Arrest proved truly confining for Darling and Gettis and several others, but average citizens such as Henry Krause received lighter treatment. "Mother & sister knew the Capt. and Leutenant (as they were men that had lived here but had deserted to the other side)," remembered Maria Louisa Daegenhardt. "So they alowed my brother in law to come home to his meals so sister could then see him, but he was guar[d]ed by too big negro men every time."[29]

By evening on the sixth, quiet prevailed as the United States flag flew over Tampa. Officers posted pickets to guard access to the town, and others settled in for meals, talk, and the renewal of acquaintances after a remarkable day. A naval officer chose that time to visit the place. He found the town charming, although he witnessed firsthand the toll taken on its residents by years of war. Of the experience, he wrote:

> It was a very neat, pretty place with small white painted houses, and beautiful beds of flowers in the front yards with seashell borders very neatly arranged and very attractive, while the atmosphere was redolent with rich odors from the flowers and the highly scented magnolias. After walking about some time we strolled down to

36. This cozy Tampa home belonged to Christiana Perkins. Her husband, Capt. George T. Perkins, had purchased the old Tampa billiard hall from Odet Philippe. Captain Perkins served as a civilian pilot on a Union gunboat and was lost at sea. Mrs. Perkins lived with her children at 401 Lafayette Street and the family owned the west half of the block east of city hall. (*Tampa Tribune*)

37. Mrs. Christiana Perkins. (Julius J. Gordon)

> the fort, where we saw the ruin which the gunboat had made with her guns. . . . I also saw a number of old men, women and children standing about some public building and they were a very poor, dejected looking lot of people and were only about half decently clothed.[30]

If not earlier, Tampans would have learned during the evening that the Union troops would not stay beyond the following day. "It is not intended to retain possession of Tampa, as it is a place of no strategic value," explained a correspondent. "To hold it would be to help the rebels play their old game of evacuating unimportant places to reinforce their large armies, and divide the Union army by distributing its troops among such insignificant posts." Woodbury, Fellows, Crane, Green, and Hart probably were among those who discussed what to do to protect the pro-Union people left behind. They decided to release most of the prisoners in the interest of local harmony, but to make clear to several that the wrath of the United States would descend upon them should harm befall any loyal persons. "[I was] held to the close of the war," recorded John Darling, "as a hostage for the safety of certain Union men."[31]

The departure went off as scheduled, with only a minor surprise challenging the Union plans. On the morning of May 7 Tampa bustled. The troops and sailors spent much of their time loading prisoners, freed slaves, Fort Brooke cannons, and other captured properties onto transports. As they were doing so, Jacob Summerlin's stepson Aaron Gideon Zipprer appeared under a flag of truce. Word of the occupation having reached James McKay, Jr., at Fort Meade, he had rushed to the scene with thirty-five men. He then spent the night collecting reinforcements so that, by morning, his force amounted to seventy-five "men and boys." Now, he dispatched Zipprer to tell Henry Crane and Jim Green that he wanted his family released and that he would not attack for twenty-four hours.[32]

The threat posed by McKay's message meant little to his opponents. "The Federals declined to permit either the men or my wife to

38. Edward A. Clarke. (TBHC)

leave the town and held them until they evacuated the place," McKay recalled. Rather, the servicemen continued their loading duties. About dark, they neared completion. Then, as Colonel Fellows recorded, "The picket returned in good order at the signal of firing a musket, and all were soon on board the boats." Subsequently, Captain Green led five men and ten horses through McKay's lines on their way to Fort Myers. As McKay acknowledged, his men "permitted them to pass without challenging."[33]

Where the May 6-7, 1864, occupation of Tampa had played out in a relatively peaceful fashion, the tone of the conflict quickly turned bitter. On May 19 essentially the same Union force that took Tampa seized and burned the cattle gathering center at Fort Meade. Ten days later, naval forces raided Senator David Levy Yulee's Hernando County plantation, torching several buildings including his home. With a little time taken for preparation, the Second Florida Cavalry and its associated black troopers landed at Bay Port in early July, preparatory to a march on Brooksville. At Bay Port they captured Tampa merchants Edward A. Clarke and Christopher L. Friebele, who were serving in a coast guard company and would spend the war's remainder in a Union prison camp. Leroy G. Lesley and John T. Lesley's cow cavalry companies confronted the Union soldiers during the incursion, as a result of which one of John T. Lesley's men—or, possibly his own father—shot and wounded him in the arm. Blockade vessels punctuated the raid with assaults upon salt works throughout the bay area, including operations close to Tampa. And, on August 3, the village of Manatee endured temporary occupation.[34]

Even though the Union successes demoralized local Confederates, as the summer's months passed the Cow Cavalry organizations grew stronger and soon reasserted a degree of authority in a large part of southwest Florida. Much of the credit goes to a former Confederate congressman, Charles J. Munnerlyn of Georgia. Designated by President Jefferson Davis to command the "First Battalion, Florida Special Cavalry," he possessed special gifts of administrative ability and leadership. With his second in command Captain William Footman, Munnerlyn pressed for cattle shipments and attacks upon Union forces. His efforts resulted in a misguided attempt to take Fort Myers. From a Tampa base, Footman set out in February 1865 with John T. Lesley's company and with James McKay, Jr., heading up Francis A. Hendry's unit. The hapless escapade, resented and resisted by some of its participants, ended in fiasco. "The whole thing had been a failure," one veteran of the march declared, "and . . . the whole command was demoralized."[35]

The Hard Life

Through the events of 1864 and into 1865, Tampans—most of them, anyway—ached for the coming of the conflict's end. From the period's beginning, they had grappled with the basics of survival. "64 was a very hard year for all here," Maria Louisa Daegenhardt recalled. "My Mother worked hard to keep us all together." Daegenhardt added:

> We could buy so little here. She gave $25.00 for one bushel of sweet potatoes & I remember her giving $5.00 for 10 yards of Calico. We had no flour or coffee for 4 years. But Mother had her garden and raised near all we eat. She had a cow, chickens & a few pigs. My Mother was a wonderful woman, a devoted Mother and a good manager, very economical and taught us all to lead a christian life. In her garden, she allway[s] tri[e]d to plant all the corn she could, as that was our main stay. She would watch it closely & when the corn would tassel, she would [take] the most perfect of them, put them throug[h] a selution of Alum a[nd] dry, for the triming of Hats. For my sister Amelia braided & sewed the bleached Palmetto & the fine silky shucks of the corn for her work. Besides she was the main hand at weaving.[36]

Maria Louisa Daegenhardt's reminiscences, such as those quoted above, have preserved for us an exceptional window through which Tampans' daily lives during the war's final year or so may be glimpsed. Adding further detail, she recorded:

> When the corn matured, [Mother] would pull off all the ears of corn (what we did not eat green) and let them dry. Then she would take the stalks and leaves dry & put them away for feed for the cow, even the roots she would save as they could burn under the pot. Then in time we children would help take the shuck from off the corn. The coarse ones, she used for making mats & mattresses & that was a happy time for us children for we would take the corse shucks & a fork & split them up in shreds, then tie in nots & then dry & when opened up, they made a very springy mattress. Then the corn was shelled from the cob and ground up in a very large hand mill that Mother had. Then it would go through a seive and the coarse husk on top was taken and parched for coffee, and some times Mother would parch Peanuts on little cubes of sweet potatoes, and added to it and it did make a wonderfull drink as coffee. Then the corn was sifted again and the corse was used for a sereal (hominy). The fine meal was for bread. Even the cobs of the corn was used (for we could get no baking powder then) and Mother would carefully burn them, save the white ashes, & use with the juice of a Lemon or lime or sour Orange, and it would answer so well for baking soda.
>
> How I would love to go in the woods with Mother to gather herbs & branches for dyeing purposes for our homespun dresses (as we spun & wove our own cloth) & sometimes we would get the leaves of the sweet bay tree & sasafras root and Lemon leaves to make our tea. It was a healthy drink and we all liked it. And anoth[er] happy time with me was when Mother would make her own soap. Then we would go out in the woods & gather oak bark or small oaks & burn them, get the ashes & bring [them] home, put [them] in the old wo[o]den hoppe[r], keep wet so always what driped through in the trough would be the lye from which she made the soap by adding old grease saved up from time to time.[37]

The shelling of the town by blockade vessels naturally compounded the difficulties of day-to-day survival, but even that trial eventually settled into a routine, however terrible, for residents. Those who could simply departed as soon as warning was received or the first shells began falling. "Each morning, while danger threatened," an interviewer wrote of Nancy Collar Jackson, "she, with her pony, betook herself and younger children to the home of a friend, a few miles distant, to spend the day, where Mr. [Robert] Jackson remained to watch lest a shell might fire the house."[38]

Most families fled to a spot near the Hillsborough River not far from the abandoned McKay sawmill. The Daegenhardts, according to daughter Maria, sought refuge in that vicinity at the home of "an old negro woman." Anne Givens Harrison remembered that her family made about the same trek. "Whenever the gunboats bombarded the city we used to gather up food and clothes and go to a long wooden house up on the river, where the water-works Park is now," she related. "I mean the women and children and a few of the older men who were not soldiers." Her brother Darwin Givens added detail. "When the Yankees shelled Tampa . . . ," he observed, "our family, with others, would naturally undertake to get out of the shelled district." He continued, "There was a large double house, known as the 'Campbell house,' where Hal Scarlett built his home on Seventh avenue, and we generally camped there when our little village was under fire." Tampans would not forget William J. Campbell's generous offer of a safe haven during those troubled times.[39]

As if their cares were not of sufficient magnitude, local people fretted constantly about the fate of their loved ones in the military; the news from home distressed soldiers, as well, a process that ground away at everyone's morale. This had been the case through the war, but the return of invalids and news of deaths heightened concerns as the South reeled from setback to setback in 1864. John Edward Spencer wrote his friend William G. Ferris, Jr., in February, days after Ferris suffered serious wounds at the Battle of Olustee. Although both young men were away from home, the yearning for better times expressed in their correspondence spoke volumes for the sentiments of Tampans generally:

> Billie, I am so unfortunate as to be cast away from friends aboard a C.S. Steamer,—"a gunboat" at St. Marks don't you sympathize with me? I can't see any one here that I can call a friend, especially one that I cherish as a friend from my boyhood days as your self. Ah! Billie, still fresh in my memory is our boyhood days, where we enjoyed life together—little did I think . . . four years ago when we were together in our dear little city of Tampa that our fate would have been what it is at the present time. Ah! time tells us what is in the future. Billie, the way I console myself now . . . I tear myself away from all society—such as we have her—and get off to myself and ponder over the happy days gone by. I still live in hopes that ere a long while, we will all meet our dear friends at our happy homes—and oh! what a joyful time that will be! I have not heard

from home in two months. I am troubled about home[.] on receipt of this if you are able—write me all the news.[40]

As Spencer's letter suggested, if anything bothered more than hearing bad news, it was hearing no news or, worse, hearing unfounded rumors. In a town where newspapers had not been published for two years or more, the mails served as a lifeline. When the stagecoach arrived, anxious residents crowded around the driver and new arrivals, eager to pour over any newspaper or, possibly, savor a personal letter. By March 1864, the stage and the mails had been suspended. More often than not thereafter, they failed. "I have no chance of hearing from Mr. McKay," Pleasants W. White observed of the typical situation, "except by private hands." It actually may have been easier after the Union occupation in May to communicate with Key West and the North. Catharine Hart delighted, for example, in writing to her family at their New Jersey home.[41]

Evidence of the strains of Tampa life by 1864 struck visitors and local people alike. "The appearance of Tampa is desolate in the extreme," noted General Daniel Woodbury in May. "There are very few men in the place," he continued, "hardly one able-bodied man between eighteen and fifty years of age." Five months later, conditions had not improved. "Owing to the broken up state of affairs in the County," Sheriff and Tax Collector William S. Spencer explained to state officials in September, "I have not been able to send up my Tax book as yet." Spencer added: "The persons are . . . Much opposed to paying any Tax at this time as our County are soe often disturbed by the Enemy." A Methodist minister followed up Spencer's remarks with his own in October. "Notwithstanding the difficulties we have had to contend with in this [circuit] for the past eight months," he wrote, "the work of the Lord has prospered." He concluded, "Money is very scarce in this part of the country, and people are not doing near as well toward the missionary cause, as they have done heretofore."[42]

With the opening of the new year in January 1865, even religious faith had ceased to offer the comfort that it had in earlier times. "I do so long to see you all once again; and to mingle with you all, as in days past," Catharine Hart cried to her distant family on the fifth, "but *when* will that day come again; when will this unnatural war be over, when will peace and prosperity bless our distressed country again." Hart continued: "This the fourth year of war has dawned upon us; and still the two sections of country stand in antagonism toward each other. Sometimes I am led to think God has forsaken us, and intends to let us destroy each other; wickedness of all kinds prevails, on the right hand and on the left." Little wonder then that, when word of General Robert E. Lee's surrender filtered down in April, Cow Cavalry Captain Francis A. Hendry could exclaim only, "Thank God it is over with one way or the other." He spoke for most everyone.[43]

39. General Grant and General Lee meet at Appomattox Courthouse. (LC)

"suffering exists at Tampa and vicinity"

Peace Which Passeth All Understanding, 1865-1867

The peace that settled upon the South in the aftermath of General Robert E. Lee's April 1865 surrender at Appomattox Courthouse, Virginia, proved unlike the expectations of almost all Tampans. White Loyalists believed that they now would govern the state, while freedmen excitedly embraced their liberty and what they felt was an ironclad promise of a stake for their new lives, the fabled "forty acres and a mule." Defeated Confederates assumed the worst as far as their role in affairs was concerned, many of them happy simply to be alive and returning home. All knew that one man more than all others held the key to whatever the future would bring. The victorious president of the United States Abraham Lincoln would decide matters. But, everyone misjudged the scene. Unknown to them, surprising twists of fate awaited as the calendar unfolded toward the future.

The peace crawled slowly toward Tampa. The first inkling of the possibility came in April's first week or ten days when word filtered down that a despairing Governor John Milton had chosen self-inflicted death by shotgun over surrender. After General Lee abandoned the war on April 9, the news took eight days to reach Jack-

40. Private James H. Stephens. Seen here in his Confederate uniform, Stephens served both sides during the Civil War.

sonville. By the twelfth Key Westers were reading of the northern victory, and within a few days the cannons of the Tampa Bay blockading squadron were booming in celebration. Not until the second week in May, though, did Union authorities accept the state's capitulation at Tallahassee, an act that did not become official until May 20.[1]

The post-war Union occupation of Tampa arrived on May 27. To signal the event, the United States schooner *Matchless*, most recently of Cedar Keys, passed up Hillsborough Bay carrying on board Company A, Second Florida Cavalry. This was Captain Henry A. Crane's company, although Crane, his fellow captain James D. Green, Lieutenant John A. Miller, and several other regimental officers from southwest Florida had been discharged in February due to resentments held by northern-born superiors. Within the company's ranks still served several Tampa Bay area residents. Sergeant James R. Hay and Privates Abraham Hay, James H. Stephens, and Levi S. Whitehurst stood among them.[2]

A sad sight greeted the war-tested veterans. "Tampa was a hard-looking place," remembered James McKay, Jr. "Houses were in bad order," the former Confederate officer continued. "Streets and lots were grown up mostly with weeds and the outlook certainly was not very encouraging." Baptist minister and teacher Samuel C. Craft saw things similarly. "Tampa was once a *City*, with a name and fame abroad," he wrote, "But she is no longer a *City*, for she has no incorporation." He added: "Everything, almost, upon which the traveler casts his eyes is calculated to *repulse*, rather than to *attract*." By way of examples, Craft noted "the decaying and tottering wharf" and the "disgracefully neglected grave yard." In fact, residents had taken to digging graves in the "streets" of what would become Oaklawn Cemetery, anxious to dispose of decaying remains and ignoring any rules the town or county might once have imposed.[3]

The reception accorded to the occupiers ran the gamut of personal response from elation to begrudging acceptance. For a brief time most Confederates, relieved at the hostilities' end, declined to show resentment and some welcomed the conquerors as a sign that life could begin to get back to normal. "The Rebellion was a supreme folly," acknowledged John Darling, "disastrous in all things alike to the victor & vanquished." Local Union men naturally were overjoyed. Ossian B. Hart reported one incident that symbolized for him "the spirit and temper as well as the sentiments of the people." As a newspaper reporter related of Hart's story, "Soon after the occupation by the Union forces . . . a large delegation of the country people visited the town, and on catching sight of the old flag once more, which was 'floating in the breeze,' each man with one accord reverently lifted his hat, and greeted the return of the starry emblem of their country's greatness and honor with every token of respect and delight."[4]

Their reception may have avoided the unpleasant, but, at Fort Brooke, the United States soldiers discovered a situation far less than desirable. Repeated naval bombardments had reduced the once beautiful outpost to ruin. Until suitable structures could be rebuilt or erected new, the troops were required to live in tents. Officers viewed this alternative as acceptable only for the time being, but three years afterward the problem remained to trouble the garrison. "Slabs of which other Posts are built, cannot be obtained here," explained one general officer as late as February 1868, "the troops lived under canvass expending $6,000 during the past two years, lumber was estimated for to erect temporary huts at an expense of about $2000, but all applications and estimates were disapproved."[5]

Confusion reigned as the United States soldiers attempted to organize the peace. They suspended civilian government in the form of the county commission as of May 29, but a tantalizing five-page gap in the commission's minutes suggests some resistance might have greeted the move. The bluecoats formally paroled Cow Cavalry veterans at Bay Port on June 5 and accepted the surrender of other Confederate military personnel in the region at Tampa three days later. Meanwhile, some Confederates took advantage of the associated chaos to assist Confederate officials attempting to escape capture. Most notably, the defeated nation's secretary of state Judah P. Benjamin passed through seeking passage to the Bahama Islands. Cow Cavalry captains Leroy G. Lesley and John T. Lesley aided in guiding the distinguished former United States senator from Brooksville to Manatee, where he obtained a sloop and crew. James McKay, Jr., insisted that he saw Benjamin in disguise upon his arrival at Hernando County's seat. "We soon found out who he was," McKay recorded, "when he was sent on down the line." Family lore indicates that Major McKay furnished the secretary of state a week's refuge in his Tampa home, but the assertion has not received verification.[6]

The Explosive Potential of Repopulation

May's confusion persisted through the summer of 1865, with unfounded rumors still circulating in September that Florida-born Confederate general Edmund Kirby Smith was leading a holdout army into the peninsula. Conditions at Tampa had appeared, at first, to be settling down as the soldiers restored order. Then, an influx of returning residents collided with newcomers to create the types of problems that needed only a catalyst to cause them to erupt into open violence. The easy tempers of young Rebels unwilling to accept defeat combined with raw sensitivities and the oppressive heat of summer easily could have provided the spark. They almost did.[7]

The soldiers and prisoners of war came in a steady stream. Even though the Cow Cavalry men received parole in June, many had straggled home weeks before. The soldiers of the Army of Tennessee and the Army of Northern Virginia followed. Half-starved and shabbily clothed, they came south by the thousands. Some had given up before the surrender, compelled to steal food and wearing apparel to survive on the road home. These "gray locusts" created a climate of fear that forced greater hardships on those who came later. Not a few hobbled on one leg or else lacked an arm, an eye, or worse. All hovered near exhaustion. Most would not fail to perceive, once at home, the horror and pain in loved ones' eyes after a look at their condition.[8]

The prisoners of war, too, turned their feet toward home at the first opportunity. Tampans had endured internment in numerous Union camps. Ship Island, Mississippi, for instance, had hosted Edward A. Clarke, Christopher L. Friebele, and Henry Krause, while

Camp Douglas had detained John F. White. Released in late April, they reached New Orleans in early May. Among the lucky ones, they made it to Tampa within weeks thereafter.[9]

No social service system welcomed the veterans home; rather, they encountered a splintered community in which resentments ran deep. Almost to a man, they discovered much of their property gone or destroyed, money worthless, and family suffering from deprivation and poor nourishment with no one to turn to for help. Even had they money, they found it virtually impossible to purchase necessities. With two exceptions, Tampa's stores stood shuttered and some displayed unrepaired damage from artillery shells. Two drugstores formed fortunate exceptions. The senior one, operated by Dr. Franklin Branch, had managed to remain open through the conflict. The second belonged to a relative newcomer, Claiborne R. Mobley. In late 1861 he had invested a small fortune in local real estate, although he remained in Ogden, Kansas, over which he presided as mayor. Mobley may have joined a Union regiment in his home state, but, within two years poor health had prompted his relocation to Florida. It seems possible that Branch catered to Confederate-leaning Tampans, while Mobley waited upon neutral and Unionist families. The former Kansan certainly resented neighboring Rebels, whom he remembered as a "penurious hypocritical set of men . . . bent of my destruction, that they might pecuniarily [benefit] by the enjoyment of what was my own."[10]

In the footsteps of the United States troops, a small number of additional Union men and families arrived. Matthew P. Lyons, for one, relocated to Tampa after his farm in today's Hardee County burned during the war and he had obtained release from confinement as a Cow Cavalry prisoner of war. A son-in-law of Hillsborough County pioneer James Alderman, the forty-five year old Irishman harbored anger at leading Tampa Confederates for events occurring in 1856 during the Billy Bowlegs War. The Civil War's trials merely added kindling to the fire. Others intended to profit from the garrison's presence or else from official position. Henry Albury, for instance, quickly opened the "Louvre Eating & Drinking Saloon," as well as a billiards parlor. John H. Jenks came to enforce federal laws as deputy United States marshal. On September 21 he also received appointment as postmaster.[11]

A few individuals who had been held in slavery at Tampa also returned, to supplement the limited number of African Americans

41. Dorcas Bryant. (Tony Pizzo Collection, USF)

who had remained. As noted in Chapter IV, most local slaves either had sought sanctuary within Union lines or else had left the town in May 1864 in the wake of the temporary Union occupation. It appears likely that among those already present when news of the peace arrived were Isaac Howard and Sarah Clarke, slaves of the McKay family; Wade Smith, who belonged to William J. Campbell; Sarah Hanes Brown and Lula Walker, servants of the Lesleys; and the Prine family's Dorcas Bryant, with her sons Samuel and Peter. A few additional freedmen and freedwomen surely remained, as well. Sarah Brown chose to depart briefly for her old South Carolina home following the peace, but she would return to marry Samuel Bryant. Samuel's brother Aaron, who had joined the Second Regiment, United States Colored Troops, in May 1864, also came back to his family. Cyrus Charles probably returned to his job in the sawmill business.[12]

These few families or individuals would become important to Tampa's future, but the tiny number of black residents did not stay tiny for long. Some freed slaves from the countryside made their way to town, and others found themselves there unwillingly. As to the latter group, Sarah and Samuel Bryant's daughter Emma explained. "Many plantation owners . . . not wishing to callously shut the gates on their newly-released former charges," she remembered, "brought them as far as Tampa and 'dumped' them as the ex-slaves put it." Where Tampa's slaves had tended to live near their owners' homes or else their places of work, the newcomers, who could not purchase property and had no one to take them in, made camp on the Fort Brooke reservation. Because soldiers were occupying the part of the reservation south of Whiting Street, the "squatters" usually opted

42. At ninety years of age, these Hillsborough County pioneers were living history when this photograph was taken in 1923. Left to right are Aaron Bryant (Samuel's brother), Isaac Berry, Steven Harvell, and Nathan Tucker. (*Tampa Times*)

for sites beyond East Street and north of today's county courthouse. Known as the "Scrub," the area became home to dozens of individuals and families within a few years.[13]

With individual exceptions, Tampa's black residents recognized early on that an abyss almost impossible to cross lay between them and most local whites. Even area Unionists, the greater number of them anyway, had not embraced the former slaves or acknowledged a responsibility for their welfare, much less reached out in the spirit of brotherhood. The main hope of the new citizens was that the government that had freed them would offer assistance. Rumor had it that in the towns on July 4 officials would distribute land and farm animals. Mary J. Cardy preserved a memory of that day in Tampa. As an interviewer related, Cardy's story began, "It was Fourth of July and the first parade was being held." It continued: "There were no white men in this parade, none but the negro farm hands, recently made free and rejoicing in their freedom. Celebrating the nation's birthday, they marched through the streets bearing flags procured from the colored companies then in the town." Tragically for the marchers, all the government had to offer that day was one thing, the loan of the flags they carried on parade.[14]

The freedmen clearly façed great obstacles in gaining community acceptance and understanding, but they shared with many of Tampa's white inhabitants the need to fight to stave off starvation. Without stores in which to purchase food and little in the way of money in any event, a down-at-the-heels town that suddenly had tripled or quadrupled its population simply could not feed its residents nor could they feed themselves. Compounding the problem, "intensely hot" weather sapped whatever energy remained to the hungry. By August conditions had grown so bad that military officials in Tallahassee decided to take action. "I understand that suffering exists at Tampa and vicinity among Refugees and freedmen," one authority informed another officer. "It is in my opinion important that you should proceed there and issue [rations] to these persons." The food permitted most to survive until the times improved, but the improvements did not come fast enough for some, especially freed people. The sad case of Henry Hamilton illustrates the point. A Polk County slave who had been "dumped" by his owner at Tampa, Hamilton was seen as "one of the very best members of our colored population." In early 1866, according to one account, "he was struck down by disease" and had been "unable to make anything to support himself and family." By July, without hope or expectation of support, one Sunday morning Hamilton drowned himself.[15]

Another factor added itself to the local equation in July and August. To replace departing Second Florida Cavalry troopers, the state military command directed a company of the Ninety-ninth Regiment, United States Colored Troops, to Tampa. As if the presence of black soldiers did not pose enough of a challenge to white Tampans unused to blacks in positions of authority over them, the bluecoats came with orders to "stop all sales of liquor, and [to] post a guard over the article so that none shall be sold or distributed in the place." Since Tampans traditionally had enjoyed their libations, these orders increased local resentments, a fact that facilitated misunderstandings and created the potential for serious problems.[16]

Maria Louisa Daegenhardt recorded the details of one encounter she had with the black soldiers, a story that illustrates the conflicts sparked during their sojourn. "They were so impudent and would often, meeting a child in the street, would threaten to shoot them," she recalled of actions that, probably, had been intended by the soldiers as innocent fun aimed at Rebel children. Daegenhardt continued:

> I can't forget at one time what a fright I got taking our cow & pigs out at the edge of Town where there was so many acorns & berrys for the pigs and green grass for the Cow, passing some soldiers (negros). One said ["]Let us kill a pig & take it to Camp. ["] I told them they must not shoot those pigs & he aimed his gun at me & said a little more ["]I will shoot you.["] And he did shoot one of the pigs, threw it over his shoulder & went to the Garrison. I ran home & quickly told my Mother and she went down to the Garrison & told the Commander. He said they should be punished. He gave her $5.00 for the pigs.[17]

The presence of the black troopers—when piled on to old resentments, the heat, the hunger, fear of unknown faces, a breathtaking sense of loss, racial divisions, and uncertainty about the future—came very close to igniting deadly passions. By way of background, James McKay, Jr., led a small group of young, headstrong former Confederate officers and soldiers who increasingly resisted encroachments on the old way of doing things at Tampa. In one instance, according to an army legal affairs officer, they molested a Unionist who had served early in the war in a local Confederate company.

"James McKay now at Tampa was leader of a party who hung up by the neck one Allen Lowe also at Tampa," recorded the officer, "& otherwise abused him." The officer added, "McKay acknowledged this."[18]

By August, McKay and friends prepared to challenge authority directly. The black soldiers had initiated the ban on liquor sales and also had begun passing out amnesty forms required for presidential pardons of the wealthier or more-powerful Confederates. McKay left his own account of subsequent events. "It was not long before the troops became overbearing," he wrote, "and in some instances threatened arrests of our citizens." McKay noted further, "I was one that was to be brought before a military court, for the destruction of papers and documents." Given the "excited condition of the country," a bloody confrontation could have ensued. Fortunately for Tampa, McKay backed down by fleeing. "Getting uneasy over the many reports coming to me," he explained, "I, with my brother Donald, mounted our horses and laid out in the woods for six weeks."[19]

Eventually McKay's father tapped powerful contacts to save his son from prosecution, but the idea of resistance, even violent resistance, had been planted in some minds at Tampa and at other places in the region. The idea translated itself into gunfire in September. "Only a few weeks since a party of . . . men [determined to offer south Florida relief against the detested Yankees] visited Tampa, and attempted to assassinate a deputy marshal, whom they had been told had come to execute the Federal laws, collect taxes, &c.," reported the *New York Times*. "Two shots were fired at him in the darkness, one of which passed through his cap." Although he survived that attempt unscathed, the incident hardened Marshal Jenks's attitudes toward the defeated southerners. "Mr. Jenks spoke of them as actuated by the most malignant intentions," a senior United States officer recounted, "and instanced in his own case an illustration of their murderous designs." The officer added, "He said that he was hunted by that class of men day and night."[20]

Soon reports circulated of the resistance movement's growing organization. "I discern . . . a very strong feeling of hatred among the class formerly in the Rebel Army, against those who entered the Union Army from the rebel forces, and those who fled to avoid conscription," an investigator reported in December. "This feeling has given rise to, or revived an *old* organization called "Regulators," whose purpose appears to be to drive out these two classes of persons; and that they contemplate resorting to extreme measures to accomplish this purpose." Six months later James D. Green found conditions deteriorating. "I very much regret to say that the greater portion of the Rebels treat the Union people with the utmost *contempt*," he commented, "threatening to drive them from the Country so soon as the Soldiers are withdrawn from the Country." Reflecting back to the Regulator violence at the Billy Bowlegs War's close, one participant offered his perspective. "The regulatory band went out of commission in 1858, but the repetitions of like conditions came at the close of the Civil War," he asserted. "Murderers, rogues and rascals soon took possession, but we let the situation adjust itself."[21]

Promises to Keep

While his son indulged in Regulator activity against northerners and local Unionists, James McKay, Sr., weighed more important concerns. His business enterprises were in shambles, Tampa real estate essentially had become worthless, he had lost his small fleet of ships to the war, and local people once again were depending on him to find them a way out of the wilderness. Luckily, McKay had secreted an ace in the hole. Having honored his wartime commitments to the United States government as best he could, the captain believed that he was due a reward for services rendered that would permit him to restart the Cuban cattle trade and revive the local economy.

McKay knew that he needed to act quickly. First, he hurried to Tallahassee during the summer of 1865 to meet with Provisional Governor William Marvin and Major General John G. Foster, then commanding United States forces in Florida. Likely courtesy of Foster, the entrepreneur soon found himself in Havana where "friends" sent him on to New York. According to James McKay, Jr., "old merchants" who had worked with his father then staked him to certain purchases. The "old merchants" apparently held employment with the United States. Before he knew it, McKay had claimed title to the *U. S. S. Honduras*, a steamer valued at $72,000 that had served in May 1864 as the headquarters ship for the Union occupation of Tampa. The captain also came into possession of $24,000 in goods and inked a contract with the government to transport workers from New York to Key West. Coincidentally, military officials ordered a detachment of troops to guard the McKay and Summerlin loading dock at today's Punta Gorda. Other government benefits proved forthcoming in a matter of only a few months.[22]

Having to ride out a hurricane along the way, McKay had steamed his new ship—renamed the *Governor Marvin*—to south Florida by November. From Punta Gorda, he and Jacob Summerlin managed to transport 722 head of beef to Havana before year's end. Complications slowed down operations in 1866, although the captain's good luck in obtaining another United States warship, the *Southern Star*, opened up the possibility that 1867 would see the cattle trade take off and local fortunes begin to build. It seemed by then that nothing could stand in McKay's way.[23]

Back at Tampa, certain businessman had begun to prepare for business revival during McKay's 1865 journey to New York. One-time merchants John Darling, Madison Post, and Edward A. Clarke joined with William B. Hooker, William C. Brown, Erasmus M. Thompson, John A. Henderson, William S. Spencer, and McKay's son-in-law Robert B. Thomas in seeking presidential pardons that would ease their way in business dealings with the government. "I now acknowledge my error," Thomas informed the president in a typical statement. "I acted conscientiously and now ask to be allowed to become a good and loyal citizen." Just how much information McKay had shared with some or all of these men is not known. The position which he then occupied in the community, on the other hand, is well established. "Full of energy and enterprise[,] he gives to Tampa whatever of life and business it possesses," commented army colonel George F. Thompson, "in fact we find that the people of that place dated and regulated about every thing by McKay's movements." Thompson observed further, "If they were to clear a piece of ground or plant a patch of potatoes it would be contingent upon McKay's bringing the necessary implements and seed from Key West or Havanna."[24]

Presumably, the revival of Tampa's commercial houses can be traced from the captain's late November return with the stock of goods he purchased in New York. The first store to open its doors was blockade runner Samuel Mitchell's whiskey and dry goods establishment. Having amassed a tidy sum from sales of cattle and other commodities during the recent conflict, Mitchell had begun investing in Tampa property by 1863. Within six months or so others had followed Mitchell's lead. William J. Campbell inaugurated his mercantile emporium at Franklin and Lafayette [Kennedy] Streets. Edward A. Clarke and David Hughes partnered in a store, while William B.

Henderson and Jackson S. Redbrook sold groceries. C. L. Friebele & Co., together with Kennedy & Darling and E. P. Grant and Co., soon operated, as well.[25]

Interestingly, two former Confederate associates of McKay also saw the potential for regional prosperity with the cattle industry and cast their lot with Tampa. By the spring of 1866, onetime state commissary officer Pleasants W. White and Cow Cavalry commander Charles J. Munnerlyn, along with retired superior court judge Alexander A. Allen of Bainbridge, Georgia, had hung out their shingles for the practice of law as "P. W. White & Co." The men also operated a general store at the corner of Washington and Marion Streets. "Quick Sales & Small Profits" became their motto. As fate would have it, they experienced more small profits than quick sales. The firm dissolved in January 1867, with Allen buying out his partners.[26]

Truth was that too many stores opened too quickly, based upon unreasonable expectations of how quickly the cattle shipping business could swing into high gear. Cattle abounded on the prairies representing untold wealth, but until they reached the dock at Havana they put no money into owners' pockets. In the broader Tampa Bay and Peace River regions, new settlers also abounded. By late spring of 1866, reportedly, a "tide of immigration" had begun to flow into Hernando, Hillsborough, Polk, and Manatee Counties. Unfortunately, most settlers were impoverished Confederate veterans who held little money with which to buy luxuries or necessities. Unlike the cattle grazing families that proceeded them, though, they knew farming and, at the least, could offer crops in exchange for goods. "There were several stores on Washington Street, all doing good business, for there was good country trade, the farmers coming to Tampa from a distance of 50 miles or more," explained an early resident. "They never received any money for their produce," she added. "It was a rare thing to see money."[27]

The Meaning of Law and Order

In an economy in which money remained so scarce, the creation or revitalization of community institutions proved an extremely difficult task. Credit especially should given to freedmen for making progress under the most difficult of circumstances. The Methodists who had separated from the Methodist Episcopal Church, South, in

1863 had coalesced by 1865 into one of the state's first congregations of the African Methodist Episcopal Zion Church. A onetime Fort Meade slave, the Reverend Joseph Sexton, had brought the church's message with him from Key West early in the year. Sexton probably already knew many resident African Americans and helped them to form what would become Mt. Sinai AME Zion Church. At about the same time, several Baptists withdrew from the First Baptist Church to organize their own assembly, the Beulah Baptist Institutional Church. Their motivation, a church historian reported, was the "quest for freedom of worship and dignity of the individual."[28]

43. Father Henri Pierre Clavreul. (*Tampa Bay History*)

The white churches seemed to enjoy less success. Until late in 1865 no regular services were held by any of the three denominations. No priest received a regular assignment to St. Louis Parish from early 1863 until 1869. Occasionally, Father Henri Pierre Clavreul arrived to minister to local Roman Catholics, including the John Jackson, Andreu, Masters, Leonardy, Haskins, Collier, Bouguardez, Laurenti, and Ghira families. Until February 1866, according to preacher Sam Craft, "the providences connected with the late war" kept the Baptist church from reopening. After it did, the membership remained small with Craft straining to raise enough funds to defray his $200 annual salary. The Methodists fared somewhat better. William C. Jordan, who had pastored in Hillsborough County in 1860, returned just at year's end 1865 to replace the deceased William L. Murphy. Remaining until 1867, Jordan was aided after his first year by the appointment of William E. Collier as the district's presiding elder. At the time of Jordan's departure for Polk County, the local congregation numbered some eighty-three persons, making it by far the town's largest.[29]

Schools endured the same ups and downs as did the churches. Tampa and Florida had never enjoyed a true public school system up to that time, nor was any serious attempt made in the immediate post-war years to erect one. Late in 1865, a private school for boys and one for girls began sessions for about eighty white children. Minister Craft conducted classes for the boys under a stern regiment at the Baptist church, while the other teacher, a Mrs. Hawkins, likely pursued a more-easygoing approach. Craft's philosophy ultimately failed. So few youths enrolled in his academy by mid-1867 that he shut it down. His sister, widow Arabella Craft Nunez, thereupon picked up the challenge. Using softer methods, she succeeded where her brother had faltered.[30]

The revival of another community institution afforded the versatile Sam Craft work to fall back on when his school closed. In late April 1866 the Spencer family undertook once again to publish the *Florida Peninsular* newspaper, able to defray the expense because the town's recently opened stores desired to advertise. Its amateurish appearance reflected the rough conditions then found in town, but over time the paper improved in quality under Craft's editorship. John E. Spencer served as publisher until war-related disabilities cut short his life on June 30. His brother Thomas K. Spencer then stepped into the publisher's office. During 1866 and most of 1867, the paper with this leadership team expressed a moderate approach to the new order. Its motto "tempora mutanter" meant that "times have changed."[31]

44. Thomas K. Spencer. (Jim and Martha Ferman)

Not everyone felt the same way as did Sam Craft and John E. Spencer about times having changed, a fact that evidenced itself quickly when it came to breathing new life into another set of community institutions—state, county, and town government. Where Loyalists throughout Florida had believed that President Abraham Lincoln would place the reins of government in their hands, his successor President Andrew Johnson essentially passed local control back to the same elements that had taken the southern states out of the Union. His appointee as Florida's provisional governor, William Marvin, telegraphed to one and all in speeches delivered in most parts of the state that no radical changes lay in store. Marvin knew this would be true since the president had permitted most former Confederate soldiers to vote while denying the ballot to any freedmen.[32]

The first local test of President Johnson's reconstruction plan came on October 10, 1865, when Hillsborough County voters chose delegates to a state constitutional convention. Ossian B. Hart ran on a platform of the immediate grant of all civil rights to adult freedmen, while the pro-Confederate James Gettis opposed him. Hart summarized Gettis's philosophy as "my friend Col. Hart wants to put the nigger on a level with the white man and I don't." The Marvin administration had chosen elections officers from among the old Rebel faction. "A good old acquaintance of mine," the Loyalist candidate recalled, "who had been hanged [during the war], not quite to death, to make him tell [Confederate conscription agents] where his sons in the swamps were, and who with them succeeded in reaching the Union lines, and returned after the victory, went to one of the Johnson elections." Hart added, "I met him sadly returning, and was told by him that the chief officer of the election was the man who hung him."[33]

The elections ended in an activist Confederate triumph and dismal defeat for Loyalists. In Hillsborough County, many Union soldiers remained in service at stations elsewhere and could not vote. In the end only 181 men made it to the polls. Gettis accordingly crushed Hart, who soon departed Tampa in disgust for his childhood home of Jacksonville. The constitutional convention thereafter took the minimum steps suggested by Governor Marvin for readmission to the Union. In turn, the governor on November 10 restored civil authority in the state. Elections for legislative and county offices followed on the twenty-ninth. With Regulator violence spreading through the region and resentment at Fort Brooke's black troopers simmering, the former Confederates achieved victory, consolidating power over local affairs. William I. Turner bested C. R. Mobley for the state senate, and John A. Henderson received a majority for the state house. John T. Lesley took control of law enforcement by ousting William S. Spencer from the sheriff's office. John Darling assumed the presidency of the county commission by election as probate judge. The greatest prize went to James Gettis. Newly returned from the Tallahassee convention, he now donned the robes of circuit judge.[34]

Gettis and Lesley, once in office, accepted responsibility for maintaining "law and order" at Tampa and throughout the county. Since court did not convene until April 1866, Lesley initially carried much of the burden. In fairness to the two men, disorder ranged widely during the period. Hunger prompted burglaries, and the breakdown of civil authority during the war had undermined respect for "civilized" ways. By summer 1866 the *Peninsular* declared, "Our families cannot even go to church without leaving someone at home lest on our return we find our places robbed." Editor Craft still was complaining months later of street brawls "almost daily" and of the seemingly constant discharge of firearms in the streets. Young boys, always a challenge to authority, led in causing trouble. Particularly galling to some leading citizens including Craft, the ruffians even began disrupting church services.[35]

The citizenry generally could applaud a return to law and order where these types of crimes were concerned, but Lesley and Gettis took matters further in an attempt to turn back the clock based upon their conservative political philosophies. They refused, for example, to allow Loyalists access to the circuit court for suits against former Rebels for the return of stolen property. Naturally, their stance enraged Loyalists and heightened tensions. Complaints to military authorities led by November 1866 to a suspension of the circuit court's authority in such matters and the creation of a claims court by the Freedmen's Bureau, a federal agency headed locally by C. R. Mobley. "There are now thirty *cases* pending adjudication by this *Court*," reported the commander of the Fort Brooke garrison on December 17, "they are all claims for damages sustained by Union soldiers and refugees during the war." He added, "The claimants affirm that they cannot obtain justice in the State Courts."[36]

The Gettis court also administered the roughest sort of justice to African Americans, especially when it came to individuals who demanded political rights or criticized the local power structure. "Some are taken to the whipping post for the most trivial offenses and lashed by the officers of the law until the blood trickles to their heels, or thrust into the pillory," declared a petition of Union men signed in March 1867. The judge focused his principal ire on Tom Clarke. Aged about twenty-four in 1866, he perhaps was Sarah

Clarke's son and thus would have been well known to Sheriff Lesley and Judge Gettis. Outspoken, Clarke came to Gettis's official attention almost immediately. In April 1866 the judge tried him for "burglary," an offense that Freedmen's Bureau agent Mobley doubted Clarke had committed. Gettis ordered "his ears nailed to a post." When Clarke did not mend his ways, Lesley arrested him some months later for "stealing a gun tube," which the defendant claimed "to have found in the yard of his own house." As Mobley reported, Gettis did not permit Clarke "to bring any witnesses before the court." This time, the judge sentenced him "to receive thirty-nine lashes." The Fort Brooke commander noted, "Judging from the condition of his back, the sentence was executed in a very brutal manner."[37]

An additional community institution—municipal government—revived when it became apparent to a number of Tampans that Sheriff Lesley's capabilities had been spread too thin and that, despite his best efforts, the town's crime problems persisted. Urged on by the *Peninsular*, they attempted on August 28, 1866, to elect town officers based upon the 1855 incorporation. Madison Post headed a ticket of local businessmen determined to rid the place of malefactors. The election did not meet the test of state law, though, and another took place October 25 under the superintendence of John A. Henderson, John A. McKay, and Sam Craft. For reasons not entirely clear, Edward A. Clarke now substituted for Post as mayoral candidate. His ticket won, seemingly without opposition.[38]

The new town government, meeting in a room of the county courthouse, moved with dispatch to organize and legislate. Its first ordinance banned disorderly conduct (broadly defined) and made the crime punishable at the mayor's discretion. The councilmen also created a "city watch" composed of "all white male persons over the age of 18 years." They criminalized houses of "ill fame" and "nuisances." The latter category included "the practice of throwing the carcasses bones offal or refuse parts of animals or fish into the streets"; "the practice of half grown men and boys exhibiting their persons in a nude state about or on the wharf and on the banks of the river in this city, in daylight"; "the assemblages of boys of both or either color in the streets for the purpose of play, upon the Sabbath day"; and "the practice of men or boys congregating about the steps or doors of, or Street near, Churches, during time of service therein and talking, whispering or laughing so as to disturb persons in the church."[39]

Responsibility for executing the ordinances rested with Mayor

45. Sarah Wall Clarke (Mrs. E. A. Clarke) found herself a "first lady" of Tampa as wife of a successful businessman and mayor. (TBHC)

Clarke and Marshal Louis Bell, Jr. The marshal, who purchased Madison Post's river wharf and business property soon thereafter, seemingly resigned to be replaced by John B. Robles. His instructions from Mayor Clarke, historian Tony Pizzo related, were to "act tough." Of the results, Pizzo noted, "Robles, following strict orders, soon had the Negro problem under control."[40]

Uncertainties of the Future

Tampans faced a myriad of uncertainties by late 1866 and early 1867. They depended ultimately for economic well-being on the health of the cattle shipping business, but no one could tell just when it would begin to prosper. Community institutions were reviving, but finding the funds to support them taxed virtually everyone. Merchants opened business establishments, but their customers had no money. County and city law and order campaigns combatted crime on the one hand, while ignoring Regulator acts of violence on the other. State authorities empowered courts that federal officers suspended. Blacks and Unionists had begun to demand a say in governance. Former Confederates used government to block them. Where would it all end?

Even Mother Nature proved contrary. The "intensely hot" weather of summer 1865 gave way to the "long drought" of spring and summer 1866. In August the natural calamity changed to typhoid fever. Over 200 cases were reported in the town. "It was quite an epidemic here then," recalled Maria Louisa Daegenhardt. "So many of the younge people had it[,] so many died," she continued. "I was very low, they thought I could not live, but I was so afraid to die."

Daegenhardt concluded: "I became unconcious. The next day came too screemin for I thought their were wild horses chaceing me & I had to jump the fence. Then I became convalescent & God in his great Mercy spared me."[41]

In some respects the fortunes of William B. Hooker, once the area's largest cattleman, seemed to parallel those of Tampans generally. Having lost much of his wealth during the Civil War, Hooker relocated to his old Tampa home from Hernando County in the spring of 1866. His wife had passed away during the war, and his new bride Nancy Josephine McCreight Hooker encouraged him to turn their Madison Street mansion into an accommodation for visitors. Facing large debts, Hooker accepted the suggestion. In April he advertised the Orange Grove Hotel's opening. "This house, having just been renovated, and refitted, is now ready for the reception of boarders," he proclaimed. "Regular and day boarders will find this

"O RANGE GROVE" HOTEL,

TAMPA, FLORIDA.

W. B. HOOKER, Prop't'r.

THIS HOUSE HAVING BEEN THOROUGHLY renovated and refitted, is now open for the accommodation of visitors. Persons visiting Tampa will find this house a pleasant stopping place, where they can enjoy a climate unsurpassed in the State. The table will be furnished with all the delicacies of the season. In connection with this establishment is one of the finest Orange Groves in the Southern Country.

Tampa, Fla, Augnst 17th, 1867. 17-tf

46. This 1867 ad announced the opening of the Orange Grove Hotel. (*FP*, Aug. 17, 1867)

47. Samuel E. Hope. (*Sunland Tribune*)

a comfortable and convenient house, and every attention will be paid to the wants of travellers." So few visitors took the owner up on his offer that he began selling off other assets in desperation. That fall, Judge Gettis entered an order of foreclosure against the hotel property at the behest of William B., John A., and James F. Henderson. Hooker's son-in-law Samuel E. Hope kindly purchased the Hooker home and returned possession to his father-in-law. The county's once wealthiest man thereafter struggled to keep what he had, a battle that ended only with his death on June 11, 1871.[42]

So, too, did other Tampans struggle, waiting for better days, waiting for the uncertainties to fade into benevolent truths. New Year's 1867 brought hopes that a new day might be about to dawn. Prospects for the cattle business looked better than they had. The fever had gone, and the rains had come. Crime was down. The United States Congress had passed a homestead act that might give poor people, black and white, a chance to make a life for themselves. The circumstances required some luck, sure, but the chances seemed good. At that point, though, the excesses of the conservative reaction to the war's end were set to trigger their own reaction, with evil deeds coming back to haunt those who had seized the reins of power. And, the United States Congress was about to work social and political revolutions the reverberations of which have yet to fade.

48. The view looking down Franklin Street toward Fort Brooke. (TBHC)

"I would arm every crocodile in the swamps of Florida"

Reconstructing Tampa, 1867-1869

In the spring of 1867, the United States Congress acted in response to reports of widespread violence against freed peoples and Loyalists in the South by overturning President Andrew Johnson's mild reconstruction plan and substituting its own "radical" program. Now, African American men would enjoy voting rights for the first time, and the Republican party would grasp political power throughout the region. At Tampa, where divisions and frustrations already simmered hotly, the social and governmental revolution would ignite vicious political warfare. While local people invested their energies in the conflict, other forces twisted once-promising possibilities into nothing more substantial than teases. Within two years, the town and its residents would find themselves again exhausted and searching for any light to guide them toward the tunnel's end.

The irony looms too great to pass without mention. The dramatic revolution of Congressional or "Military" Reconstruction might not have happened had not some of the South's—and Tampa's—most vociferous former Confederates too eagerly and greedily grasped power in 1865 and 1866 under President Andrew Johnson's reconstruction plan. Seemingly, they intended to ensure that Civil War defeat meant nothing greater than technical freedom for slaves. In some respects, they may be forgiven for thinking so. The president certainly encouraged them by his actions. Meanwhile, Johnson's political opposition had manifested itself as so extreme that northern voters refused to back their radical agenda. "I do not believe there will be any peace until 347,000 men of the South are either hanged or exiled," Wendell Phillips had declared in 1865. The next year W. P. Brownlow added in a similarly strident style: "If I had the power I would arm every wolf, panther, catamount and bear in the mountains of America, every crocodile in the swamps of Florida, every Negro in the South, every devil in Hell, clothe him in the uniform of the Federal Army, and then turn them loose on the rebels of the South and exterminate every man, woman and child south of Mason and Dixon's line."[1]

Quickly, though, the climate of national opinion swung toward endorsement of Radical Republican ideas, with Tampa events and Tampa people aiding the movement along. The process began with President Johnson basking in popular support during the summer of 1866. As he did, a southern Loyalist convention gathered at Philadelphia to warn northern voters of the tragic events then occurring within the old Confederacy. Florida's involvement could be traced to a Tampa meeting held on March 15. There, "with most of the counties in South Florida . . . largely represented," delegates created the Union Party of Florida to oppose the one-time Rebels who had taken over state and local government. William A. Lively, Wesley Mansell, and Claiborne R. Mobley numbered among local men present. Perry G. Wall represented Hernando County. Although he remained at Jacksonville far from his old Tampa home, Ossian B. Hart stood foremost in the Unionists' eyes as their leader. Not surprisingly, Hart, Wall, Mobley, and others quickly appreciated the important opportunity presented by the Loyalist convention. So that the "bitter" happenings at Tampa and elsewhere in the state could be related, they organized a Florida delegation with Hart as chairman. At Philadelphia in early September, he won election as a convention vice president. As Hart explained, he also "stood out boldly for our great principles of equal suffrage and rights."[2]

The Southern Loyalist Convention garnered much attention in the North, but its impact increased exponentially when delegates created a "traveling committee" to hound the president's trail as he made a campaign swing through the North and Midwest. Congressional elections would be held in October and November, meaning that voters had begun to focus on political questions. Johnson hurt him-

49. William Lee Apthorp. (TBHC)

self by appearing drunk and losing his temper at a number of stops, but the traveling party's recitation of southern horror stories stirred strong emotions against the president's policies. Hart brought to the process a basketful of Tampa area memories. He shared them effectively. "Hart's speech was the 'plain unvarnished tale' of a man of sound common sense and won greatly upon the audience," one newspaper observed. Partly as a result of Hart's and the traveling committee's efforts, the Radical Republicans mastered their opposition and emerged from the elections with majorities in both houses of Congress. They could pass new laws and override expected presidential vetoes.[3]

The Radical Republicans set to work with a passion following their electoral triumph. The Reconstruction Acts of April 1867 and subsequent months called for earthshaking changes in the South's way of doing business. For the time being, the United States Army would supervise affairs in most of the old Confederate states, pending the writing of new constitutions and elections for new officers. The laws specified that adult African-American men could vote in the constitutional convention elections and implied that new state constitutions would guarantee that right permanently. Military authorities appointed O. B. Hart as superintendent of Florida voter registration to oversee the contests. For Hillsborough County he designated a registration board consisting of Matthew P. Lyons, one-time Union army officer William Lee Apthorp, and Frederick D. Newberry, a black man likely brought to Tampa by army service. By November, they had recorded the names of 211 whites and 87 blacks on registration lists.[4]

The Reconstruction Acts produced another result, the supersession of the Union Party of Florida by the Republican party. O. B. Hart spearheaded that action in his Jacksonville law office on March 27, 1867. The event's echo soon sounded at Tampa. "The Refugees and Union men are jubilant," reported Fort Brooke's commander in May, "they are Industriously at work perfecting their organization as a political party [and] they have entire confidence in their ability to select Loyal Union men to Office when the proper time comes." He added: "A meeting of Union citizens white & colored was held at Tampa on the 11th Inst. Resolutions expressive of Love for the Union and a determination to stand by the Government under any and all circumstances were passed."[5]

The Republicans' potential for political clout manifested itself in succeeding months. For one thing, Tampa's city councilmen found themselves compelled in late June to suspend the "city watch" of "all white male persons over the age of 18 years" that they had mandated the previous November. On July 4 came a more-public demonstration. "The fourth has been mildly celebrated to-day," a disapproving townsman related. "The troops marched under arms to the Court house, and such of the citizens, while and colored, as cared enough about it, gathered there and listened to the reading of the Declaration of Independence by Mr. [Henry] Albury," he continued. Not only did C. R. Mobley and freedman Handy Williams speak but Judge James Gettis felt it necessary to address the gathering himself. "As far as the effect on the audience," the townsman added, "the colored speaker rather surpassed the others." The occasion's energy refused to die down. "Toward night," it was noted, "a party of freedmen paraded the streets with a flag and fiddle, and gave vent to their patriotism in songs and shouts."[6]

The Republicans got directly to the point at a large public gathering held on August 30. They agreed to demand of military authorities that Judge Gettis suffer removal from office "because we do not think the well-being of the people requires the holding of any more Circuit Courts in this Circuit at this time." Those in attendance also insisted on the dismissal of all other county and municipal officers. Instead, they argued for new appointments, including: Matthew P. Lyons, judge; James R. Hay, sheriff; Henry L. Crane, clerk of court; Joseph Brownlow, Joel Knight, and Daniel Gillett, county commissioners; and B. C. Leonardy, mayor. Blacks in attendance, objecting to some of the names, insisted that Frederick

Newberry substitute for Gillett on the county commission and that Cyrus Charles, L. G. Covacevich, and Charles Carter make up the town council. They also desired a black man, John Forrester, to act as town marshal. The Fort Brooke commander subsequently decided that he preferred Newberry for marshal, but otherwise sided with the freedmen.[7]

Military officials dodged implementation of the Republican demands as the Reconstruction saga continued to unfold. Sheriff John T. Lesley, who remained in office but labored under supervision of Fort Brooke's commanding officer, helped to organize the conservative opposition. To oppose C. R. Mobley's candidacy for constitutional convention delegate in a district that included Polk and Manatee Counties, he and his associates nominated Fort Meade cattleman William Marion Hendry. Passions built to a fever pitch as the two factions maneuvered for support. The tensions spilled over to the town's newspaper in late September. Publisher Thomas K. Spencer deemed Sam Craft too moderate in his opposition to the revolution then ongoing. Spencer ousted the editor in favor of his own brother-in-law Henry Laurens Mitchell, a former Confederate officer and state legislator who had studied law under Judge Gettis and was allied closely with Sheriff Lesley. The political heat commenced to sizzle in the *Florida Peninsular*'s columns.[8]

The convention election went off as scheduled during November 14-16, 1867, with charges and countercharges of corruption bandied about on all sides. Mobley insisted that the Democrats (or Conservatives) had played dirty tricks and that their ballots should be discarded. H. L. Mitchell, in turn, claimed Republican tampering with the results, venting his particular ire at registrar William Lee Apthorp. "The registrars opened the ballot box, stole out Democratic and put in their place Republican votes," Mitchell argued. Fort Brooke commander Richard Comba believed all the charges nonsensical. "There was some excitement for a short time after the Election in November," he reported to superior officers, "but purely of a party character." Comba added, "The citizens conducted themselves in a quiet and orderly manner." Since most whites declined to vote, the county turnout amounted to only 191 ballots cast out of a potential 320. Mobley won 115 of the votes, enough to give him and the Republicans a first taste of victory.[9]

Sunshine Through the Clouds

The eleven months that led up to C. R. Mobley's November 1867 election win had seen Tampans' spirits rise and fall with a volatility every bit as intense as the political feuding associated with the Reconstruction process. It is well to remember that, even at the period's beginning, the town had yet to recover its prosperity from wartime disruptions. Future county judge Charles E. Harrison recorded how the community's down-at-the-heels appearance struck him upon first sight. "It was certainly a little village," he began. Harrison continued:

> The village of Tampa in 1867 was confined entirely to the area lying between Whiting Street on the south, about Tyler on the north, East street on the east, and the river on the west. This area was not by any means closely built up. The humble wooden houses were very much scattered, there being many vacant lots and unoccupied spaces lying between them. The principal business street was Washington, not Franklin. There were, of course, no pavements. Neither were there any sidewalks that deserved the name. Only here and there was there a little stretch of boards laid down by some enterprising citizen or a few yards of oyster-shells or saw-dust. The streets were uniformly of the deep sand for which Tampa has been famous for many years.[10]

One Tampa eyesore symbolized for Harrison and many others the town's continuing depressed condition. Of the "Jackson Street Gully," he wrote:

> At the time of my first acquaintance with Tampa, and for a number of years afterward, one of the most conspicuous physical features and vexing municipal problems was the Jackson street gully. It will be observed even now [c. 1912] that the street is the lowest of those intersecting Franklin, all of the streets running at right angles with it sloping towards it from both sides and thus draining into it. There was also—and still is—considerably low lying land near its head. All of this during the rainy season drained into Jackson street.
>
> All of these things combining let such a flood down Jackson street that it was washed out, making a deep and wide canyon occupying all the width of an ordinary sidewalk on each side—only there were no sidewalks only places for them. Innumerable attempts were made to close and fill up this gully; but with only temporary success, it being washed out again when the next rainy season came.[11]

50. This photo, taken in the early 1880s, shows that the Jackson Street gully remained an unsolved problem for residents. (TBHC)

Tampans drew strength to continue under the troubling circumstances from hope born of a belief that prosperity lay just around the corner. Most townspeople looked to James McKay, Sr., to reap it for them from cattle sales. "The McKays then held full swing in all this part of the country," explained a local man. "It seemed as if they owned and controlled everything," he continued. "They had plenty of money, and money is here, like everywhere else, king." Unfortunately, McKay's task of re-establishing the shipping trade to Havana had proven more difficult than the captain had anticipated. He would handle about 7,000 head in 1867, but problems kept cropping up. Plus, McKay's local reputation took a tremendous blow in September when his steamer *Southern Star* under Captain Archibald McNeill transported yellow fever from Key West to Tampa Bay. The tragedy presaged others to come.[12]

Another aspect of Tampa's economy also offered hope in early 1867. James D. Haygood some months earlier had resurrected the local lumber industry by opening the "Tampa Mills." The combination saw and grist mill created jobs while giving the town some semblance of industry. John T. Lesley recognized opportunities in the

51. William Hester Brown. (TBHC)

Tampa Mills' success. With partner William Hester Brown, he purchased from C. R. Mobley machinery "which belonged to what was known as the Bell Mill," a concern moribund since the Civil War's beginning. Having invested considerably in new facilities, Lesley and Brown prepared to open for business by late July. The *Florida Peninsular* delighted in the coming reality of "two Steam Mills daily turning out their thousands of feet of lumber." The concerns' sounds and routines gave Tampans the punctuations of their days. "At morning, noon and night the ear is saluted by the merry whistle of the engines," remarked one visitor, "not of the Rail Road trains, for the cars have not yet arrived, but of the Tampa Saw Mills."[13]

Local merchants, happy to hear cash registers ring from sales to salaried mill hands, looked as well to new customers to fatten their receipts. Population totals in the Tampa Bay area, if not in town, were rising. "The tide of emigration which has flown so steadily into this section of Florida for the past ten months, still continues, but not in such numbers," the *Peninsular* reported in March 1867. One month earlier its editor had insisted that "about one thousand families have settled in the four Counties of Hillsborough, Polk, Hernando, and Manatee since the war closed." Most looked to Tampa for supplies. "Stock [i.e., the cattle industry] absorbs every thing and consequently the supplies of the people have to be bought and brought from elsewhere," observed a correspondent. "A merchant asserts that something near twenty thousand dollars worth of corn and other articles of food were sold in Tampa [in 1867]."[14]

Of considerable importance to the area in the years to come, a federal program encouraged many of the new settlers—in addition to some longtime residents—to claim their own parcels of land. The

Southern Homestead Act, approved by the Congress on June 21, 1866, had opened up homesteads on easy terms to persons "without distinction of race or color" who could take a loyalty oath, with rations supplied in some cases by the government. Within the year, the law's terms were relaxed to permit onetime Rebels to apply. The statute required a proper application, five years' subsequent residence on the land, payment of a small fee, and the farming of a portion of the property.[15]

The homestead law carried with it significant implications for Tampa's future. Since freedmen, Loyalists, and women could take advantage of the program before former Confederates were permitted to do so, the best available lands surrounding the town (including Hillsborough River frontage) presumably would end up in hands other than those of former Rebels. Some white conservatives chafed at this possibility and other changes homestead settlements would bring. "There are many [freedmen] who wish the coming year to go upon Homesteads," Lieutenant Comba reported in June 1867, "and I think there will be many next year who will be able to start out quite well, those few that have already started are doing much better than I expected, and the others are taking encouragement from what they see them doing." He added, "White people are generally decidedly opposed to it, and will do nothing to favor, or assist, them forward, but upon the contrary they tell them there is no Gov't land and circulate other false statements among them to dissuade them from making any efforts." The lieutenant concluded, "The only reason I can see for it is they fear they will loose their labor should they work upon land of their own."[16]

Notwithstanding resistance from whites, individual freedmen and Loyalists desired to enter Tampa area homesteads as soon as they could. The law's implementation proceeded slowly. The *Peninsular* finally published the Interior Department's rules of May 18, 1867, on June 29. Clerk of court John J. Givens attempted to assist with applications, but not until the arrival of locating agent William Lee Apthorp in July was the process facilitated. A later chapter will discuss the specifics of Tampa growth in light of the homesteads. Suffice it to say here that among early applicants staking claims close to the town limits were Nancy Collar Jackson, Augustus Santhorant, S. P. Haddon, and freedpersons Cyrus Charles, Benjamin Taylor, and John Matthews.[17]

A Tendency Toward Disaster

Cattle sales, mill jobs, frontier expansion, prospering commercial houses, and homestead grants combined to offer Tampans a small measure of optimism during the spring and summer of 1867, but the ill fortune of recent years nonetheless continued to haunt local people just as the impact of the Reconstruction Acts began to hit home. A harbinger of things to come arrived in April with news that the schooner *James E. Price* of New Orleans had wrecked at Mullet Key. Merchant Edward A. Clarke and publisher Thomas K. Spencer barely survived, while the ship's cargo of supplies for local stores was lost in its entirety. Tampans suffered accordingly. "This is a melancholy affair and a calamity to the whole country, inasmuch as there are no provisions to be got in the country," editor Craft declared. "There are many families here in town entirely out," he explained. "Much suffering must inevitably result."[18]

Calamities thereafter piled one upon another. In May fire destroyed the homes of freedmen in "the Scrub" before sweeping through large areas of the town cemetery. Fears of yellow fever contagion spurred authorities to quarantine Tampa in early June. The next month mail service suspended. When the steamer *Alliance*'s captain James McKay, Jr., announced a few days later that his vessel no longer would call, a local man observed, "We shall be about as secluded from the busy world as was Alexander Selkirk or Robinson Crusoe, or as the Man in the Moon."[19]

The sense of isolation caused by the absence of mail service continued until September and, doubtlessly, enhanced the hardship of subsequent events. For one thing, rains came beginning in June, drenching the town and region almost incessantly for months. By August's end they had poured so much water upon the land that it no longer could hold the bounty. What farmers normally prayed for, they now cursed. "The crops are quite poor," an army officer remarked. "The corn and the cotton crop this year will probably be a failure," he continued. "The country has been flooded with water and the roads are almost impassible."[20]

With the "Stormy & Extremely Wet weather" came "billious fevers" that struck scores of local people. When James McKay, Sr.'s *Southern Star* touched at the Manatee River with yellow fever aboard, a sense of panic ensued at Tampa. It appears that the dreaded "yellow jack" failed to reach the town, but whatever ailment beset the

52. This striking photograph portrays Maria Moore Post (Mrs. Madison Post) in old age. It permits the reading of local pioneer history on the face of a former mayor's wife and helpmate as the wooden homes of oldtime Tampa fade into the background. (TBHC)

community persisted. Several persons perished, including onetime mayor Madison Post. "We have had a great deal of sickness in this place, and throughout the Country," William G. Ferris lamented on September 15, "undoubtedly occasioned by the excessive rains, the like of which was never before known here." He appended, "It is a hard struggle for the best to get along."[21]

By the time Ferris took his pen to hand, the flooding had intensified, a fact that contributed to making all of the other problems worse. For 100 miles or more northward into the peninsula editors bemoaned the onslaught of precipitation. "Since 1848 the water courses of this State have not been so high as within the past week," the *Ocala Banner* proclaimed in mid-October. "The results may be briefly summed up in this sentence: The flat woods and swamps are under water, wharves, bridges, and causeways washed away, many farms hidden and crops drowned and general ruin staring some of the proprietors." Many of Hillsborough County's flimsy bridges gave way, including the one over Six Mile Creek. During rainy periods, wagons would not be able to access Tampa from the thriving farm and cattle country to the east for one year or more.[22]

October's flooding slammed Tampa merchants, brought a renewed attack of the fevers, and compelled many residents to flight. "Considerable sickness still exists in town, four deaths reported in town within the last ten days, and has caused some alarm among the people," Lieutenant Comba recounted on October 31, "some families have left town in consequence, yet the Doctors declared the disease nothing but a malignant Type of Bilious Fever, others who appear to have a knowledge of the disease also, declare that it is yellow fever." The officer added: "Whatever the disease I am satisfied that it originated here, and has existed here more or less since the first of August, it was not thought much of until within the last month, in which time about twelve cases have proved fatal." To compound the grim assault's toll, children seemed to suffer disproportionately, sending wails of anguish into the night from many homes. Such was the case, for instance, at C. R. Mobley's residence on October 31, when the fevers claimed his eight-year-old daughter Maude.[23]

With these circumstances offering context, the emotional intensity of the political campaign and November delegate contests becomes even more understandable, but the elections proved insufficient to fully expend the pent-up anger and frustration because bad news kept blanketing Tampa in the months thereafter. Where rain waters had rotted crops in the summer and fall of 1867, for example, drought accomplished the same purpose in the spring of 1868. Farmers ached as corn burned in the fields by June. They then watched on Christmas Day as a hard freeze made the point that their trials remained far from over.[24]

The most important of the ill tidings related to happenings in

Cuba. Creoles on the island were pushing early in 1868 for independence from Spain and, perhaps, annexation by the United States. The possibility of armed conflict sent the Cuban construction industry crashing, thereby drastically reducing the demand for lumber. Since Tampa's mills shipped much of their product to the island, this posed a major problem. As a visitor noted in February, "The saw mill business has not prospered." The owners attempted to switch their operations to cotton ginning, but serious damage had resulted to their enterprises and the local economy.[25]

The next blow struck at the cattle industry. Preparing for revolutionary conflict, Cuban officials set about raising revenues wherever they could. Among other initiatives, they imposed during the summer of 1868 an import fee of $7 per head of live cattle. This levy priced Florida beef well out of the range of most Havana residents. Sales plummeted. For the entire year Florida sellers managed to dispose of only about 3,000 head in Cuba, less than half the previous year's totals and far below expectations. The next year brought more of the same, as shippers such as James McKay, Jacob Summerlin, and others desperately searched out new markets from New Orleans to New York City.[26]

The jackhammer blows pounded Tampans until the community's fabric began to unravel. By the time young Kate Barnwell arrived with her family from Alabama in December 1868, the place had become "terrible looking." She recalled, "Tampa was a very small little town with only two or three stores, and a very few people, and no streets at all but only sand roads with palmetto roots and high scrub-oaks on each side of the roads." Cash had disappeared. Two months before Barnwell's advent, lawyer John A. Henderson had noted just how critical the problem had become when discussing a $7,000 debt owed by an area merchant. "There is hardly that much cash in this whole country," he had declared. Eight months earlier a traveler had noted, "Business done now is a barter trade."[27]

Spreading economic collapse reduced many local residents to penury. Hardest hit were freedmen. "[They] are by no means in a prosperous condition," concluded one correspondent in February. "How many of them make a living is yet unexplained." In the circumstances, a rash of robberies hit local grocery and dry goods stores. Merchants demanded a quick dose of law and order. Lieutenant Comba, insisting on recognition of basic rights in judicial proceedings, objected to harsh measures. Soon, he withdrew authority to try "slight" offenses from local courts. In their place, he created committees of freedmen to hear cases and impose punishments. Tempers rose between the town and the military to the point that, in June, Mayor Edward A. Clarke resigned along with the town marshal.[28]

With Tampa's plunge, Fort Brooke's fortunes rose and its facilities improved. General John T. Sprague, who had commanded its forces in the late 1840s, took up its cause with his superiors in early 1868. "This is . . . a most important post," he insisted, "its remoteness, the character of the population, a large number of Freedmen, a resort of refugees from justice, the vagrant thoughts and habits of a frontier settlement, the absence of law, the protection of union citizens, and the reckless and uncompromising conduct of men engaged in the Confederate cause for ten years past, all contribute to render Fort Brooke the most exposed and important post in Florida." Thanks to the general's influence, allocation of long-sought funds for repair and construction received approved. "Under Instructions from the Chief Qr Master 3rd Mil Dist, this post is being rebuilt," Lieutenant Comba reported on May 31, "work commenced on the 20th Inst & in which the troops are taking an active part."[29]

Politics and the City's Demise

During prosperous times, changes of the political magnitude of those wrought by Congressional Reconstruction could wrench the soul of any community. Tampans found themselves in circumstances far less advantageous. In point of fact, they grappled unsteadily with the hottest of political issues while also attempting to deal in a very close and closed environment with calamity after calamity. Under the circumstances, wounds opened that generations would fail to heal.

The year 1868's political events commenced with the constitutional convention held at Tallahassee in January and February. A faction of delegates, mostly black and known as the Mule Team, seized control at the outset only to be displaced amid a great deal of excitement and maneuvering by a somewhat more moderate group headed by O. B. Hart. Tampa Bay delegate C. R. Mobley sided with Hart's forces to write a constitution that granted immense powers to the governor. Among them, the state's chief executive could appoint all county officers except constables and state legislators.[30]

The constitution's completion signalled the beginning of an election season looking toward May approval of the new charter and election of officers. The Republicans backed onetime Wisconsin editor Harrison Reed (who was President Johnson's man in the state) for governor, while Conservatives divided over participation in what many believed to be an illegal process. From Tampa came firm support for opposing the Republicans. "Wherever I have been I have found but one opinion among the conservative people," John A. Henderson informed state party leaders in late March, "that is that [it] is best to fight them on every line, that we ought not and must not accept the constitution, because it is bad, and that, because it might be worse, is no reason that we should endorse or ratify the objectionable features proposed."[31]

Soon, Tampa found itself awash in politics besides all of its other mounting problems. The voter registration board resumed its work in a controversial manner, opening its rolls for new voters from a table in C. R. Mobley's drug store. Mobley, at the time, proudly carried the Republican nomination for the state senate seat that included Hillsborough (now Hillsborough and Pinellas) and Hernando (now Pasco, Hernando, and Citrus) Counties. A host of Republican luminaries came to town on April 17 to keep the political fires burning. Constitutional convention delegates Green Davidson, Charles H. Pearce, and Jonathan C. Gibbs, among others, filled the African Methodist Episcopal Zion church and stirred those present with a passion for radical politics. Conservatives were not to be outdone. "We are all united and enthusiastic," John A. Henderson reported two days after the Republican rally. "We will send a good report," he added. "Keep the ball in motion."[32]

The political crisis touched the nation, the region, the state, and Tampa's local people. Against the backdrop of President Johnson's impeachment by congressional radicals, the sharpest of emotions burst forth. "The late Rebels show more hatred toward the Govt. at the present time than I have noticed at any time during the past two years," Fort Brooke's Lieutenant Comba observed on April 30. "The political Campaign now in progress in this part of the State has brought to the surface some of the worse men of both parties, who deem it their province to stir up the passions & prejudices of the people," he continued. "An honest appeal to their intelligence is not thought of, not to be a Radical, is to be a Rebel, & to be a Radical is to be a traitor and an enemy to his state." Comba concluded, "All Classes of the people have taken sides on these questions, and the consequence is that the community are kept in a continued state of excitement, which is likely to continue until after the Election or until politions are compeled to confine themselves to discussing the Great political questions at issue instead of indulging in personal and party abuse."[33]

The clamor reached its climax with polling on March fourth through sixth. So much emotion had been packed into the campaign that little remained for sparking troubles on election day. "The election . . . passed off very orderly," Comba informed his superiors, "not an angry word could be heard at the various voting places during the entire election." The lieutenant noted further: "'Politicians and grumblers generally' seem to have lost their occupation. No more street harangues, or abuse of this, or that candidate, all appear to have acquiesced in the result and have quietly settled down to their legitimate business." The county voted Conservative and against the constitution by about forty votes out of almost 300 cast. Charles Moore took Hillsborough's seat in the state house of representatives, although Republican C. R. Mobley—who lost in Hillsborough—nonetheless took the senate seat. Statewide, Republicans captured the governor's office and control of both houses of the state legislature.[34]

The local setbacks stemmed Republican euphoria not one whit. Senator Mobley threw a series of biracial parties at his home. Neighbors, angry at the turn of events, complained of "loud music and dancing by colored people" but found that they now could do little to curb the celebrations. On May 20 the parties moved outdoors briefly when Lieutenant Governor-Elect William Gleason happened into the port on his way to Tallahassee. "The old Town Hall bell sounded forth the fact that some unusual event had taken place," a correspondent declared, "and soon the gathering masses knew that they had a live Lieutenant-Governor among them, and they gave him an old-fashioned welcome at the residence of their Senator elect." Three days afterward a "May Celebration and Picnic" brought African Americans together again for public rejoicing. In doing so they evidenced greater maturity than that displayed by some of their white political opponents. "Upon special call brief speeches were made by several colored men," commented the *Peninsular*, "all of which were in the right spirit, expressing sentiments of respect and true friendship for the whites, desiring their friendly counsel and co-operation in the pursuits of life, and for their prosperity."[35]

During the summer and fall, both sides of the political divide organized and prepared for the future. In opposition, county Conservatives

53.-54. Jeanette Collar Haskins and William Thomas Haskins. (*Tampa Bay History*)

met on a number of occasions beginning in July to plan future strategy. Taking a leading role were men who made up the cream of Tampa's professional and merchant class. They included John T. Lesley, Henry Proseus, John T. Givens, Alexander A. Allen, Edward A. Clarke, William G. Ferris, William B. Hooker, Joseph Robles, James D. Haygood, Vincent Leonardy, William T. Haskins, Robert Canning, John Jackson, Joseph Grillon, Thomas Fisher, Samuel C. Craft, Domenico Ghira, Henry L. Mitchell, D. Isaac Craft, Louis Bell, Jr., Samuel Mitchell, Wesley Mansell, William E. Sweat, John A. McKay, and John A. Henderson. John T. Lesley emerged as party chairman. It would be said of him in later years that "no man in Florida displayed more bravery and fidelity in the long and trying fight to relieve the state from 'carpetbag' rule and Negro domination."[36]

Beyond party building, the Republicans faced the task of creating state and local governments. At first, C. R. Mobley exercised the greatest influence when it came to Tampa and Hillsborough County. With the senator's guidance, Governor Reed in August and September filled all county appointive offices. William Lee Apthorp emerged as county judge, with Matthew P. Lyons taking office as county clerk. Henry Albury assumed duties as sheriff. James R. Hay did the same as tax assessor and Bartholomew C. Leonardy as tax collector. James A. Thompson controlled the purse strings as county treasurer. Frederick D. Newberry presided as the county's first new justice of the peace. Creating the greatest stir, the new county commission included two black men, Mills Holloman and Cyrus Charles, and three whites, Joseph P. Brownlow, Charles Armor, and Henry H. Keen.[37]

When it came to filling two final offices, Governor Reed frustrated Senator Mobley's will and created a rivalry that would rend the Hillsborough County Republican party. The governor had grown close to James T. Magbee and designated him to serve as circuit court judge. The former Tampa lawyer and Democratic powerbroker had been serving as state senator at the time of secession. Magbee had appeared, at first, to support the Confederacy, but ultimately he had adopted a stance more pro-Union. As a result, the senator had suffered removal from office in 1862. Subsequently, Magbee had relocated to Wakulla County where his wife owned a plantation, had run for and lost the office of Florida secretary of state in 1865, and thereafter had practiced law at Tallahassee. Aware that Magbee's appointment as judge would put in place a rival for power in Hillsborough, Mobley advanced himself as a candidate for the position. As it turned out, Reed opted for Magbee and offered Mobley only the job of state's attorney. In the circumstances, Mobley accepted.[38]

By October 1868 the new Republican officeholders had taken up county government's reins, with James T. Magbee assuming greater authority than C. R. Mobley was prepared to concede to him. The two men soon locked horns. Initially, Magbee enjoyed support from *Peninsular* editor Henry L. Mitchell, who dismissed Mobley as nothing more than a "border ruffian." When the judge immersed himself in Republican party-building efforts, though, Mitchell used the paper to denounce him. Particularly, the editor ran a scathing article written by William B. Henderson (who also had married a sister of publisher Thomas K. Spencer). In response, Magbee fined Henderson $100 for contempt of court and launched his own newspaper from a courthouse office. Named the *True Southerner*, Tampa's newborn Republican organ debuted October 10, 1868, with Edward O. Plumbe as editor and Charles L. Newhall as publisher. Since the judge designated his own paper to carry legal advertisements, the *Peninsular's* financial underpinnings suffered accordingly. Editor Mitchell thereafter adopted a political posture even more extreme than his previous Conservative stance.[39]

The escalating newspaper rhetoric destroyed whatever chances Tampa possessed for a peaceful Reconstruction. For their part, black residents deeply resented white intransigence and race-based hatemongering as purveyed by the *Peninsular*. They seethed also upon learning that President Johnson had appointed the paper's publisher Thomas K. Spencer as deputy United States marshal, making the former Confederate the region's chief federal law enforcement agent. Thomas E. Jackson recalled that, when news of Ulysses S. Grant's presidential election reached town the same month, the Republicans took out their frustrations on Tampa's sole black Democrat, a onetime William W. Wall family slave. "A group of the Negroes caught Bill Duncan at the intersection of Franklin and Washington Sts. and mobbed him," Jackson declared. "Capt. [James] McKay, just landed from a trip to Cuba," he continued, "saw the crowd, and on being told that old Bill was in danger of being killed by the mob, he pushed his way in, pulled several off the prostrate man and struck one who was choking Bill, killing him with the single blow of his fist." It seems highly unlikely that James McKay actually killed anyone that day, but the story otherwise may reflect actual events.[40]

On the other hand, Conservative emotions hit new low after new low as Republicans consolidated their rule. Among the happenings, William Lee Apthorp assumed duties as Tampa's postmaster in August. Former Union army officer Ansel A. Watrous of Bay City, Michigan, who had arrived from Key West in May as the new federal revenue collector, succeeded Apthorp as county judge in October. Then, *True Southerner* editor E. O. Plumbe took over as judge from Watrous in January 1869. The same month a "black and tan" meeting of white and black Republicans held at the county courthouse took upon itself the right to nominate replacements for county officers. "This is a very pretty little scheme worthy of the fertile brained Mobley," mockingly declared the *Peninsular*, "and worthy the party which he carries in his pocket."[41]

Something as simple as the opening of the town's first school for African Americans, which occurred in fall 1868, added fuel to Conservative fires. This was the case since the classes were held in

55. Acting from his Conservative convictions, Henry L. Crane joined the ticket that would dissolve the town he had long loved and helped to build. (TBHC)

the courthouse, which Conservatives viewed as a visible symbol of their lost power now being defiled by Republicans. "Heretofore the Sheriff always had charge of our Court House, but our present County Commissioners have taken it out of his charge, and this public building is now under the control of no one we suppose," lamented Henry L. Mitchell in January 1869, "as it is appropriated to every purpose [except] that for which it was intended." The editor added: "A Printing office, negro schools, negro preaching and negro balls are all allowed at the Court House! Who pays the taxes to keep up the Court House? The white people of Hillsborough county."[42]

When the legislature met in early 1869, Republicans took a further step that proved for many of Tampa's Conservatives the straw that broke the camel's back. On February 4 a proposal requiring the reincorporation of all municipalities received final approval. Anticipating that occurrence, a bi-partisan group led mostly by Republicans gathered on January 28 to call for a municipal reorganization election. Bartholomew C. Leonardy headed the gathering's slate as candidate for mayor on a ticket that included, among others, Matthew P. Lyons, and William H. Harrison.[43]

The Conservatives would have none of it and determined to abolish Tampa's corporation. Given the difficult straits facing townspeople at the time, they acted partly from resistance to the idea of new municipal taxes added to other financial burdens. But, there was more. As Theodore Lesley observed, "This was done . . . to keep the city government from falling into the hands of the carpetbaggers and Republicans." His grandfather John T. Lesley, who ran on the "No Corporation People's Ticket," told Theodore Lesley that he acted to keep the city "from falling into the hands of corrupt adventurers," whom he defined as "the former slaves of the South, abetted by northern guns and Southern renegades, [who] filled every public office with controlled henchmen." Joining the ticket with Lesley were Henry L. Crane, Josiah Ferris, Ferdinand Wade, John F. Fletcher, Lawrence E. Masters, John A. McKay, James Williams, and County Commissioner Cyrus Charles, who may have owed his livelihood to employment at the Lesley saw mill. On March 1 the Conservatives prevailed, terminating Tampa's existence as an incorporated municipality. As the city closed its books, though, much of the story remained to be played out. Political turmoil at Tampa had only just begun.[44]

56. James T. Magbee was Hillsborough County's first permanent, full-time lawyer as well one of Hillsborough County's most prominent political figures from the 1850s to the 1880s. Noted for a love of, but low tolerance for, alcohol, Magbee endured public condemnation by his political enemies for his drinking, as well as numerous mean-spirited pranks. He found the reins on his buggy cut in Brandon; a gray jackass was found strapped to his judge's chair in the Brooksville courtroom; and when he "fell dead drunk in the sand street at Franklin and Washington" in Tampa, he was covered with molasses and corn and rolled about the streets until most of his clothes came off. Artist Gene Packwood depicts him in this sketch from D. B. McKay's *Pioneer Florida* being ridiculed by men in a local saloon after all the wheels have fallen off his wagon. Despite such torments, Magbee remained a respected lawyer and editor, as well as an influential politican, until his death. (Leland Hawes)

"when the keepers of the house shall tremble"

Industry, Impatience, and Injunctions, 1869-1872

In March 1869 residents watched as partisan politics doomed Tampa's municipal corporation, an event that occurred as the town's economic fortunes ebbed disastrously. Political fervor split the community with bitter repercussions, but, over time, its harsh results also prodded many Tampans to understand that their hopes for the future depended upon cooperation, rather than conflict. This new way of thinking, born in good part of desperation, in turn opened doors of salvation that otherwise would have remained tightly closed. Subsequently and against most expectations, some local people would combine unexpectedly to aid a one-time Tampan's election as governor. That man, they thought, would craft for them the key to the future.

The symbols of Tampa's ailing condition stood everywhere to confront townspeople in the spring of 1869. On Washington and nearby streets commercial houses were boarded up as the less well-established businessmen bankrupted, sold out, or gave out. Alexander A. Allen packed up and moved back to Georgia in February, for example, while Captain John Miller waited until April

57. Captain John Miller. (Grismer, *Tampa*)

to set off for Pennsylvania. The problems grew worse that month as heavy rains pummeled area farms into mud pits. Meanwhile, federal officials reacted to demands for cuts in military payrolls by reducing Fort Brooke's garrison. By May only 21 men remained to occupy its newly constructed buildings and, more importantly, to patronize local businesses. In September these few soldiers, too, received orders to depart. The post, garrisoned for most of the previous forty-five years, rested in the care of a lone quartermaster's agent.[1]

The single most striking symbol of the town's ill fortune arose when the Florida Hotel burned. Tampa's most comfortable antebellum accommodation, it had remained a familiar rest stop and meeting place under owner James McKay, Sr., and manager James Williams. Then, on Saturday evening, May 29, flames erupted from its kitchen. "The citizens generally, and the officers and soldiers from the garrison were soon on the ground and did all that could be done under the circumstances to extinguish the fire," reported the *Florida Peninsular*. Unfortunately, the municipal corporation's demise had spelled the end of its fire fighting capability. "There being no fire engine, no hooks, no ladders, in fact nothing to work to advantage with, the flames soon reached the Dining room, and then the Hotel itself," the account continued, "and in a short time that stately building went down before the destroying element." The tragedy even highlighted the town's racial problems. "When the fire broke out there was a little colored girl sleeping in the kitchen (her mother being absent)," the reporter observed, "and during the height of the fire her screams were distinctly heard by people outside, but it was impossible to save her, and after the kitchen fell in and the fire abated her remains were found, near where she had been put to bed, dreadfully burned and disfigured."[2]

It is not beyond the realm of possibility that arson lay behind the fire, although the identity of the person who struck the match is open to question. Details are hard to come by, but three days earlier a "riot" had resulted in the arrest of at least one young black leader, Peter W. Bryant. Circumstances suggest that Sheriff Henry Albury intended merely to protect Bryant from the tender mercies of a lynch mob. The sheriff designated Bryant's friend Thomas Clarke to guard him, for one thing, and he set the place of confinement as Fort Brooke. Also, it appears that Bryant won release without trial. Given the favorable light in which military authorities viewed the wishes of the hotel's owner Captain McKay, perhaps his intervention to protect Bryant prompted the vigilante action, with the property destruction intended as a warning.[3]

If so, the incident formed part of a trend toward violent vigilante action in the Tampa Bay region just as Fort Brooke's garrison diminished and, finally, departed. On July 25, for instance, Manatee County's black voter registrar John Lomans was whipped at Fort Ogden. A few days afterward, another black leader, Coleman Willis, and his nephew were lynched at Brooksville. Into 1870 similar events repeatedly occurred. While Tampa avoided the lynchings, it nonetheless witnessed related incidents. "We have heard a vague rumor of a law and order party having been organized in Hillsboro County," reported the *Tallahassee Sentinel* in August 1869. Within months, several African American leaders suffered prosecution based on trumped-up "larceny" charges. After Thomas Clarke and Bob Roach were convicted of that crime in fall 1869, to cite two examples, they received executive clemency from the state. Clarke returned the following year with the governor's commission to raise a company of black militiamen to balance the white Regulators' power.[4]

While these events played out, some Tampans were benefitting from the new political order and others were beginning to rethink their attitudes and affiliations. The former group consisted in good part of Republican leaders who, especially after President Ulysses S. Grant took office in March 1869, were reaping the plums of office. For one, State Attorney C. R. Mobley, already one of the town's most affluent residents, soon enjoyed the benefits of federal employment. This provided Mobley with a distinct advantage over most local people since the United States paid generous salaries in cash whereas the state and county advanced only depreciated scrip. First, the former state senator accepted the powerful position of United States

Attorney for the Southern District of Florida. Subsequently, he held office for a brief period as deputy collector of customs. Meanwhile, Bartholomew C. Leonardy stepped into the role of deputy collector of internal revenue and Matthew P. Lyons succeeded John F. Fletcher as postmaster.[5]

As avowed and aggressive Republicans assumed office under President Grant, they opened up employment opportunities in federal service to some local African Americans. This fact attracted quite a number of men to Tampa during the 1870s, while affording several longtime residents the protection of official United States government position and the financial security afforded by the nation's payroll. Isaac Howard's experience offers a case in point. Having arrived in town as a James McKay family slave in 1846, he secured—likely with McKay's assistance—a customs service job by 1870. Remaining a government employee for most of the remainder of his life, by 1889 Howard had amassed a personal estate estimated at $10,000. Other men associated with federal employment included Peter W. Bryant, Thomas McKnight, Solomon Sally, G. A. Sheehy, and L. R. Thomas.[6]

The financial rewards of federal and county government employment—coupled with good wages paid to laborers and shiphands due to a shortage of capable workers—permitted members of Tampa's African American population to advance their community from the destitution of the immediate post-war period. Isaac Howard and his wife Polly, for instance, welcomed African Methodist Episcopal minister Thomas W. Long to town in June 1870 to found a congregation. With a small number of others, they soon constructed a brush arbor with guidance from minister John Thomas. Within two years the AME members had purchased land and begun erecting a sanctuary. They called their church Mt. Moriah at first but later adopted the name St. Paul AME Church. One year before the AME church coalesced, the local AME Zion congregation had undertaken the building of a new church building. With the Reverend Joseph Sexton's assistance, Samuel Bryant superintended construction of what eventually would be known as Mt. Sinai AME Zion Church. A fair conducted from Christmas Day 1869 to New Year's provided funds necessary to complete the project.[7]

The cause of education within the African American community also advanced. Already in mid-1867 its members had desired to act on their own. "I have spoken to the freedmen about their school," reported a Freedmen's Bureau agent, "they are quite willing to raise money for the purchase of a building and site, among themselves, if they can have a Teacher paid for teaching, as their means for paying a teacher are very poor, as they seldom get money for their crops when disposed of." Classes for the children had commenced in the courthouse in fall 1868. Neither the county nor the state thereafter accepted responsibility for providing a suitable building to continue the school. In 1869, the local Freedmen's Bureau office—located at the corner of Washington and Monroe Streets—served the purpose temporarily. Finally, in May 1870 a bureau agent arrived to oversee erection of a proper building. "It was located on Harrison street between Morgan and Marion," remembered Iola Brumick. "It was [twenty-five feet by thirty feet], one room with no partitions and few windows," she added, "but it was very dear to the hearts of colored people." On September 1 the bureau deeded the new structure, together with its site (Block 2), to a board of trustees consisting of C. R. Mobley, William F. White, John Williams, Peter W. Bryant, and Pady Richards.[8]

Railroads and New Blood

While the Republican advent had assisted some black and white Tampans toward a more secure economic footing, it also served to bring the Republicans together with some conservative whites in the interest of getting the town on its feet again. Since the early 1850s, pretty much everyone who had given the matter much thought had believed that the building of a railroad to Tampa Bay offered the only permanent solution to Tampa's economic malaise. C. R. Mobley had grasped this fact quickly. As a constitutional convention delegate in early 1868 he had pushed a resolution to mandate such a line as a part of the state's new charter. When the legislature met that summer he again took the lead in securing state assistance. Mobley achieved passage of a suitable law only to see it vetoed by Governor Harrison Reed.[9]

The railroad question offered political enemies a subject on which they could agree. Senator Mobley and Judge James T. Magbee, for example, saw eye to eye on the subject. They worked on the governor until, in late spring 1869, he endorsed construction to Tampa "and finally Key West." On June 24, 1869, the legislature followed Reed's lead by approving generous state grants "for the purpose of building a railroad from the waters of Tampa Bay and Charlotte

58.-59. Mary Eugenia Spencer and her husband, Henry L. Mitchell. He served as Florida's governor and as a railroad advocate. (Norman Stallings and Baynard Angle)

Harbor, on the Gulf, by the way of Ocala, and ending at Gainesville, on the Florida Railroad."[10]

For most white Tampans, the potential of a railroad for building Tampa prosperity far outweighed animosities born of partisan politics. While the legislature considered the railroad bill in June, many town leaders reached out across the political divide to unite in pushing the measure. At a courthouse gathering, prominent conservatives Franklin Branch, Edward A. Clarke, W. T. Haskins, D. Isaac Craft, Thomas K. Spencer, and William G. Ferris linked their names with those of Republicans Mobley, W. H. Harrison, Matthew P. Lyons, Ansel Watrous, and Edward O. Plumbe. When a similar group convened on July 24 to organize a qualifying railroad, Henry L. Mitchell, Christopher L. Friebele, John A. Henderson, and Henry Proseus participated with the others, as did Judge Magbee. Economic self-interest definitely had produced some strange bedfellows.[11]

Reverberations of the newfound cooperative spirit sounded in numerous ways. Governor Reed, who labored under the threat of impeachment for much of his term in office, thought that he had stumbled across new political support. His thinking likely reflected the influence of the county's new Conservative senator John A. Henderson (Senator Mobley lost his seat with appointment as state attorney).

60. Governor Harrison Reed. (FSA)

In any event, in June 1869 Reed named D. Isaac Craft as county treasurer. For a short period in 1870, he permitted Samuel Mitchell and John A. McKay to serve on the county commission. In March 1870, he also tapped Perry G. Wall, a prominent Hernando County Republican whose sons-in-law included Edward A. Clarke and Christopher L. Friebele, as Hillsborough County Judge. The governor tended to run hot and cold on such initiatives, though, and he soon dismissed Mitchell and McKay.[12]

The cooperative spirit gave birth, as well, to a bipartisan attempt to resurrect the municipal corporation. Urged on by Republican Sheriff Henry Albury, more than a dozen local leaders—including Domenico Ghira, John P. Andreu, Henry L. Crane, John Jackson, Franklin Branch, James McKay, Ansel Watrous, B. C. Leonardy, Louis G. Covacevich, C. L. Friebele, E. A. Clarke, J. F. Henderson, and Thomas K. Spencer—met on November 5 to consider whether townspeople, rather than the county commission, should govern in Tampa. In this instance, the cooperative spirit proved insufficient to reach the desired goal. Unable to agree on a suitable approach, the men decided not to call for an election until some later date.[13]

The railroad developments produced additional unexpected results. Intrigued merchants from other parts of

61. Edward O. Plumbe. (TBHC)

Florida and elsewhere realized that railroad construction to Tampa and the railhead's proximity to the cattle ranges could yield fortunes for suitably daring entrepreneurs. The first individuals to take action were George Blum and his New Orleans partner David Kloppenburg. They opened a general store in August 1869, pioneering in the process a radical innovation for a postwar business community that had depended upon the barter system. The two men, contrary to the practice of the "old merchants," promised to pay "the highest market price *in cash*" for local produce and hides. Within months a second partnership had followed Blum & Kloppenburg. Comprised of New Yorkers Gustave Lewinson and Edward Bettman and Fernandina resident Isidore Blumenthal (with New York backers Simon Hackes and David Forchheimer), the partnership premiered a very large and well-stocked dry goods and general merchandise store in December. After a business reorganization in 1870, the firm carried the name I. Blumenthal & Co.[14]

The commercial revolution spurred by I. Blumenthal & Co. and its predecessor extended beyond the retail merchandising business to a much-needed revitalization of the timber and milling industry. The company leased James D. Haygood's Tampa Mills from its then owner Joseph Robles and also constructed its own new sawing facility on the Hillsborough River's eastern banks just above Lafayette (now Kennedy) Street.[15] The *Florida Peninsular* fairly gushed when it described the new operations in December 1869:

> This extensive manufacturing establishment, which is now in successful operation, running ten circular saws, and sawing out Cedar boards for export to Germany at the rate of 1,000 gross per day, has been kindly shown us for inspection by Mr. G. Lewinson, and we were surprised to see an establishment of such magnitude far beyond our expectations.
>
> Within the short space of three weeks there has been erected a most substantial building three stories high, 25x45 feet, divided in the different departments of sawing from the log through the crosscut, rip saw and small saws, assorting, dressing and packing in boxes of about 7 cubic feet ready for export.
>
> The machinery itself is perfect in all its details, running as smooth as clock-work, and there being a perfect system of labor, every employee at his post, attending to the work assigned him, unequaled by any manufacturing establishment North.[16]

NEW YORK OFFICE, Hackes & Forchheimer, 472 BROADWAY.

ISIDORE BLUMENTHAL & CO.,
General Merchandizing and Cedar,

Tampa Bay, Florida, August 24 1871

My Dear Governor

I hereby have the honor most respectfully to tender to you my resignation as County Commissioner of Hillsborough Co. I find it impossible to perform the duties without neglecting my Business. Thanking you for the confidence in me, believe me to be very truely Your friend

I Blumenthal

His Honor Judge Magbee will in due time recommend a suitable person, in whose recommendation I will join. Bl. —

Under Hon. J. C. Gibbs Secty of State given this in absence of the Governor, please to accept resignation without delay Bl. —

To His Excellency Harrison Reed Governor of Florida

62. This 1871 letter from Isidore Blumenthal to Florida Governor Harrison Reed is written on the letterhead of his merchandizing and timber business in Tampa, with a seal affirming its affiliation with New York. The text reads, "My Dear Governor! I hereby have the honor most respectfully to tender to you my resignation as County Commissioner of Hillsborough Co. I find it impossible to perform the duties without neglecting my Business. Thanking you for the confidence in me, believe me to be very truely Your Friend, I. Blumenthal." (FSA)

The transformation of Tampa's business community had only begun with Blum & Kloppenburg and I. Blumenthal & Co. Another entrepreneur, Gustave Oppenheimer, arrived on the same boat with Lewinson, Bettman, and Blumenthal in November 1869. Within two months he had pioneered an entirely new style of eating establishment for the region. His Riverside Restaurant and Oyster Saloon—situated on Water Street near the Jackson Street ferry—promised "to entertain customers in first class style." The proprietor advertised oysters "in Fulton Market style" and further offered "game, fish and all the variety of a well selected bill of fare." Isolated and depressed Tampans had never experienced anything like it.[17]

Not surprisingly, expectations of a railroad and the jolt of energy administered by the recently arrived businessmen ignited new life and infused new energy on the local scene. That fall, the *Peninsular* detailed for eager readers the improvements going on all around. It seemed that every store and home was soaking up badly needed coats of paint, while a few families built new homes (W. C. Brown) or new stores (E. P. Grant & Co.) Manager Henry L. Crane spiffed up the Orange Grove Hotel, now the town's main hostelry, in anticipation of a flood of visitors. Probably sparking the most delight, some merchants undertook to construct wooden sidewalks along sandy (or muddy) commercial ways. "We like to see this going on," the *Peninsular* proclaimed. "It is a sign of returning prosperity."[18]

From these beginnings, a sense of what must have approached euphoria built during the first eight months of 1870. The African American community joined in. Mill jobs had brought workers regular paydays (in cash), while others had begun to prosper on homestead claims. Two black men, Cyrus Charles and Mills Holloman, sat on the county commission. By June a volunteer militia company would reach full organization, providing a mechanism for protection and reinforcing a sense of security. An Emancipation Day parade on January 1 allowed an occasion to express long withheld emotions in public. "Forming a procession, they marched through the streets to the Court House, where they were harangued for a couple of hours by speakers of their own color," observed jaundiced editor Henry L. Mitchell. "They wound up their show by singing 'Old John Brown,' &c."[19]

Excitement ran even hotter among whites. The Gustave Lewinson and Isidore Blumenthal cedar mill shipped its first load to Germany in January, giving concrete evidence of future profits. The following month the legislature created two new railroads that might build to Tampa. The Great Southern Railroad, backed by Republicans, aimed to run from Palatka on the St. Johns River "to the most southern available harbor on the coast or keys of Florida." John T. Lesley, who had declined to participate in earlier bipartisan plans, joined as a director of the Upper St. Johns, Mellonville, and Tampa Railroad. As its name suggested, this line planned to tie the upper St. Johns River near Orlando directly with Tampa.[20]

It seemed at the time as if the entire peninsula suddenly had come alive to business possibilities. The Constitution of 1868 had mandated appointment of a state commissioner of immigration. Appointee J. S. Adams had produced a "vast and widely distributed correspondence" that had aided Florida in adding 40,000 new residents within three years. Now, not only were Republican legislators promising millions of acres of public lands in support of railroads, but wealthy northerners also had begun to take a serious interest in the state. One of them was Harriet Beecher Stowe, author of the world-famous *Uncle Tom's Cabin*. She had settled at Mandarin near Jacksonville from where she penned a series of letters extolling Florida to her brother Henry Ward Beecher's New York newspaper the *Christian Union*. Journals throughout the North and Midwest soon reprinted her words. Another famous northerner, Union army general Henry S. Sanford, purchased 1,200 acres on the upper St. Johns in 1870 "to build a thriving town in this delicious climate." Rumors had other wealthy investors acting likewise.[21]

No wonder that, by May, Tampans had become positively giddy with excitement. The *Florida Peninsular* was insisting, against the tide of all-too-recent experience, that "a first-class hotel is much needed in Tampa." Within a few weeks Isidore Blumenthal had bought John T. Lesley's saw mill, expanding his operations considerably. Shortly, he moved his large store into even larger accommodations. In July, the good times led to another—and more serious—attempt to reincorporate the town. This time, though, the bipartisan spirit flickered dimly, a sad portent of problems to come. Reinvigorated and confident Conservatives encouraged by Franklin Branch and W. T. Haskins sought a town government with Senator Henderson serving as mayor and C. L. Friebele, Wesley Mansell, John A. McKay, Dr. Branch, and E. A. Clarke as councilmen. The men misjudged the temper of the times. Their initiative came to nothing.[22]

The Slide

As it turned out, many Tampans by mid-1870 were misjudging the times, a dynamic that, according to critic David Nolan, has occurred often in Florida's history. The dynamic has involved the repetition of an often vicious cycle. "The sounds emanating from Florida were two," Nolan noted, "Boom! Pop!" He continued: "Take the dreams, the influx of newcomers, and money, money, money. Mix them together and you have a boom." Sadly, the good times never lasted. "The booms were invariably punctuated by the revenge of God, man, and Mammon," Nolan wrote, "hurricane, frost, yellow fever, insect plague, war, and financial panic." He concluded: "One bit of conventional wisdom holds, 'If a man comes to Florida poor, he stays poor. If he comes rich and stays long enough, he gets poor.'"[23]

The bubble burst at Tampa well before local people prepared even to consider the possibility, and some might say that greed or envy started the process. The incorporation attempt certainly illustrated that good times brought desire to some to seize power as quickly as possible. Plus, envy at others' success soon entered the picture. The town's new dynamism had originated with a small group of newcomers, most of them Jewish, well-to-do, savvy in the ways of business, and of northern or foreign origins. They would have been considered "carpetbaggers" by many southerners, and they were Republicans. Still, their original reception had been warm and enthusiastic. Clearly they were making great strides at uplifting the town, yet five or six months later some merchants began to realize that these new men had stolen their customers. At that point subtle and not so subtle criticisms, especially of I. Blumenthal & Co., began appearing in the *Peninsular*, reflecting talk around town. Nothing too serious, mind you, at least not so long as the good times persisted.[24]

The problem was, the good times persisted only until the fall. The tumble commenced in September after Prussian troops invaded France, launching the Franco-Prussian War. The conflict shut off continental ports to shipping. The German market for Tampa cedar dried up almost overnight. Isidore Blumenthal quickly shifted his operations to cotton ginning, providing competition for Captain John Miller, who recently had returned and opened a gin on the riverbank. Both firms staggered as commodity prices plunged throughout the world. Blumenthal shut down some operations and laid off workers, while attempting to cover basic expenses through sawing pine lumber and

63. Judge Perry G. Wall. (TBHC)

processing sugar cane. The local construction business collapsed, though, leaving him in increasingly tight circumstances.[25]

The parade of ill tidings continued. On October 1, J. C. Rockner & Co.—a partnership of cattleman Rockner and Jewish entrepreneur Jacob R. Cohen—opened general stores at Bartow and Fort Meade. This, together with the already opened commercial house of Sherod Roberts and Cornelius B. Lightsey at Fort Meade, gave the cattle industry centers in southern Polk County two major retail outlets. Tampa business drained into the interior. The town's ties to the cattle shipping business suffered, as well. On October 26, James McKay's steamer *Governor Marvin* wrecked and sank off Key West while trying to maneuver out of a storm. "We hope the vessel is not a total loss, as reported," mourned the *Peninsular*.[26]

Politics joined natural disasters to bedevil townspeople. In 1870 Conservatives had launched a major effort to capture Florida's congressional seat, the lieutenant governor's office, and the legislature. Nomination of Alachua County's black state senator Josiah Walls for the congressional seat heightened an already tense situation. Somehow, a melee erupted at Tampa on election day, presumably between black Republicans and white Conservatives. Hauled before Judge Wall for "assault and battery" were Republican leaders Thomas McKnight, Aaron Bryant, and Samuel Bryant. About the same time another black man, Alex Wilson, found himself charged with "grave misdemeanors" after fatally stabbing James Prevatt in a set-to at the Blumenthal mill. Wall wisely dropped the charges against McKnight and permitted low bail for the Bryants. When he declined to release Wilson, others

64. These pioneer Tampa Bay area residents of the post-Civil War era are, left to right: Peter Nelson, Isaac Smith, Monroe Messer, Samuel Bryant, Manuel Stillings, and Andrew Johnson. Sam Bryant, along with his brother Aaron, was one of the Republican leaders arrested for "assault and battery" during the 1870 elections. (*Tampa Times*)

stepped forward to resolve the matter. "The prisoner had been heavily ironed," editor Mitchell reported, "but by assistance from friends he managed to release himself."[27]

The bad news of December struck far more deeply than did Alex Wilson's knife in James Prevatt's body. Governor Reed's battle against impeachment had led him into a deal with former United States Senator David Levy Yulee. A giant in Conservative circles, Yulee agreed to supply anti-impeachment votes in the legislature. For his part, Reed acquiesced in Yulee's desire that the state not contest issuance of a federal court injunction that would prohibit Florida from granting lands in support of railroad construction. Effectively, the pact left Yulee's Florida Rail Road—which tied Fernandina with Cedar Keys—without competition as the only rail connection between the Atlantic Ocean and the Gulf of Mexico. Known as the Vose Injunction (Francis Vose, a disgruntled debtor of Yulee's line, had filed the original action), the court order also knocked away the financial underpinnings of all the proposals to build rail lines to Tampa Bay. It would remain in effect, with disastrous consequences for Tampans, for a decade.[28]

If 1870's eventualities burst the bubble of optimism, 1871 brought misery. The year began with a hard freeze in January. By then law enforcement within the county had lapsed after Sheriff Albury, doubtlessly frustrated by continuing political opposition, quit his job and relocated to Key West. Perhaps his absence did not matter so much, though. Circuit Judge James T. Magbee's court had not met during 1870 while the jurist stood suspended due to an impeachment attempt. Not until March did Massachusetts-born Union army physician Dr. Francis James Gould succeed Albury (by then Magbee had been reinstated). Gould lasted but a month or so before giving up the job. An interim followed before another Republican and Union army veteran, William McFarland, took the oath in July. His tenure barely would outlast Gould's.[29]

May produced economic catastrophe when the boiler at the I. Blumenthal & Co. cedar mill blew up. "The whole of the brick work was thrown down," explained a published account, "the boilers thrown up and across one another, and the roof lifted and almost demolished." This calamity combined with labor unrest caused by threatened payrolls tore the partnership apart. Blumenthal managed to retain control, with Gustave Lewinson separating to open his own grocery store. Meanwhile, the Franco-Prussian War dragged on, squeezing the life out of Tampa's timber industry.[30]

Politics resurfaced to take a toll after Governor Reed, with Senator Yulee's assistance, survived impeachment in January and February 1871. The governor and his ally Judge Magbee resented the lack of support that they had received from C. R. Mobley, Matthew P. Lyons, and their followers. Reed and Magbee decided to rectify matters. First, they determined to remake the county commission. Commissioners Daniel Gillett, Cyrus Charles, Ansel Watrous, and Mills Holloman lost their seats, to be replaced by Loyalist Robert J. Whitehurst, AME minister John Thomas, black jailer Robert Johnson, and Isidore Blumenthal. In May, Magbee—with Thomas and Whitehurst backing him up—attempted to wrest control of the county Republican organization from his opponents during a lively party conference. He failed. "Mobley and Lyons rule the Republican camp in Hillsborough," observed an onlooker.[31]

Conservatives, viewing these and other political events, grew at once concerned and emboldened. Concerns arose, for instance, when members of the local black militia company elected Thomas McKnight as their captain. In doing so, they telegraphed boldly their intention to pursue a hard-line position when it came to local race relations and protection of rights. Outraged whites demanded of state officials that they be allowed to organize, as well, but the pleas met with rejection. Out in the hinterlands, a lack of official military

65. Dr. John P. Wall. (*Sunland Tribune*)

organization hindered white reaction little. Regulators lynched and attacked in Manatee, Polk, and Hernando Counties. Given the Republican rupture and law enforcement difficulties found throughout Hillsborough, an onset of violence there appeared all too likely.[32]

Short periods did occur during the depressing slide when Tampans briefly could believe that the worse had passed. Late June and July 1871 offered such a time, but its major events suggest just how difficult affairs had become, seemingly in the wink of an eye. The first such occasion came in the form of a "commercial convention," held at the courthouse on June 30. In the midst of sudden economic ruin, bipartisanship re-emerged. White leaders from across the spectrum joined to plead for a state grant of 100,000 acres of public lands to facilitate railroad construction. C. R. Mobley and John T. Lesley, James T. Magbee and John A. Henderson, C. L. Friebele and Isidore Blumenthal, and many other unlikely pairs worked to craft appropriate resolutions. Of course, the effort came to naught as the Vose Injunction remained in force.[33]

The convention's failure already may have sunk in when many of the same Conservatives met at the abandoned Fort Brooke hospital on July 24 to organize their own church. The first Episcopal services had been held at Tampa in 1868, but no serious effort toward establishing a congregation had ensued. Circumstances had changed by 1871, with more people requiring the ministrations of a faith with which they could affiliate comfortably. The Parish of St. Andrew's Church resulted. Founding vestrymen included Henry L. Crane, Henry L. Mitchell, William G. Ferris, Josiah Ferris, Edward A.

Clarke, Thomas K. Spencer, and Charles Hanford. Crane and Spencer served as wardens, with Hanford acting as secretary. The Reverend R. A. Simpson ministered to his tiny congregation of from six to twelve communicants for the next two years.[34]

66. Ariana (Anna) Eliza Givens. (Samuel Givens Harrison III)

St. Andrew's joined Tampa's Methodist, Baptist, and Roman Catholic churches just in time, for in August the slide continued. In their severity, the events that followed must have compelled residents to contemplate the Biblical plagues and their meaning. They began early in the month when red tide afflicted Hillsborough Bay. "We learn that the beach from Hooker's Point to the mouth of the Six Mile Creek is strewn with dead and dying fish of all kinds known to our Bay," the Peninsular informed readers. Within days another affliction descended. This time, a severe storm lashed town and countryside, dealing a "heavy blow" to crops and farmers' hopes. Heavy rains in September completed the work of agricultural ruin.[35]

By that time, greater fears distracted attention from crop damage. In late August or early September, Dr. John P. Wall had attended an ailing seaman on board a vessel moored in the bay. Unaware that he was treating yellow fever, Wall somehow spread the disease to his wife Pressie and his fourteen-month-old daughter Julia. Matthew P. Lyons's daughter Mary Ann contracted the malady about the same time. By September 8 the three were dead. The next week the "yellow jack" claimed Nancy Crawford, a Mrs. Spaulding, and Sheriff McFarland. A report of September 30 noted "a number of new cases" and "quite a few persons have left town." Jakob F. Geisinger and Charles Cooper succumbed the next week, and so on.

67. *Frank Leslie's Illustrated Magazine* used this drawing by Matt Morgan to illustrate Florida's tragic battle with yellow fever during the early 1870s. (FSA)

The fever's threat loomed so great that those who remained behind to nurse the sick earned respect that lasted for a lifetime. Judge Magbee, for example, revered young Anna Givens for courageously caring for his family. The terror lingered day-to-day for almost three months. Local doctors could not signal that it finally had passed until November 25.[36]

During that chaotic fall of 1871, the actions of a number of Tampans made little sense and sometimes lapsed into the inane. In the yellow fever epidemic's midst, for example, Conservatives suddenly called an incorporation election. Apparently, the brazen attempt to capitalize on the departure of scores of residents appalled many who remained. The measure met with defeat "by a small vote." Also in October, Conservative pranksters attacked Judge Magbee. Likely with a sense of relief that his family had survived a close call with the fever, Magbee proceeded to get good and drunk, ultimately passing out in the shade of a tree that stood alongside a downtown street. Charles Wandell, described by a friend as "a wag and a practical joker," poured shell corn over the jurist and then set pigs lose on him to the amusement of the prankster's fellows. Editor Mitchell took the incident, exaggerated it wildly, and published the account, knowing that Conservative newspapers throughout the state would pick it up. Whether the incident disgraced Magbee, Wandell, or Mitchell the most remains open to question.[37]

The new year 1872 brought little relief to weary locals. To the good, free state- and county-funded public schools operated for the first time beginning in January. Republican School Superintendent William F. White had labored long and hard against local white resistance to the idea of tuition-free education. His work now resulted in two Tampa schools, one for children of each race. Edward A. Clarke, William B. Henderson, and D. Isaac Craft presided as the white school's trustees. It met in the courthouse. Matthew Hooper, Peter Bryant, and Isaac Howard carried out the same responsibilities on behalf of African American children. Their classes convened at the Freedmen's Bureau school. Meanwhile, also at the courthouse a county commission majority of Chairman Isidore Blumenthal and black members Bob Johnson and John Thomas attempted to implement the beginnings of effective local government. The men strove to deal with matters ranging from jail construction to water supply, health regulations, and transportation infrastructure. Economic stagnation, though, meant low revenues. Plus, Conservatives resisted Republican innovation. Most initiatives, accordingly, died aborning.[38s]

All the while, Tampans found themselves again struggling with and within a community in crisis. The town showed it. "The place looks broken down from sheer weariness of trying to be a town," wrote one visitor in February 1872. "Its decaying structures and dilapidated fences remind us of old age, 'when the keepers of the house shall tremble.'" He added, "We do not take leave of this place as a dear friend." By the time Bill Neeld came on the scene in September, the town had settled even deeper into slumber. "Tampa was little more than a trading post," he recorded, "supplying our back country."[39]

The people displayed a "broken down" spirit, as well. Someone began the year by stealing the county's first deed book. At the same time, Baptists fell to feuding over the issue of expelling women for dancing. By mid-summer congregation members had halved the Baptist minister's salary and agreed to hold services only every other month. Hungry for financial support, the minister at one point rented out the sanctuary for a "road show." In May, the Spencer family gave up on the *Florida Peninsular*. C. R. Mobley took it over as a Republican organ. It lasted four months before suspending. Mobley revived the paper in October to further Republican electoral prospects. It closed permanently soon thereafter.[40]

The weather yet again turned an angry face to the community, finding a difficult and complicated situation and making it worse. Drought in the spring led to floods in the fall. At one point a funeral procession attempted to pass from the Orange Grove Hotel to the cemetery. On the way, it encountered water two feet deep. "The coffin was transported on a dray, for there were no hearses in Tampa at that time," recalled Darwin B. Givens. "Just as the cortege reached a small cleared place both horse and dray bogged down," he continued. "The horse began floundering around, [and] the coffin slipped off the dray." Givens concluded: "The Masons had to place planks under the side of the horse and pull him out. They were then forced to 'tote' the coffin to the graveyard on their shoulders." Doubtlessly, William Powledge had longed for such downpours as he watched his store burn that year. The conflagration, for a time, endangered the entire downtown business district.[41]

Gold Doubloons and Political Possibilities

Although, as a rule, Tampans faced dire concerns by mid-1872, this situation—as usually proves the case with most rules—allowed for exceptions. Beginning in 1870, the long-awaited launch of the Cuban cattle trade finally had occurred. Shippers landed over 7,000 head on Havana's docks that year, over twice the rate of the previous two years. The trade doubled again in 1871. By 1872 shipments ran to over 21,000 beeves. As a result, Spanish gold seemed to pour into southwest Florida. "Most people in this county and country had stocks of wild cattle which found a market in Cuba at a doubloon per head for 4-year-olds," explained Bill Neeld of 1870s life as he remembered it. "A doubloon was a Spanish $20 gold piece—worth about $16 in American gold," he continued. "This money was sufficient to pay taxes and buy shoes, calicoes and a hundred geegaws, gimercracks, oil lamps, and kerosene oil." Neeld added: "In fact, most cattlemen were rich, in that they had no way of spending their incomes—except to buy one another's stocks of cattle."[42]

Tampans beheld this blessed event with mixed emotions. Unlike country folk, most townspeople did not own range cattle. Some, though, held thousands of head, and others profited by serving as middlemen for the trade. In fact, during 1869-1874 the largest shipper of cattle from Florida to Cuba was the partnership of John T. Lesley and William B. Henderson. Others with local connections such as Henderson's business partner John Miller and his brothers John A. and James F. Henderson, Perry G. Wall's merchant son William W. Wall, onetime blockade runner Samuel Mitchell and his brother Henry L. Mitchell, and, of course, the McKays benefitted amply. According to historian Joe Akerman, some fortunes mounted rapidly. Take the case of John T. Lesley, for example. "Revele Anderson, a black cowman who worked for Lesley," Akerman related, "remembers seeing a wash tub full of gold coins in the bedroom of John T. Lesley."[43]

The greater number of Tampa's merchants found it difficult going to take advantage of the cattle industry's sudden prosperity. Many of the principal owners concentrated their families at or near Fort Meade, while some others grouped at Bartow or Fort Ogden. As seen earlier in this chapter, merchants such as Sherod Roberts, Cornelius B. Lightsey, Julius Rockner, and Jacob R. Cohen quickly catered to their trade by opening for business on the cattle frontier. With shopping so easily accomplished near to home, many cattle families stopped making their accustomed periodic treks into Tampa.[44]

One Tampa entrepreneur with family connections to the frontier merchants fared better than did some of his competitors. Charles Slager had emigrated from Germany to Jacksonville in the early 1850s. He prospered there with a retail store until the Civil War intervened. A Loyalist, Slager emerged from the conflict a Republican. Before coming to Tampa in late 1870, he had served on Jacksonville's town council and school board and had risen to high office in the state's Masonic orders. His winning personality endeared Slager to Tampans, with his prewar residence in Florida relieving him of the burden of the "carpetbagger" status that weighed heavily on the town's other Jewish businessmen. Slager's family network extended to Jacob R. Cohen through Cohen's brother-in-law and store manager Philip Dzialynski. Probably with their help, the new Tampan realized that a commission business geared to servicing the stores of the cattle

68. Merchants such as For Meade businessman Sherod Roberts drained revenues from Tampa's commercial houses during the early 1870s. Later in the decade Roberts would construct the telegraph line that, at long last, would connect Tampa with Fort Meade and the outside world.

frontier offered possibilities more lucrative than a simple retail trade. He had transformed his business in line with those thoughts by August 1871. As of that time, the merchant had served Tampans for four months as their postmaster. In two more, he would fill the vacancy left by the yellow fever death of Sheriff William McFarland.[45]

One major dilemma confronted cattle industry people and merchants such as Slager who depended upon them. It involved the reliability of the Cuban trade. Experience had proven its volatile nature, and area men were farsighted enough to seek out more-stable markets. The growing industrial cities of the North and Midwest served that need perfectly, leaving transportation as the only obstacle. Effectively, a railroad into south Florida offered the only option. The Vose Injunction blocked the state from backing construction, and without that support no lines could be built. The cattlemen thus needed a governor who would lift the Vose Injunction.[46]

Here, interest, relationships, and politics coincided. During Governor Reed's term, turmoil had marked the day. By summer 1872, the state's surviving Loyalists and many black Republicans believed supreme court associate justice Ossian B. Hart to be the man to provide honest and effective government for Florida. Although standing for radical reform ideas, Hart's personal and business ties ran deep into south Florida. His longtime friend Jacob Summerlin remained "king" of the cattlemen. Summerlin, in turn, associated closely in business affairs with Jacob R. Cohen and Philip Dzialynski. Their friend Charles Slager had known Hart well at Jacksonville and had helped him to found Florida's Republican party. Most of Tampa's merchants and many of its other citizens, black and white, also held personal acquaintance with the jurist and former townsman. For John A. Henderson this was even more the case than for most. Now a Conservative leader in the state senate and acting as the political voice of the cattle industry, Henderson's ties with Hart and his wife Catharine were personal indeed. When the senator's young wife had died in the Civil War's closing months, the widower had asked the Harts to care for his child. Flora A. Henderson remained with the Harts in Jacksonville.[47]

So, in the summer and fall of 1872, many—although certainly not all—Tampans and other area settlers came to see the election of Republican Ossian B. Hart as governor to be essential to the future of their town and their region. Hart knew their problems, just as he knew how to use government to solve them. He held the key to unlocking the future by overcoming the Vose Injunction and building a railroad down the peninsula. Some prepared to help him overtly, while others acted quietly and outside the glare of public exposure. The contest might be a close thing, but they knew few alternatives. It all came down to the question, could Hart be elected?

69. The buildings at Fort Brooke, formerly the site of military operations and the core of the pioneer community, remained a central part of Tampa after the Civil War. The military vitality and sense of purpose, though, soon were eroded by a slipping and uncertain economy, which threatened decay and abandonment. (TBHC)

VIII

"fears are entertained of serious results"

The Panic, 1872-1875

The growth of southwest Florida's cattle trade after 1870 teased Tampans as golden wealth spread its warm embrace through the region's frontier settlements. Although a few local people benefitted from transporting and marketing beef, the town's prospects for the most part had declined. Its economy remained dependent upon a cedar industry subject to volatile fluctuations. Plus, the timber business and its profits rested firmly in the control of "Yankees," "Republicans," and "carpetbaggers." It seemed for a while to some Tampans that the 1872 elections miraculously might wipe away obstacles of racial, political, economic, and legal natures. Delivery appeared close at hand, and would that it had been so. As residents would learn, though, recent local history offered a clearer glimpse of the future. Fate held unexpected and less than agreeable plans in store for Tampa.

The desperate grasp at political salvation in 1872 originated when onetime resident and town councilman Ossian B. Hart pursued the Republican gubernatorial nomination. Rejecting corruption and disorder associated with carpetbag rule, the supreme court associate justice promised honesty, integrity, and efficiency in government. To further Hart's plans, the candidate depended upon Tampa area support. A signal that his hopes would not be frustrated came at the Republican state convention when former Tampa slave Peter W. Bryant placed Hart's name in contention. That November, Hillsborough Countians gifted the candidate with but 152 of their

70. Jacob R. Cohen. (TBHC)

488 votes. Still, the governor-elect's victory had come with crucial help from southwest Floridians. Especially, key leaders of the cattle industry—Jacob Summerlin and State Senator John A. Henderson prominently among them—quietly had aided their old friend.[1]

Details of understandings between Hart and prominent Tampa-area residents remain nebulous, although they certainly involved mutual responsibilities. As to the governor, the agreements would have presumed two things: Hart's good faith efforts to lift the Vose Injunction, which prohibited most state support for railroad construction; and his encouragement of railroad building down the peninsula. The plans' first stage centered on the opening of train service to Orlando, a village that Summerlin was developing in cooperation with his merchant friend Jacob R. Cohen. Cohen, in turn, invested in Tampa shortly before the election by opening a commercial house of his own. There, other longtime acquaintances and associates of Summerlin, Cohen, and Hart awaited the fruits of the new leadership. Republican sheriff Charles Slager, particularly, would have helped to prepare local people to take advantage of the election and its results. Presumably, the second stage of everyone's plans anticipated that cattle money would finance a railroad extension to Tampa Bay, once the steam engines reached Orlando. The cattlemen also would provide some financial assistance during the electoral campaign and, more importantly, political muscle in favor of the governor's legislative agenda.[2]

The pact produced favorable results at first. Within days of taking office in January 1873, Governor Hart initiated negotiations aimed at resolving the Vose Injunction and laying the groundwork for state backing of the Great Southern Railroad, a line intended eventually to run from Georgia to the Florida keys. Meanwhile, Senator Henderson, who maintained personal ties with the Harts beyond his role as the political voice of cattle interests, maneuvered behind the scenes to insure legislative approval of the governor's programs, including Florida's first civil rights act and a revamping of state finances. The weeks consumed by the legislature's session saw Hart achieving win after win with Henderson's assistance, but they also revealed the complexities of Reconstruction politics. Henderson might discretely labor on behalf of the Republican agenda so long as the benefits ran to south Florida, but others were not so pragmatic. For example, one of the senator's friends and fellow Tampa attorneys, State Representative Henry L. Mitchell, fought the governor almost at every step.[3]

Once the legislature adjourned and as the Vose negotiations proceeded slowly, Hart took the time to place his personal stamp on Hillsborough County's government. He punished Republicans who had strayed too close to the most fervent Democrats (as Conservatives again were coming to be called). In this regard, the governor removed Charles Hanford as county clerk and replaced him with William F. White, a Union army veteran who had relocated from Illinois to Tampa in 1869 and then served as tax assessor and superintendent of schools. Matthew P. Lyons stepped in for White in the assessor's job. Hart also relieved some staunch Republicans of responsibilities so that they could concentrate on business challenges, while rewarding other solid party backers with jobs. Loyalist James R. Hay, for instance, succeeded Charles Slager as sheriff, while Robert J. Whitehurst took over the merchant's duties as tax collector. In the same spirit, Hart relieved his close friend Perry G. Wall of the county judge's heavy burden. C. R. Mobley filled in for Wall temporarily before Samuel D. Chase put on the judicial robes.[4]

Mostly, Hart endeavored to bring stability to local government; that is to say, he selected men who would pursue governmental responsibilities with commitment and a sense of pragmatism. A look at his county commission designations aids in making the point. The four Republicans chosen by the governor served out their two-year terms, with three of the four remaining for a second term. They were Matthew Hooper, Charles Moore, Joseph P. Brownlow, and Mills Holloman's son Adam Holloman. These individuals' appointments reflected geographical and racial diversity. The governor attempted to

71. Judge Charles E. Harrison with his family. (Samuel Givens Harrison III)

ensure some political diversity, as well. In one of his first changes, he placed his old Loyalist friend Henry A. Crane's son Henry L. Crane, a moderate Democrat, on the board. When Crane resigned for personal reasons in January 1874, Hart then turned to an old adversary, John Darling. The former arch-secessionist and Rebel, now sixty-five years of age, had mellowed with time's passage. He had accepted Baptist baptism in 1868 and had served the church with dedication, earning the title "the Deacon." When he stepped onto the county commission, Darling—the longtime cornerstone of Tampa masonry—was serving one of his numerous terms as worshipful master of Hillsborough Lodge No. 25, F. & A. M.[5]

The new officers earnestly attempted to fulfill the governor's expectations, although they faced enormous obstacles. This particularly was the case at Tampa, over which the commission exercised jurisdiction in the absence of a municipal government. The town had deteriorated in appearance and attitude. Trash lay on unused lots, many homes stood empty, and thickets of weeds served as home for wild and not-so-wild animals. Charles E. Harrison recalled that, "sometime before" January 1873, someone had dumped a steamer's smokestack in the middle of Tampa Street, leaving it there to obstruct the sparse traffic that passed the site. County facilities added to the town's shabby appearance. "Hillsborough County has no jail house, and the court house is in a very dilapidated condition," one influential regional newspaper reported in March, "and none of the public roads have been worked since the war."[6]

The fact that Hillsborough County and Tampa possessed no jail helps to illustrate an additional—even critical—problem of the times, that of crime. Regulator defiance of authority and the sudden appearance of wealth in traditionally poor southwest Florida had helped to spawn a violent crime wave. Sheriff Slager had battled the menace with mixed success, a crusade that his successor Sheriff Hay also embraced. Unfortunately, even with assistance of a deputy or two, the lawmen could not reach out to protect every spot in the huge county. They could not even begin to provide the constant law enforcement presence required by Tampa's situation.[7]

Several incidents occurred that impacted seriously on the community and that point out to us the immediacy of the dilemmas of violence and crime, as well as limitations on the ability of area sheriffs to combat them. The first case stemmed from Judge James T. Magbee's responsibility to hold court on November 16, 1873, at Pine Level, the rural seat of old Manatee County located ten miles west of Arcadia. After the day's adjournment, the judge walked over to a boarding house where he planned to spend the night. That evening, Regulators struck. "He . . . was sitting in the parlor," a correspondent noted, "when some person fired through a window at him." The account added, "No clue has been found as to the would be assassin." The judge found himself waiting for a return visit by the perpetrators. His alarm soared in August 1874 when Sheriff Hay's black deputy Dick Roach was murdered "by some unknown person" while sitting in a chair at his home "in the suburbs of Tampa." With the sheriff unable to guarantee his safety, the frontier jurist took

72. Sheriff Charles Slager.

matters into his own hands. "We are informed that suspicious persons have been seen, at the dead hour of night, lurking about Judge Magbee's premises," observed one townsman. "The judge is on alert, and has contrived such defense as will blow all rascals into eternity who invade his yard."[8]

The second example involved an outlaw who avoided killing as best he could, a person who would gain renown with time's passage as "the Robin Hood of South Florida." As would be expected from his nickname, John W. "Hub" Williams specialized in relieving some of the area's wealthier residents of what he considered to be their ill-gotten gains. Early in 1873 Hillsborough County's sheriff, likely Charles Slager, nabbed the felon for stealing horses. With no jail in which to house his prisoner, the sheriff confined him in a rotting hulk moored in Hillsborough Bay under the care of jailer and former county commissioner Bob Johnson.[9] We know something of Hub's experience in the Tampa jail because, among other talents, he enjoyed the ability to express himself in poetry. A few verses survive:

Bob Johnson came around about nine in the night,
And in his right hand he held a small light.
He tapped on the door and gave me a hail,
To see if I was safe in the Tampa Bay jail!

When breakfast came around it was a hunk of cornbread,
As hard as a rock and as heavy as lead,
And a cup of cold water from a dirty wooden pail,
And I dam near starved in that Tampa Bay jail!

Now, dear ladies, I've sung you my song.
I know damn well I have sung nothing wrong.
I was always fighting, and I never was afraid,
But I'll never enter another jail gate![10]

Hub's desire for freedom ultimately outweighed the capacity of Hillsborough County law enforcement to restrain him. On at least one occasion, he succeeded in fleeing his floating prison. As a surviving partial verse proclaims, "I jumped through the window and escaped from the boat, and swam ashore to shoot an old goat." Recaptured, Williams faced a county jury in October 1873. Convicted, he never gave up hope. "Sheriff Hay and son, who undertook to escort young Williams to the Penitentiary lost the scamp somewhere on the railroad en route to his destination," a local man recorded. "Williams, it is said, leaped head foremost out of the car window in the night time, while the train was in motion, making his escape in a dense swamp where pursuit was impossible." The man added a little more detail. "Williams was hobbled with a chain but managed to free himself, whereupon he disappeared without saying good-by," he continued. "In the jump his head plowed the ground like a spent cannon ball."[11]

A Community in Change

Given the era's problems, Hart administration Republicans set about making a difference as best they could. For example, with the limited resources available, the county commission launched a clean-up campaign. In July 1873 it authorized courthouse repairs and began a bidding process for painting, while furthering the work of its predecessor board in supporting public schools, making efficient use of public property, encouraging development of Tampa's riverfront, improving roads, and aiding bridge construction. Early the following year board members strove to furnish the county with a suitable jail to be erected on the courthouse square's northeast corner. Although delays of one sort or another kept contractor John J. Givens from completing the two-story, oak-plank and cypress-shingled structure until January 1875, board members nonetheless could tote this as one of several solid accomplishments.[12]

Republicans were advancing local development in other ways. Bartholomew C. Leonardy, for one, decided to offer African Americans the advantages of a regularly laidout subdivision. In 1871 he had purchased from freedpersons Thomas and Ellen Jackson an eight-acre portion of their homestead that lay in the Scrub region along Tampa's northwestern boundary. During summer 1872, Leonardy and county surveyor William F. White staked out streets and marked property lines for ten town blocks. In doing so, they established the grid for Tampa's future growth. Where the town's streets going back to developer Augustus Steele's late 1830s plans roughly had run parallel to or at right angles to the Hillsborough River's lower course, Leonardy's scheme adopted a north-south, east-west axis. Accordingly, he turned Morgan, Marion, Monroe (Florida), and Franklin Streets northward, while creating two new public ways above Harrison Street. The first he named Magbee Street after his friend the judge. Subsequent generations would call it Royal Street. Just to the north

73. Constant Bouguardez. (Pizzo, *Tampa Town*)

came Wall Street, after one-time Judge Perry G. Wall. Future Tampans would know it as Fortune Street for freedman Benjamin Taylor's widow Fortune Taylor, whose homestead lay just to the east along the riverfront. Though unnamed by Leonardy, the street at the northern limits of his subdivision—Constant Street—would adopt the name of an-other homesteader, Constant Bouguardez, whose lands lay on the river just above the Taylor place.[13]

Having created "Leonardy's Addition to the Town of Tampa," the owner transferred much of it to other hands. A Roman Catholic, he donated block number one, situated at his property's northeastern corner and directly north of Tampa's burial ground, to his church as a grave yard. St. Louis Cemetery resulted. Similarly, he gave lot two, block eight (at the corner of Monroe Street and Magbee) to the African Methodist Episcopal Church through trustees Henry Hopkins, Henry Blair, Lewis Henderson, Henry Bell, John Green, and Tom Blige. He sold them the adjoining lot on Monroe Street, as well, for $25. On the plots arose Tampa's first AME sanctuary built as such. "This lot was covered with palmettos," church historian Andrew J. Ferrell, Sr., reported. "The men cleared and burned the palmettos at night while the women sold coffee, fish, chicken and rice, and ice cream," he added. "With the land cleared a church was built 40 by 60 feet, and they named it Mount Moriah [later St. Paul]."[14]

Mt. Moriah AME Church's comforting presence drew to Leonardy's Addition over the next year and one half several of Tampa's leading African American families, enabled to purchase lots and build homes by decent-paying government or cedar mill jobs. Church member Lewis Henderson may have been the first. He bought lot one, block eight, next to the church for $18 in January 1873. Henderson soon added two nearby tracts to his holdings. As months passed, Wade Taylor and Isaac Howard became his neighbors. Other families likely settled on the property during this period with Leonardy's permission, hoping in the future to accumulate the price of purchase.[15]

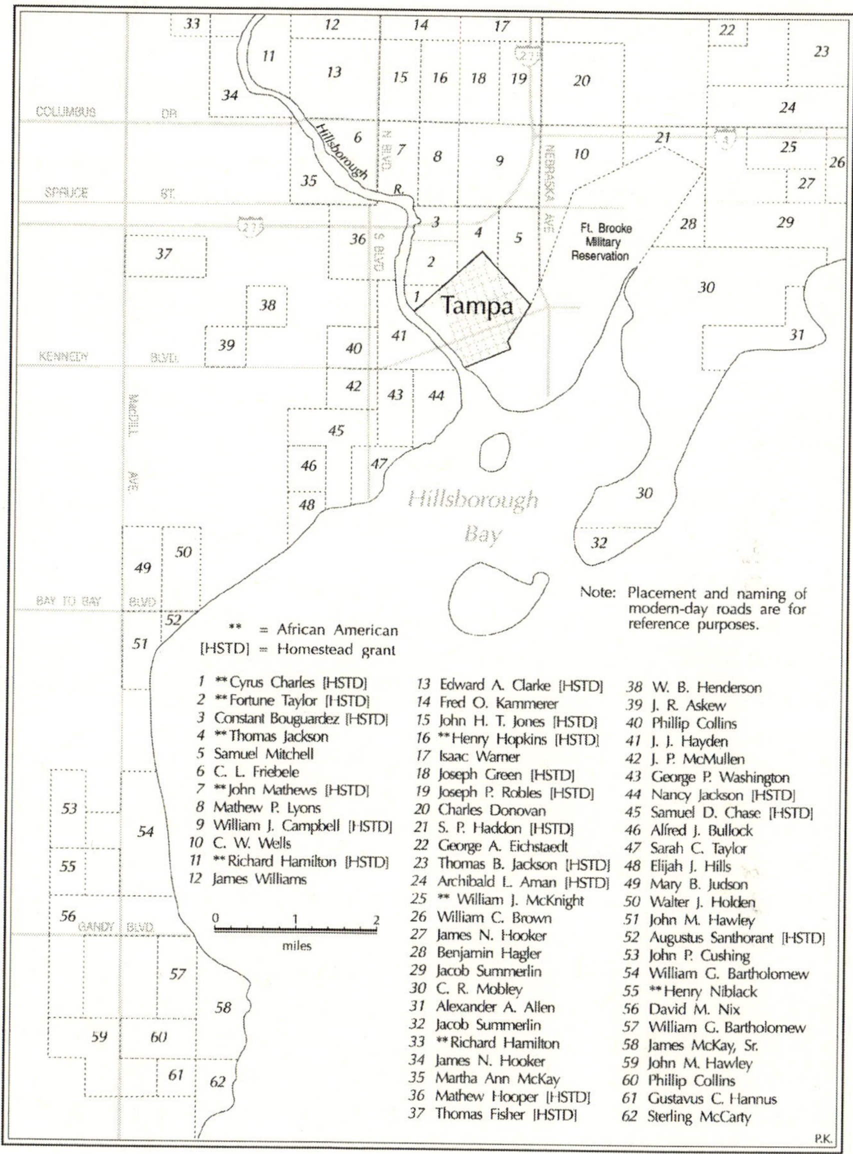

74. This map by Florida State University cartographer Peter Krafft illustrates how title to lands surrounding Tampa came into private hands in the post-Civil War era. Especially, note that the property of black homesteaders Cyrus Charles, Fortune Taylor, Thomas Jackson, and John Mathews ringed Tampa's northern boundaries and limited its ability to expand.

Leonardy's Addition may have served another purpose for Tampans in 1873, beyond providing homesites for black families. Local white businessmen could see from its example that their town was changing and not, from their perspective, for the better. Increasingly, African Americans and northern-born Republicans were gaining influence over the town's future at a time when the number of old-line white families actually may have been dropping. The count of newcomers needed to reverse the local balance of power ran fairly low. Hillsborough County's population grew from 1867 to 1870 by 64 percent to 3,215 persons. In that year, African Americans amounted to 17 percent of the whole. On the other hand, Tampa's residents totalled a mere 796 individuals, 28 percent (222) of whom were black. If white Democrats held their own, the addition of a mere 200 blacks or other Republicans would have honed a decisive edge in the local electorate.[16]

When assessing whether they could hold their own, white Democrats discovered unsettling facts. For persons not involved with the cattle or cedar industries or else employed by the government, nonfarm employment was becoming ever more difficult to obtain. The bust that commenced with the Franco-Prussian War of 1871 had persisted and deepened as trade flowed out of Tampa. Mercantile houses now operated on the Pinellas peninsula. A. A. Archer, L. O. Bennett, and Henry Thomas conducted business at Clear Water Harbor by 1870. Three years later that community boasted its own newspaper, the *Clear Water Times*, something that Tampa could not then claim for itself. Even more importantly, bustling stores in the cattle towns of Polk and Manatee Counties took away many of the gold doubloons for which Tampa storeowners yearned. Accordingly, opportunity, when it beckoned for many at Tampa, beckoned elsewhere. When Ephraim L. Harrison lost his job with Gus Lewinson, he relocated to Fort Meade. His son Charles—newly minted as a lawyer and wed by Methodist minister Edward F. Gates to Anna Givens—saw few possibilities professionally speaking. He first tried Brooksville but soon followed his father to Fort Meade. "There was more business to do," he explained. Harrison's friend and fellow young attorney Stephen M. Sparkman took the same path at mid-decade. He simply could not make a living as a lawyer in Hillsborough County.[17]

This slow population drain continued as more blacks and Union army veterans were arriving at Tampa and in its immediate vicinity, drawn mostly by the availability of cheap land well adapted for growing citrus. Relatively speaking, this industry rated as a new one for the town. Prior to the Civil War, one or two small groves at Sarasota Bay, Odet Philippe's "orchard" at today's Safety Harbor (where the proprietor introduced grapefruit to the state), and Louis Lanier's modest planting at Fort Meade comprised the largest area holdings other than for the trees planted by William B. Hooker around his Tampa home. Following the peace, Hooker's trees—now mature and bearing fruit—took on an importance far greater than their numbers. Every traveler who stopped in town saw the oranges and many assessed their potential. "The cultivation of fruit is attracting much attention in south Florida, and is destined to be an important element of commerce," commented the *Florida Peninsular* in 1868. "There are some very handsome trees in Tampa," its article continued. "Capt. Hooker, at the Orange Grove Hotel, has beautiful trees and delicious fruit."[18]

African American homesteaders properly could claim to be among the first postwar residents to understand the economic potential of citrus culture. Cyrus Charles, for instance, selected in 1867 a pie-shaped five-acre homestead wedged between Tampa's northwestern boundary, the Hillsborough River, and Benjamin Taylor's homestead. When Isidore Blumenthal and James McKay attested to Charles's settlement a few years later, they asserted that he immediately "built two houses, dug a well [and] planted [orange] trees." According to witnesses, Benjamin Taylor, beginning January 20, 1868, "built a house [on his homestead] and planted seventy Orange trees and Guava, peach and plum trees." Numerous other black farmers established homesteads stretching eastward from Tampa as the years passed, most of them following the lead of Charles and Taylor. Former county commissioner Mills Holloman, to cite an example, proudly noted in support of his homestead application that he had "more than 20 bearing Orange trees & some other fruit."[19]

Northerners anxious to improve their health by relocating to a more congenial climate quickly joined with some resident whites in seeing citrus as their own economic salvation. Michigan's Chauncey W. Wells, to name one, arrived in 1869 with $20 to his name. He painted houses while homesteading a large tract situated between Tampa's eastern edge and the Fort Brooke military reservation (roughly, the acreage bounded by today's Columbus Drive on the north, Nebraska Avenue on the west, and Nick Nuccio Parkway on the east and south). By decade's end, Wells's six-acre grove had afforded him financial security and community recognition. Similarly, David M. Nix settled close to Ballast Point, claiming land on Hillsborough Bay east of modern Himes Avenue, above Gandy Boulevard, and below Coachman Avenue. Nix planted his own grove but, with the passage of time, hit upon the idea of renting out citrus tracts to naval officers. By 1879, the year before his death, Nix's properties were valued at $10,000 or more, a far cry from his 1873 estate of $50.[20]

In a limited sense, the secret was out by 1873, with regional and even a few northern and midwestern newspapers carrying notices of Tampa Bay's citrus successes. "Our orange trees are bearing a large crop, and the fruit is growing rapidly," asserted one resident to readers of the *Savannah Morning News* in August. "Nothing affects this crop," he added. Two months later a Tampan informed the same journal, "We need a railroad here." He continued, "As soon as transportation can be had, thousands of oranges, limes and other tropical fruits will find a way to the markets of the world." A different newspaper observed: "The south Florida orange crop is predicted to be larger than ever before known in the history of the country. The fruit will bring this season at the groves twenty dollars per thousand."[21]

Thus, in the early 1870s citrus culture attracted new residents to the vicinity who desired to take up home places near—but not in—Tampa. They needed larger and less expensive tracts for planting trees than the town could offer them. In the circumstances, the original 160-acre townsite came to be surrounded by 1873 with land claims held or owned primarily by African Americans, wartime Unionists, and northern-born Republicans. In today's Hyde Park neighborhood, Judge Samuel D. Chase homesteaded while John M. Hawley bought out Augustus Santhorant's claim. Matthew P. Lyons purchased Uriah Collar's tract on the Hillsborough River's west bank between Spruce and Cypress Streets. Directly north of town lay homesteads of freedpersons Cyrus Charles, Fortune Taylor, Tom Jackson, and John Mathews. Matthew P. Lyons, William J. Campbell, and Campbell's son-in-law C. W. Wells controlled every acre outside the Fort Brooke military reservation that lay between today's Columbus Drive and Henderson Avenue on the north and south, and Fifteenth Avenue and Highland Avenue on the east and west. On Hooker's Point and to the east of the military reserve, Jacob Summerlin and C. R. Mobley dominated.[22]

75. William W. Wall. (*Sunland Tribune*)

Desperation and Incorporation

As each year of the early 1870s passed, Tampa's conservative white leaders fretted more urgently about trends that saw their numbers diluted to the ultimate advantage of Republicans. They had attempted to forestall the problem by holding a quick incorporation election during the yellow fever epidemic of 1871, but the scheme had fallen flat. By the time B. C. Leonardy finalized the survey of his "addition" to the town the following year, they knew they needed to try again. Hesitant to risk another election, they called a public meeting this time to consider the matter. Seventy-three persons attended, including African American voters Peter Golson, Andrew McKnight, Thomas McKnight, Solomon Stanton, Dave Anderson, Lewis Henderson, Jim Mills, Handy Williams, Wash Harrison, and Henry Brumick. All told, twenty or so Republicans contested the matter with fifty-three Democrats. By those totals, B. C. Leonardy lost the mayoral contest to William W. Wall. The defeated refused to become the vanquished. They sued in Judge Magbee's circuit court to overturn the act of incorporation. His honor complied with their petition, declaring that the requirements of state law had not been followed.[23]

The pro-incorporation forces perceived a golden opportunity in late summer 1873, ensuing events having heightened their sense of urgency. County government under the Hart administration had begun to regularize local affairs and build popularity with area voters, but the governor had left the state ailing. Many expected his death, considerably undermining Republicans' optimism. This emboldened Democrats who, coincidentally, also saw more cause for insecurity if they waited too long to act. Several more northern families had staked out land close to town. Also, the end of the five-year waiting period before the grant of titles to early homestead filers neared. This raised the possibility that the tracts might be subdivided on the Leonardy pattern, attracting even more blacks and northerners with smaller and more affordable parcels. Meanwhile, the economy had slumped further as the Vose Injunction negotiations dragged on without immediate promise of resolution. Some businessmen—two senior Republicans in particular—found themselves forced to consider giving up, closing up, and departing. Charles Slager moved to Texas, where he had passed away by year's end. Isidore Blumenthal bankrupted, and his lumber and cedar mills closed. Republican clout weakened accordingly. After some months, the cedar mill reopened under new management (about which more later), but the damage had been done. Some local whites had lost money, and jobs had evaporated. More departures of conservative white voters appeared likely.[24]

Given all circumstances, the pro-incorporation men proceeded with determination. They called another public meeting, but this time they limited participation to persons residing within the original 160-acre township. As a result, only forty-eight men gathered in stifling heat at the courthouse on August 11. Thomas K. Spencer, Joseph B. Wall, Franklin Branch, William C. Brown, William T. Haskins, Charles E. Harrison, and W. F. Burts coordinated the event. Twelve Republicans urged B. C. Leonardy's candidacy for mayor, but thirty-six Democrats carried the day for twenty-three-year-old James Edgar Lipscomb. An Alabama native who had come to Tampa in 1871 and clerked thereafter in William W. Wall's general store, Edgar Lipscomb burned with the fires of youth and the pangs of frustration at having been too young to serve the Confederacy's cause. Selected to assist him in the new municipal government were: Charles Hanford, clerk; John G. Robles, marshal; and aldermen W. T. Haskins, Edward A. Clarke, John T. Lesley, Josiah Ferris, and Henry L. Crane.[25]

It took three days to organize town government. On August 14, the council quickly approved several measures, signalling in the process that a new day had dawned, politically speaking. First, its members granted the mayor and marshal considerable authority by enacting a tough ordinance proscribing "riot or affray." The crimes included being "drunk or disorderly" or making "loud noise or vociferations" or doing "any other act or acts having tendency to disturb the peace and quietness of the inhabitants." Punishment rested in the mayor's sole discretion. Firing a gun within the town limits came within a second ban, thereby making Republican electoral victory celebrations somewhat chancy. Finally, the Democrats telegraphed their sentiments regarding the status of their political opponents when they adopted a cemetery ordinance that restricted to a particular area burials of "Strangers and Colored People."[26]

The atmosphere of conservative triumph that filled the courthouse in August dissipated as the calendar turned to September. First, heavy rains had pelted the community in August. By the next month they had turned it into a quagmire. "We have had very heavy rains and stormy weather," observed an area farmer, "which have done considerable damage to [crops]." Bridges washed away, once again segregating town from countryside and cutting merchant sales ever more drastically. Then, on the twenty-third, a killer hurricane from the Yucatan Channel slammed into the town, bringing heavy flooding and serious damage to property. Farmers saw corn, cane, cotton, and potato crops devastated. Tough times turned hard as stone.[27]

At that point, real problems surfaced. News began filtering into Tampa that the nation's economy had taken a serious tumble. By late September, in fact, a full-scale stock market crash had created general financial panic. Industries collapsed, hundreds of thousands found themselves unemployed, and ruin befell countless businesses and households. This Panic of 1873 would prove to be one of the most-severe economic depressions ever suffered in the United States, and its effects would linger in some respects well into the 1880s. The nation's industrial might trembled as its people reeled.[28]

At Tampa, the shocks kept coming. For the Democrats, an important one involved their attempts to encourage establishment in town of a conservative newspaper. At first, success attended the efforts. "R. E. Neeld, of Key West, and formerly editor of the Guardian, has removed his press and material to Tampa for the purpose of publishing a *red hot* Democratic paper for the unterrified of that section," a report noted. Sizing up his market, though, Neeld temporized. "The first issue of the Hillsborough Guardian made its appearance on 6th [September]," commented one townsman. "The people here consider it a 'weak sister' (neutral)." Still, C. R. Mobley had no intention of allowing even a "weak sister" to control local news. He announced his intention to revive the *Florida Peninsular*. That was all it took. Neeld sold out to the Republican leader, while remaining as editor. Bill and Alfred Neeld, Burns Canning, Ad Arnold, and Edgar Drew assisted in getting out the new *Tampa Guardian*.[29]

What news the *Guardian* had to cover! October 1873 witnessed the Hub Williams trial. November permitted his escape. While Williams fled, Regulators vented their ire on Judge Magbee with the assassination attempt at Pine Level. Already rattled by the close call with sudden death, the judge returned to Tampa to face the terminal illness of his friend, the paper's publisher C. R. Mobley. Although the two men once had fought for local Republican control, the battle against Democrats eventually had brought them together thanks to Governor Hart's influence. When Mobley passed away at home on December 30, the judge fell stricken with grief.[30]

C. R. Mobley's death set the stage for one of Tampa's most-celebrated exercises of municipal and judicial authority, one which appears with greater clarity given an understanding of the season's many tumultuous happenings. As he was wont to do in times of stress, James T. Magbee reacted to his friend's passing by taking to the bottle. Sensing an opportunity to embarrass the judge while evidencing to all his new-found municipal power, Mayor Lipscomb ordered acting marshal Owen Dishong (also twenty-three years of age) to arrest Magbee under the new "riot and affray" ordinance. Dishong locked his prisoner in "a small log structure standing near the river, about the foot of Lafayette [Kennedy] street." Soon, Magbee hailed a passerby and asked him to summon his wife Julia Magbee to bring him pen, paper, and ink. With the supplies, he wrote out a habeas corpus petition addressed to himself as circuit court judge. He thereupon granted the petition and issued a writ for his release. Julia took the order to court clerk William F. White, who sealed and delivered it to Sheriff James Hay. That officer then attempted to serve the writ upon the mayor at his place of employment, the William W. Wall store. According to Charles E. Harrison, "Lipscomb grabbed an axe-handle and with remarks more emphatic than elegant, chased the doughty sheriff down the street." Magbee then spent the night in jail, but the story's final chapter had yet to play out.[31]

That saga unfolded in late winter 1874. On March 18 Governor Hart died suddenly at his Jacksonville home. Exactly one week later, Magbee opened the circuit court's spring term at Tampa. Disheartened and irritated by the sad turn of events, the judge determined to take out his ire on Mayor Lipscomb and Marshal Dishong. He ordered their arrest for contempt of court. Lipscomb refused on his and Dishong's behalf to submit but agreed to appear in court the

76. Major Peter W. Bryant.

following morning. "There is much excitement," a local man reported, "and fears are entertained of serious results." When time for court arrived the next day, the defendants entered the courtroom with a crowd of supporters. Lipscomb ally Edward A. Clarke carried a shotgun. Nonplussed, Magbee thundered at the two men "on the enormity of the offense they had committed." He then sentenced them to pay $100 fines and spend ten days in jail. "Lipscomb sprang forward," remembered Charles E. Harrison, "grasped the shotgun in Mr. Clarke's hand, wrenched it from him and leveling it at Magbee, exclaimed `You d—d old scoundrel; if I'm to go to jail I'll send you to hell first.'" Harrison added, "In an instant every man in the court room was on his feet and the gun was snatched from Lipscomb's hands quicker than he had grasped it."[32]

The contretemps split Tampans into armed camps. After Lipscomb and Dishong rejected Sheriff Hay's demand for surrender, the law officer summoned a posse from the countryside. "The men came, mounted, armed and equipped," Harrison recounted, "but they rode up to W. W. Wall's store and reported to Lipscomb and stated that they were at his orders and would defend him to the last." Harrison likely overstated the posse's sympathy for the town officials. Seemingly, they and the sheriff desired to avoid bloodshed as Judge Magbee and Major Peter W. Bryant sought new governor Marcellus L. Stearns's permission to use the black Hillsborough County militia company. Communications took time, though. After a few days had passed in waiting, tempers died down. The posse disbanded and uneasy truce descended upon a troubled town.[33]

Gold Poured Into a Vacuum

Where the *Tampa Guardian* brimmed with vital news in late 1873 and early 1874, its readers endured the months that passed thereafter with little to intrigue them. Tampa's economy, flat to begin with, drifted slowly downward as the Panic of 1873's impact reached the isolated community. In summer a plague of bugs hit local citrus groves, a concern relieved only when Thomas P. Kennedy came up with the idea that "a current of electricity turned loose upon an orange tree infested with insects will destroy the vermin and revive the tree." Kennedy's plan foundered when he failed to obtain a battery that would enable him to "reduce the matter to a demonstration." As had many local businesses, the *Guardian* quietly shut its doors in September. Hungry for good news, townspeople by October had pledged $1,500 for a telegraph connection to the outside world. It was not nearly enough. So, by year's end excitement came mostly from rumors. The juiciest one had pirate treasure awaiting discovery. "A company is being formed to dig up Tampa gold, as several millions are said to have been buried there," observed a correspondent. "But one of our citizens seems to know the exact locality," continued the report, "and he is wonderfully quiet on the subject."[34]

The good news that did arrive usually involved progress elsewhere, a fact that doubtlessly offered little comfort to depressed Tampans. Cattle money fueled heady times at Fort Meade, for instance. The town, it was said, was "flourishing, busy, and bustling." A report published by state officials quoted teacher Robert LaMartin as commenting: "If the sound of the hammer and mallet is a significance of the progressive spirit that pervades its limits, it can freely claim progress. The health and water is fine, and society refined and orderly." Similar tidings came to Tampa from the west, as well as from the east. The vicinity of Clear Water Harbor pulsed with excitement. The *Guardian* spoke of wealthy Alabamians moving there to develop extensive citrus groves and bringing with them the wherewithal to attract a railroad "to Point Pinellas." The *Clear Water Times* extolled the region's attractions, while James P. McMullen founded a new town of Bay View just east of the harbor. By summer 1875 two stores, a post office, a Masonic lodge, and orange trees galore graced the community.[35]

The town government could do little under such conditions to relieve Tampans' misery, although some attempts were made at cheering through beautification. In this vein, the council in March authorized planting "trees for shade trees at any place on the center lines of the streets as well as on the lines Ten (10) feet from the outside lines of the Blocks." Otherwise, the municipal corporation soon grew irrelevant. The council suspended August elections, authorizing Mayor Lipscomb to call for balloting at his discretion upon ten days' notice. It seems unlikely that any such contest occurred until August 1876. Meanwhile, the mayor held power to appoint a clerk, treasurer, or marshal, if necessary. By October 1874, the city's impotence appeared evident to all. When "some of the Young Ladies and Gentlemen of Tampa" desired to use the courthouse room "called the Town Hall" for "giving Amateur Dramatic entertainments," they approached the Republican county commission while eschewing the Democratic town council that controlled the room.[36]

As always, of course, pockets of light shone through the general gloom. For many African Americans, for example, government jobs and maturing orange groves permitted relief from otherwise depressed conditions. Republicans still ruled Florida, with Judge Magbee holding office as chairman of the party's state central committee. Adam Holloman remained on the county commission, Peter W. Bryant exercised wide influence as a militia major, and Samuel Bryant represented the county at Republican meetings. And, beginning in late summer 1873, control of most federal employment in the Tampa Bay region rested in the hands of former Alachua County legislator Henry W. Harmon. Described as "very intelligent and alert and a very ready speaker," Harmon also served as clerk of the Florida house of representatives. Under a change in United States policy, the African American official assumed authority over Fort Brooke and its military reservation in February 1874.[37]

Some cedar mill workers also found cause for giving thanks. Upon I. Blumenthal & Co.'s collapse in 1873, they had been thrown out of work. Fortunately, Harlen P. Lovering happened to be in the area surveying timber resources for his brother J. P. Lovering, a manager for the Dixon Pencil Company of Jersey City, New Jersey. By September, the Loverings had restarted the riverside cedar mill, having already undertaken extensive repairs. They and the company would operate it for the next half decade, as the town's largest employer.[38]

The cedar industry's crucial importance to Tampa during the 1870s merits a closer look. In May 1874, the *Guardian* helpfully explained its operations. "The manufactories of cedar pencils in Germany and other European countries are indebted to this coast for the supply of most of their material," it observed. "This cedar is gotten out and hauled to Tampa in the shape of nicely-hewn logs, some ten feet in length, worth on an average fifty cents per square foot," the article continued. "This timber is then shipped to New York, sawed into slips, cedar pencil length, thence sent to Europe." The account concluded: "The cedar logs are hauled in by farmers, are in piles about town and in heaps along the river. The cedar forests up the river are almost inexhaustible, though in the swampy hammocks causeways have to be built to facilitate the getting out of the cedar."[39]

Lastly, the vacuum created by the ruin of Tampa's over-extended Jewish entrepreneurs and other troubled businessmen opened up lucrative opportunities for men who had prospered along with the cattle industry and the flow of Spanish gold doubloons into southwest Florida. Especially, it permitted the emergence of the partnership of John Miller and William B. Henderson, soon to oversee Tampa's largest retail store and to manage a fleet of ships operating in and out of the port. Other merchants such as Edward A. Clarke, William W. Wall, and Christopher L. Friebele managed to snap up desirable town properties at tax sale prices. Joining them was William B. Hooker's son James N. Hooker, who worked for Miller and Henderson. When H. L. Crane & Co.'s dry goods store greeted its first customers in August 1873, the owner could offer appreciation to his partner Hooker. Lastly, the void that existed in I. Blumenthal & Co.'s wake also placed into question control of much of the town's riverfront. Joseph Robles, James Williams, and D. Isaac Craft stepped into the picture and soon made away with the prizes that the Loverings and the Dixon Pencil Company did not want.[40]

Though little noticed at the time, one private event served as a harbinger of just how important the cattle business and its resources were to be for Tampa and all of Florida. The 1869 loss of the *Governor Marvin* and other setbacks had seen the McKay family's fortunes ebb by the early 1870s. As they did, James and Matilda McKay's daughter Almeria Belle fell in love with a Brookesville physician and farmer, Dr. Howell T. Lykes. The couple wed in 1874, in which year Dr. Lykes launched a political career by achieving election to the state house of representatives. In subsequent years, he expanded his business interests deep into the cattle industry, including the export of beeves to Cuba. At Havana in 1900 his and Almeria's sons would

77. Those who had lived through the Civil War understood well the reality of economic change. This ten dollar Confederate bill issued by the State of Florida had no value after the war. Inhabitants of the Tampa Bay area felt victimized by both history and circumstance.

found the Lykes Brothers Corporation to carry on their father's work.[41]

For most, though, 1874 ended and 1875 began without evident enthusiasm for Tampa's future. The likelihood of any turnaround glimmered faintly, if at all. The economic depression's grasp held opportunity a prisoner, destroying, it seemed, any real chance that the town would get its long-desired railroad. Of symbolic importance, by January a disillusioned John Darling joined those who had given up. That month he asked for and received a letter of dismissal from the Baptist church, stating that he was "about to leave the area." If Darling's act represented the ebb of Democrats' fortunes, February brought a blow to Republicans. Confronted at every turn by political quicksands, James T. Magbee resigned as circuit court judge. Tales of drinking and drunkeness ultimately had provided his enemies with the ammunition they needed. The king of Tampa's Republicans stood dethroned. What, everyone wondered, possibly could come next.[42]

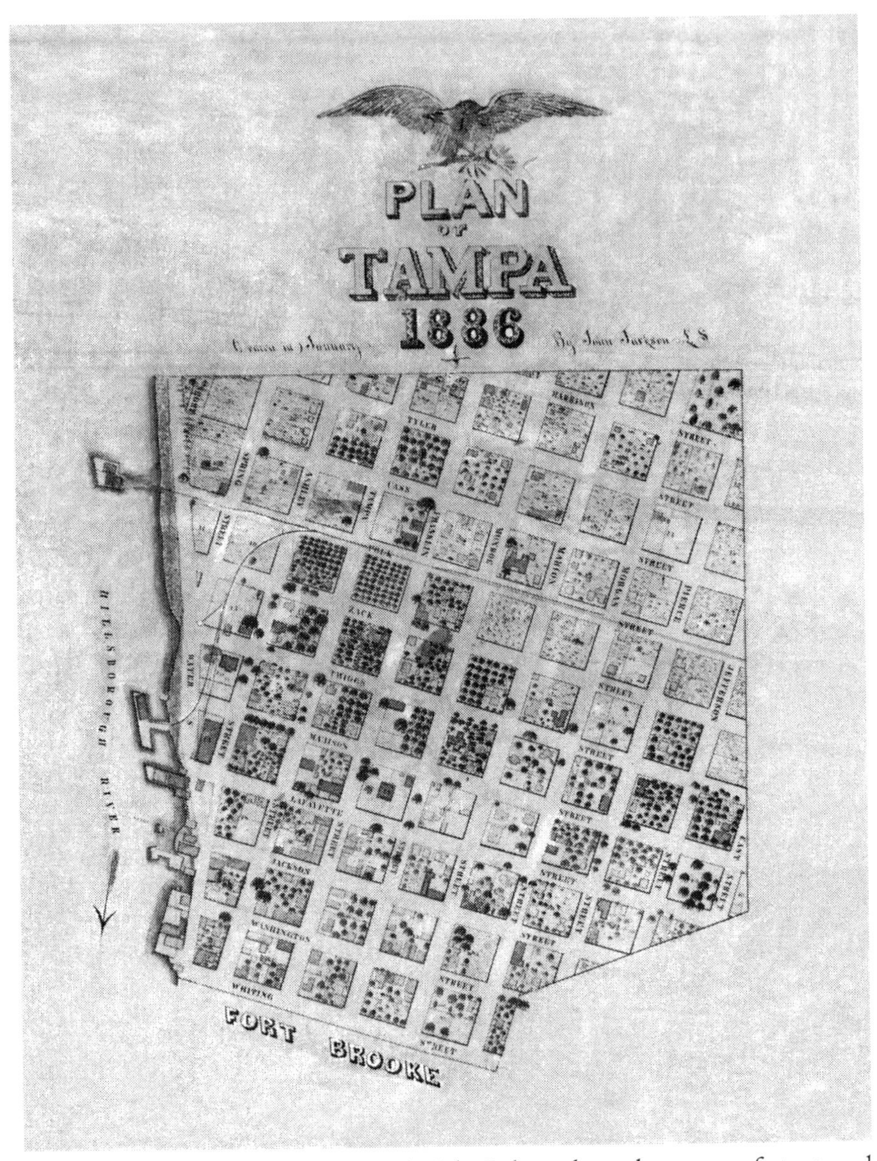

78. This plan of Tampa drawn in 1886 by John Jackson shows the pattern of streets and development that had taken shape as the era of Reconstruction drew to a close. (TBHC)

"better times are beginning to dawn"

Turnaround, 1875-1877

At mid-decade of the 1870s, Tampans disposed to ponder such things could look back upon two decades of turbulent and troubled times, a period during which their town's fortunes first peaked and then commenced to slide. In the midst of excitement stirred by what they thought would be the imminent arrival of a railroad, they had incorporated their city in 1855. Then, five days after the governor inked their charter, Indian war burst into regional conflagration, killing more dreams than combatants. Thereafter, Regulator violence, plagues, pestilence, political power plays, secession, Civil War bombardments, military occupation, racial divisions, Reconstruction fiats, floods, droughts, hurricanes, personal animosities, anger, greed, and what have you combined over twenty years to reduce the community to the equivalent of a punch-drunk fighter struggling to stand on his feet.[1] Sometimes such a fighter needs time to understand that the count has given him a victory. By the same token, would Tampans find the going difficult when long-awaited good fortune finally came calling? Would they reach out and embrace it?

Little glimpses of the possibility of better times appeared during 1875's opening months, but many townspeople, inclined by experience to expect the worse, may have missed seeing them. After all, negative signs abounded. For instance, St. Andrew's Episcopal Church had been without a minister for over one year. The First Baptist Church soon would suspend because "the church was unable to keep a pastor long." As late as December 1876, a visitor would describe the town as "the most forlorn collection of little one-story frame houses imaginable." The Dixon cedar mill's closing in late summer 1875 likely reinforced the tendency to foreboding, even though the facility reopened in November after repairs and modernization.[2]

What the spell of gloom kept hidden from the sight of many was that increasing numbers of African American and northern-born farmers slowly were building solid economic foundations for themselves, their families, and their neighbors based upon orange culture. In the spring of 1874, to cite an example, John M. Hawley relocated to Tampa from Detroit, Michigan, "for the benefit of his health." He selected a place for his home on the Interbay Peninsula. Eventually, Hawley found to his chagrin that Augustus Santhorant had preceded him, forcing the newcomer reluctantly to hand over $500 in gold coins for the land. The property, through which Bayshore Boulevard passes today, was bounded roughly by modern MacDill Avenue on the west, Palmira Street on the north, and the grounds of the Academy of the Holy Names on the south. The experience did not shake Hawley's hopes for his new home, however. He believed that Tampa Bay offered special opportunities while much of the nation endured the agonies of the Panic of 1873. So, the new owner built a cabin, planted orange trees, and waited for better health and economic security.[3]

At about the same time as Hawley invested in his land, other northerners, many anxious about health problems, sank roots in Tampa Bay area soil. One of them was William G. Bartholomew. A Connecticut native, Colonel Bartholomew had served during the Civil War as commander of the Twenty-seventh Massachusetts Volunteers. At Tampa Bay, he dreamed of starting a healthier life on a farm a mile or two below Hawley's bayshore place. The tract ran from just below Euclid Avenue on the north to about Coachman Avenue on the south. As time passed Bartholomew added holdings west of his original homestead and also behind the McKay family's Ballast Point reserve. Described by Donald B. McKay as a "courteous gentleman," the colonel easily established friendly relations with many Tampans. His closest rapport may have been with another Civil War soldier, but one who had backed the opposite side. Harry C. Culbreath had

79. More than a village but less than a town, Tampa began to claim its own identity in the mid-1870s. (TBHC)

served with distinction as colonel of the Second Regiment, South Carolina Artillery. Shortly after the Confederate surrender, he had preceded Bartholomew to the Interbay Peninsula, where he developed a homestead at what has become Beach Park. With Bartholomew's arrival, a devoted friendship ripened between the two men. When Culbreath died in 1885, his grieving fellow "placed a beautiful floral tribute on the grave." According to McKay, "Every Memorial Day thereafter as long as he lived the kindly old Northern officer placed flowers on the grave of the gallant old Southern officer who had become his friend."[4]

While Hawley, Bartholomew, and others opened settlements and planted orange groves, early homestead claims located near Tampa began to mature. On March 19, 1874, Cyrus Charles—who had prospered to the point that he and William J. Campbell jointly operated a timber business by 1870—received the county's first grant of homestead title from the United States government. Santhorant's followed on June 8, S. P. Haddon's on August 25, and Fortune Taylor's on November 11. Soon, Thomas Fisher, Constant Bouguardez, John Mathews, Samuel D. Chase, Nancy Jackson, Chauncey W. Wells, Thomas B. Jackson, William J. Campbell, James E. Morris, Edward A. Clarke, A. L. Aman, Matthew Hooper, and Joseph Green had come into final possession.[5]

80. The Watrous Family and their home. James Monroe Watrous and his wife Jennie moved to Tampa from Michigan in 1876. (Mormino and Pizzo, *Tampa: The Treasure City*)

With lands surrounding Tampa titled and to-be-titled at long last, a few local residents such as Edward A. Clarke, William C. Brown, J. Edgar Lipscomb, Bartholomew C. Leonardy, and James T. Magbee began buying up portions of large homesteads and either holding them for speculation or else reselling to newcomers. Late in 1875 a Detroit real estate firm composed of F. X. Spranger and Otto Lang entered the market. On December 6 they purchased from Judge Samuel D. Chase's widow Harriet the family homestead situated in today's Hyde Park between Rome and Willow Avenues on the west and east and extending from Swann Avenue on the north to the bayshore. Two months later the speculators resold the 150 or so acres to James M. Watrous of Bay City, Michigan, who—like so many others—was seeking improvement of his health. As it turned out, the Watrous family would react to their bay area home just as did most of their fellow newcomers. "At first the south seemed liked a desolate country[,] as it is compared with the north[,] for the country has neither the money or business here,"

Watrous's wife Jennie informed a friend. She added, "But labor and money will make a nice home in time."[6]

By mid-1875 at least one resident realized that enough new settlers could be anticipated to make it worthwhile to subdivide his holdings into smaller and more attractively priced parcels. B. C. Leonardy had provided the model a few years earlier with his "Leonardy's Addition to the Town of Tampa." Now, Chauncey W. Wells created "Orange Hill." The development, as defined by county surveyor William F. White, rested above today's Tenth Avenue on a tract wedged westward of the Fort Brooke Military Reservation. Roughly speaking, modern Columbus Avenue bounded it on the north, with Nebraska and Fifteenth Avenues limiting it west and east. To provide access to holdings, Wells laid out five east-west and three north-south streets. The former, from the south, he named Star, Logan, Liberty, Enterprise, and Wells. The latter, from the west, the owner called Orange, Olive, and Oak.[7]

Within the year, two others would repeat Wells's initiative, both on the Interbay Peninsula. In March 1876, John M. Hawley separated his lands surrounding Palma Ceia Springs into seven tracts of varying sizes. Current streets such as Rubideaux, Barcelona, and Santiago may reflect lot lines drawn at that time by surveyor White. Two miles to the south, David M. Nix carved up his homestead, situated just below the Bartholomew place, into five parcels. Two of forty acres each lay between Himes and MacDill Avenues above Gandy Boulevard. Three of about twenty acres apiece ran from MacDill to Hillsborough Bay. "Avenues" anticipated by Nix's effort included today's Villa Rosa Avenue and, perhaps, Hawthorne Road.[8]

Hillsborough's county commission proved eager to accommodate this type of growth—which, after all, swelled area Republican ranks—by encouraging development of public ways, bridges, and other needed amenities. Beginning in January 1875 it regularized the county's basic road system, specifying links that would receive public support and which, by law, residents were required to work. In March, John M. Hawley approached the commissioners to request that "a Public Road . . . be laid out from the Ferry to Gadson's Point." The board granted the request, which recognized the Interbay Peninsula's attraction to settlers, and asked W. G. Bartholomew, W. E. Sweat, and Sterling McCarty to see to the matter. Those gentlemen reported their work completed in October. The "Bay Road," as it was called, began on the Hillsborough River's western bank opposite Jackson Street. From that point, it ran southwesterly to an intersection with the north-south center line of Section 34, Township 29 South, Range 18 East; that is to say, it coursed from the Tampa ferry to modern MacDill Avenue about where that street presently intersects Bay to Bay Boulevard. From thence, the new public way led due south through the Bartholomew and Nix lands to Ballast Point.[9]

Avenues and Sand Beds

Orange plantings and road blazings brought more immigrants to Tampa Bay as 1875 wound toward its conclusion, although some did not locate where Tampans might have preferred. General John Constantine Williams of Detroit, for example, cast a wide glance over the region looking for the ideal spot to plant a colony. Tampans, eager to draw Williams closer to their orbit, attempted to sabotage his interest in the Pinellas Peninsula (as likely they also did with others). "Damn Point Pinellas!" Williams told a man who inquired if he had examined that vicinity. He added, "I was told by a gentleman in Tampa, also by one in Clearwater, that it is only four feet above tide-water!" Corrected as to the facts, Williams turned back to the peninsula, decided to make it his home, and hied himself to Detroit to collect his family. "On his return he invested largely in land," observed area pioneer John A. Bethell, "including the site of St. Petersburg." Meanwhile, other arrivals produced new citrus groves that soon dotted the land around Clear Water Harbor. "The great business of our country is the production of tropical fruits," proclaimed one resident in 1875. "To this all other branches should be looked upon only as auxiliaries, by which we would procure the necessary supplies to enable us to prosecute with vigor this more important aim."[10]

Not everyone turned away from Tampa, though. As shown by the Hawley and Watrous families' experiences, the town's surrounding lands lured a number of families from Michigan. "It is stated that a colony of thirty immigrants from Bay City . . . is expected at Tampa this month," noted a December 1875 report. The nearby state of Indiana also contributed seekers after health and fortune. One of them, jeweler Robert Mugge of Germany by way of Terre Haute, intended to find a cure for his asthma, not at Tampa but in Cuba. His boat stopped in at the town, however, and he liked it. Deciding to remaining, Mugge sent for his brother-in-law Louis Mann and family.

Mugge and Mann first opened a tailoring shop and then a grocery and general merchandise store.[11]

With all due respect to Michigan and Indiana, they could not claim the greatest credit as starting point for immigrants to Tampa in 1875 and 1876. Thanks to Dr. Henry R. and Caroline Whitford Benjamin, that honor belonged to Nebraska. At Omaha in 1874, Caroline's health declined. Henry noticed that she improved the following summer, leading him to believe that a warmer climate would revive her completely. "In September [1875], after thorough investigation of the subject, aided by such means as the profession is able to furnish to guide us in such selections," he later wrote, "we came to the conclusion that the west coast of Florida possessed the best climate, all things considered, to be found in the United States, if not in the world." The Benjamins, with their son Dr. George Nelson Benjamin and brother-in-law R. A. Whitford, got themselves quickly to Tampa once their decision had been made. On November 6, the *Tampa Guardian* advised locals, somewhat erroneously, that "three families from Omaha, Ks., arrived the first of the present week with a view of a permanent residence." Once on the scene, the Nebraskans reached back to their old home state to interest friends and relatives in cheap real estate. Especially, George N. Benjamin brokered land deals north and northeast of town. Everyone planted orange groves.[12]

The influx of grove owners-to-be piqued the county commission's continuing interest in furthering growth. Its existing attitudes in that regard had found reinforcement in November 1875, when Governor Marcellus Stearns placed John M. Hawley on the board. Thus, petitioners expected and found a friendly reception when they approached the panel in July 1876 to ask for more and better roads. In the process, the county settled on a policy that influenced, if not determined, the location of Tampa's major arteries for generations. The petition anticipated the commissioners' ultimate decision. "It is evident that as the County settles up and people fence their lands," it read, "it will be necessary to inaugurate a different system of roads from that now in vogue." The document stated further, "It is evident that the shortest distance from any point to another is a straight line between such points and . . . it is obvious that Roads should be established on the shortest lines that the nature of the case will admit of." Since lands usually were divided by section and township lines, the "best policy," where practicable, was "to establish Roads on Section and Township lines" by "using one half of the width of the road from each mans land." Since section lines lie one mile from each other, many of Tampa's principal thoroughfares may be found today to be located at one mile intervals.[13]

The public ways specifically requested of the commission in July 1876 were two in number. The future Nebraska Avenue originally was defined as "commencing at the intersection of Washington Street in the Town of Tampa, with the line of former Military Reservation of Fort Brooke Fla. running thence North Eastwardly on said Reserve line to the intersection of said line with the Range line between Ranges Numbered (18) Eighteen and (19) Nineteen, thence North on said Range line to the County line between Hernando and Hillsborough Counties." The second new route, eventually to be known as Michigan Avenue (now Columbus Drive), was "to commence at the corner of Sections 11-12-13-14 of Range 18 and run thence due East on the Section lines between Sections 12 & 13 Range 18, & 7 & 18 — 8 & 17 — 9 & 16 in Range 19 to the intersection at the N.E. corner of Section 16 with the road to six mile creek." Board members instructed William C. Brown, Joseph Robles, and William J. Campbell to lay out the routes accordingly.[14]

The names of the petition's signers, preserved in the county commission's minute book, offer identity to the long-time residents and the newcomers who were betting their futures on orange groves north and northeast of town in 1876. The men included: B. B. Lake, Henry L. Mitchell, D. Isaac Craft, E. D. McLaughlin, C. W. Wells, W. J. Campbell, S. P. Haddon, T. H. Estell, C. L. Runnels, William J. McKnight, A. L. Aman, S. F. Hewitt, Edom Gross, George N. Benjamin, H. R. Benjamin, I. W. Warner, C. C. Cook, R. A. Whitford, William H. Webb, Fred O. Kammerer, Joseph Green, S. J. Lyons, Joseph Robles, S. B. Knight, S. I. N. Branch, E. P. Grant, H. J. Madsen, William Danford, W. C. Branch, A. T. Frierson, E. A. Clarke, John T. Lesley, Thomas P. Kennedy, John R. Swingley, William W. Wall, Franklin Branch, H. Hopkins, Henry L. Crane, James N. Hooker, Alfred Neeld, Perry G. Wall, Henry Krause, William J. Hillyard, C. L. Friebele, W. B. Henderson, and S. L. Friebele.[15]

The presence of William January Prince McKnight's name on the petition eases the way to reinforcing a point made in the previous chapter. African Americans helped to pioneer the citrus industry at Tampa and benefitted financially with its success. In Prince's case, he and his wife Maria Simon McKnight relocated to town from

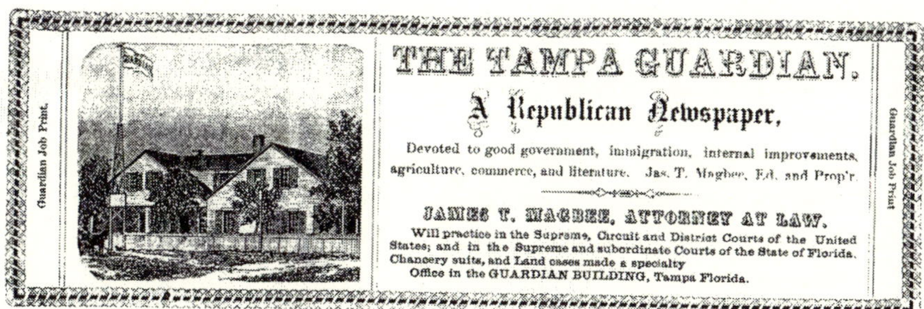

81. The *Tampa Guardian* enjoyed a renewed vigor as the economic fortunes of the area began to improve. (LC)

Hernando County in the early 1870s, homesteading and grove tending. His brother Thomas McKnight had preceded Prince on the same journey, while other brothers Elijah and Anthony followed with their families within a few years. As would be true of other such families coming to Tampa during the orange boom of the mid-1870s, the McKnights contributed to the community in ways both shortlived and longlasting. A Baptist minister, Prince came to accept the pulpit of Beulah Baptist Institutional Church. When the congregation at long last felt financially able during late summer 1875 to purchase land from Thomas and Ellen Jackson and erect a sanctuary, McKnight served with Solomon Stanton as one of its two trustees.[16]

Rewards Unevenly Spread

The same promise of prosperity that fuelled construction of Beulah Baptist Church filled many an area home, if not the whole of Tampa. Following 1874's tree infestation, the region for a time enjoyed excellent weather for growing citrus. "The orange trees at the Orange Grove Hotel are blooming a third time this year, some of the trees are nearly white with blooms," bragged the *Tampa Guardian* on September 4, 1875. "The orange tree in this climate frequently blooms and puts on fruit from two to three times in the year," its notice declared, "and the fruit matures." The paper's editor went on to note that Florida's "orange belt" had begun to move south. "Indeed it will be found [now]," the item insisted, "[along] the entire gulf coast." The *Guardian* began to chronicle shipments week to week, as they built in size. The seven days prior to November 13 saw 88,497 pieces of fruit loaded on board at Tampa's wharf. The next four weeks added

569,000 to the total.[17]

Out-of-town newspapers and journals began to pick up stories from Tampa, bringing the area a sort of exotic renown during the nation's otherwise difficult times. In this regard, the revival of the *Tampa Guardian* by James T. Magbee in April 1875 assisted tremendously. As one influential newspaperman pointed out, "South Florida is an inviting section of the State, and a well-conducted newspaper can do much towards making known its advantages." The former judge orchestrated a happy chorus of good tidings designed to captivate sufferers from northern winters and cruel economic depression. Usually the articles boasted of citrus production and quality but sometimes they lauded the salubrious climate and its beneficial effects upon recent settlers. The intensity of Magbee's cheerleading grew with the rise in immigration and grove development. "As a general thing, better times are beginning to dawn, more apparently than they have since the surrender," he proclaimed in mid-1876. "We see what improvements have been brought about in one short year," the editor continued, "and must express our gratification at the encouraging prospects before us."[18]

It should be noted, too, that Magbee balanced his *Guardian* cheerleading for growth and development with a keen sense of the need to preserve and maintain at Tampa those amenities of life that made it a special place. Given the city's unfortunate record in this regard through the years, Magbee's efforts stand out even more. Doubtlessly, at the time he was writing, his denunciations of despoliation reinforced to readers elsewhere conceptions of Tampa as a semi-tropical, if wild and remote, paradise. His sensitivity extended even to preservation of the remains of peoples long in Tampa's past. "Some one has been digging into the Indian mound in the Garrison," he noted in March 1876. "This thing should be stopped," the onetime judge insisted, "that beautiful mound should not be destroyed to gratify the foolish whim of persons who want to find buried treasure instead of working for it."[19]

As editor Magbee also pointed out, the turnaround in area prospects occurred during the year or year and one half that preceded the summer of 1876. An illustration of that fact comes readily to mind, one that involved a man who stood among the nation's best-known literary figures. In early 1875, poet Sidney Lanier researched and wrote on behalf of the Great Atlantic Coast Railroad Company a guide to the sunshine state entitled *Florida: Its Scenery, Climate, and*

82. Among the guests posing outside the Orange Grove Hotel for this photograph are Henry L. Crane and the author Sidney Lanier. (*Sunland Tribune*)

History. In doing so, he essentially ignored Tampa other than to mention how to get there and where a traveler could go from there. In 1876, though, the author's health failed. Since publication of his book he had read and heard so much about the town's healthy climate that he chose it for his recovery. Lanier and his wife stepped off the steamer in December, and they remained until April 1877. The poet delighted in the Orange Grove Hotel and other facets of town life. "The weather is perfect summer, and I luxuriate in great draughts of balmy air uncontaminated with city-smokes and furnace-dusts," he recorded. "This has come not a moment too soon; for the exposures of the journey had left my poor lung in most piteous condition."[20]

Along with his health, Lanier's spirits revived at Tampa. This (and financial necessity) led him to write numerous poems while staying in town. They carried titles such as "The Stirrup Cup," "Tampa Robins," "A Florida Sunday," and "The Bee." Within a short time he published the verses in popular, nationally circulated magazines, thereby further spreading Tampa's newfound renown.[21] *Lippincott's*, for example, carried the delightful "Redbreast in Tampa" during the summer of 1877:

The robin laughed in the orange tree;
"Ho, windy North, a fig for thee!
While breasts are red and wings are bold,
And green trees wave me globes of gold,
Old Time! thy scythe reaps bliss for me,
So blithe, so blithe, a bird can be.

"If that I hate wild winter's spite—
The gibbet trees, the world in white,
The gray sky bending over a grave—
Why should I ache, the season's slave?
No, no: I sing; and singers be
Too hot for Time's cold tyranny.

"Nay, windy North, I catch my clime;
My wing is king of the summer-time,
Whose constant touch my breast doth hold;
So laugh I through my green and gold,
With: Time, they scythe reaps bliss for me,
So passing blithe we robins be."[22]

The appearance of beauty, tranquility, and "advances" as seen through Sidney Lanier's eyes or read thanks to James T. Magbee's pen belied serious undercurrents at play in Tampa. To start with, one drawback of orange grove prosperity was that not everyone shared in the bounty. Although some old-time residents joined the trend, others were slow to do so. George W. Wells, a grizzled veteran of the region who lived at Alafia, understood the situation well. "The old settlers of this country, up to a few years past, did not turn their attention to farming and fruit raising," he explained in 1877. "If they had done so," he continued, "to-day South Florida would have been almost an entire orange grove. Wells added, "Cattle have been on the brain for many years past, but now the range is failing fast, and they must resort to other means for a support." The comments concluded: "A great many have taken the orange fever, and it seems to spread daily; and, without doubt, fruit growing in this country will pay remarkably well at a time not far distant. In fact, it is paying well now to those who own bearing groves."[23]

Having hesitated to join the rush to citrus culture, some "old Tampans" openly resented the northern newcomers' successes. Their mere presence rankled more than a few. It particularly irked one group (many of whose members were Confederate veterans) to see streets named after Yankee states such as Nebraska and Michigan. They could not, of course, stop the Republican county commission from acceding to such requests. After January 1877, though, the Democrats ruled in Florida. The disgruntled now could insist on equal consideration. Their demands eventually saw the light of day in November 1877 when Joseph Robles and sixteen others asked for their own artery into the citrus country above town. The new road would run "due North from the Northernmost terminus of Monroe Street in Tampa to the Hillsborough River." With pride of placing shining brightly, they called the street Florida Avenue.[24]

Old-line residents, who themselves were partaking in development and citrus planting ventures, at times manifested their disdain for the newcomers by engaging in sharp practices that sometimes veered toward dishonesty. What might be termed "skinning the Yankees" proved a popular game in more than a few local households. The practice did little damage to the boom as long as resentments remained private. When they emerged into public view, though, the disclosures produced widespread local embarrassment.

That happened in August 1876 courtesy of Tampa's postmaster John S. Judson. A recent emigrant from Bay City, Michigan, Judson grew so infuriated at what he considered improper treatment of himself and other northerners that he allowed his views to be published (without attribution) in the *Semi-Tropical*, a Jacksonville magazine. Edited by former Governor Harrison Reed of Wisconsin, the journal circulated throughout the North and Midwest. "It even becomes evident to a stranger who makes an effort to start any new business in Tampa, that will in any way conflict with 'the old set' of business men, that the whole are combined against him, though in his absence they can quarrel and gouge each other equal to the 'fair average' of all communities whose 'constitutional law' is mainly composed of 'personal redress' for all offences," the article declared. "When he [Judson] began to look for land for his proposed colonists, he found all the choice locations held by 'homestead claims,' by those same 'old merchants,' notwithstanding they never lived upon them, either personally or by proxy," it continued. "Yet no one dared to take one of these claims without buying 'the right,' because the whole community appeared interested in maintaining these 'rights,' notwithstanding it kept immigrants out of the country."[25]

83. George Nelson Benjamin. (*Sunland Tribune*)

Judson's charges took wing, with damage to Tampa's reputation accruing into 1877. Especially this proved the case when the *Bay City Tribune* took up its former townsman's cause in May. "We say to northern men," the paper thundered, "let such a land lie desolate and accursed, before you invest one dollar, or expend one breath, in efforts for its recuperation." Henry R. Benjamin attempted to rehabilitate his adopted home's image by contributing his own story to the *Semi-Tropical*'s columns. In July he submitted a piece entitled, "The Climate and Society of Tampa." Benjamin observed, "We came here in the fall of 1875, under very unfavorable circumstances, but we were never more kindly treated by our own kinfolks than by the people of Tampa." J. R. Askew, who came to town in early 1877 from Jacksonville, Illinois, sought to buttress Benjamin's initiative. During travels out of state, he made a point to "express himself as well pleased with that section" whenever he could. The attempts certainly did not hurt Tampa's cause, but memories of the Judson incident would linger.[26]

Battles in the Streets

Relations between the various elements of the Tampa area population during the period 1875 to 1877 naturally included a huge dose of political discord, and, as such, the town's political saga during the period offers a fitting subject with which to close this history of Civil War and Reconstruction. Violence had played a part in Tampa politics at least since 1858, with Reconstruction's last years serving to expand on the tradition. As was true elsewhere in Florida and the South, the fight for political control would witness many a good man taking part in many an unsavory deed.

The context involved the movement of people out of and into Tampa. The town, limited within its original 160 acres, had not grown with the orange boom. Its population, though, had altered significantly. Some southern whites had departed with the decline of local industry and commerce during the decade's first half. Among those who remained were individuals who had invested, by late 1875 or early 1876, in orange groves located above the community's northern bounds or else on the Interbay Peninsula. A tendency to want to live near one's grove began to emerge, with a scattering of households relocating accordingly. A few families followed to work on the new places for wages. As these Democrats lost their rights to vote in municipal elections, more Republicans claimed the privilege. African American families such as several sides of the McKnight clan had taken up residence, as had a number of the recently arrived parties from the North. An electorate that, in 1873, had seen Democratic electors outvoting Republicans thirty-six to twelve seemingly stood narrowly in favor of the Grand Old Party by mid-1876 or else inched very close to that mark.[27]

This state of affairs understandably did not sit well with the Democrats, especially when they weekly read of wonderful Republican advances and accomplishments in the pages of the *Tampa Guardian*, their town's only newspaper. As irritating as this situation seemed in 1875, it swelled in importance with the coming of 1876 when state and national elections might reverse the tide of Reconstruction. The first step for the Democrats necessarily was to bring forth their own organ. Thomas K. Spencer, long associated with Tampa newspapering, accommodated the need. In March he published the first issue of the *Sunland Tribune* to the relief of many conservatives. A Virginian, Charles N. Hawkins, edited the paper, while Dr. John P. Wall acted as associate editor. The staunchly Democratic *Savannah Morning News*, one of only two daily newspapers widely circulated in Florida, commented, "The Sunland Tribune is a large, newsy, neatly printed journal, and is edited with exceptional ability." Its editor added, "[We] gladly place it upon our exchange list."[28]

In the months that followed, the *Guardian* and the *Tribune* parried, thrusted, and jabbed at each other while stirring partisan sentiments generally. Which is not say that politics was not already a hot topic. Both state and national races appeared tight, and much depended upon the outcomes. In some parts of Florida and the South, African American voters by then had suffered violence, intimidation, or disenchantment to such an extent that they had withdrawn from the political process. At Tampa, conditions quite the contrary prevailed. Black electors signalled their intention to play full roles in the upcoming campaigns, a fact that would stoke the intensity and eventual bitterness of the contests. On August third, the men organized formally to support Republican causes by creating a "Hayes & Wheeler Campaign Club," so named for Republican presidential candidate Rutherford B. Hayes and his running mate. At the "very large and enthusiastic" gathering, numerous individuals accepted leadership roles. Elected as officers were Peter W. Bryant, president; Andrew McKnight, vice president; Henry Brumick, treasurer; John A. W. Patton, secretary; William Walker, assistant secretary; John H. Welsh, chaplain; Aaron Bryant, grand marshal; and Isaac Howard, assistant grand marshal.[29]

The campaign club's founding came as several other happenings fanned the political flames. It was just at that time, for instance, that the *Semi-Tropical*'s article containing John Judson's complaints found its way into print. Old-line Tampans seethed at what they considered the contemptible arrogance of an outsider and troublemaker. Meanwhile, the same Democrats cheered as the state Republican party struggled to heal terrible wounds brought about by infighting between supporters of Governor Stearns and United States Senator Simon P. Conover. As the party's major officeholders reeled from personal attacks and offered their own in return, elated Democrats pushed supporters to register to vote. Some also prepared quietly for minimizing the black vote by stepping up encouragement of Ku Klux Klan-type vigilantes.[30]

Plus, the Tampa Bay region's rising prosperity—thanks to modernization of the Dixon cedar mill and the promise of citrus culture—had spawned a movement to revitalize municipal government. Some practical-minded Democrats realized that they must act with Republicans or else suffer domination of the town's affairs by their opponents. So, they developed a bipartisan election ticket to contest an August municipal election. Republican Harlen P. Lovering, who ran the cedar mill, headed the slate as its mayoral candidate. Democrat William C. Brown, already town clerk, accepted nomination to remain in the post. Councilmen included Democrats Thomas E. Jackson and William B. Henderson, in addition to *Sunland Tribune* associate editor Dr. John P. Wall. Black Republican Henry Brumick, a well regarded shoe and boot maker, joined his name with theirs.[31]

The exact circumstances and events of the 1876 municipal election remain shrouded in mystery, but clearly the contest proved a fierce one. Records hint that ardent Democrats, Republicans, or both attempted to move people into town during the campaign's final days in order to swing the results. A street battle also may have ensued on election day. At least, three key black Republicans—Thomas Clarke (also known as Thomas Jackson), Elijah McKnight, and William Walker—were hauled before Justice of the Peace William C. Brown to answer to charges of willfully disturbing the peace, unlawfully entering a building, and assault. In the end, the bipartisan ticket prevailed.[32]

That a bipartisan ticket could survive at Tampa in 1876 helps to make an important point. Most Democrats did not mind Republicans participating in politics, so long as their approaches were what they (the Democrats) might have termed "sober and responsible." A "good, conservative, business-like" approach met with acceptance, where a more "radical" position sparked anger. "So far as we have been able to judge, they regard it as our right to vote as we please," explained Henry R. Benjamin. "And we believe that a man coming to this or any other part of Florida, can enjoy his political opinions, with as much freedom as in the North." Jennie Watrous added her own thoughts on the matter. "Northerners have the impression that Republicans must keep silence but that is a mistake, here at least," she wrote. "James is a Rep. and has a host of good friends among the Southerners, it is the man and not the politics that is looked at, and people can live here without any fear of molestation."[33]

Benjamin and Watrous had it right when it came to persons with perspectives that did not threaten the white southerners, but there were others whose beliefs did not so please. John Judson was one of them. The furor that resulted from the *Semi-Tropical* article would not have burned so ferociously had he not been a Yankee radical. Back home, his stand was a popular one but not so at Tampa. The *Bay City Tribune* eventually would insist, given Judson's experience, that "A Northern man cannot live peaceably in the South without giving up his manhood."[34]

Memories of one of Judson's compatriots stirred passion in at least one local man's mind seventy years after the 1876 elections. Having written of W. G. Bartholomew and H. C. Culbreath's friendship, Donald B. McKay commented on another officer newly come to town. "But there was a third colonel, also a veteran of the Civil War," he wrote, "who located on a small farm about three miles northwest of Tampa shortly after the arrival of Colonel Bartholomew and his family." McKay continued:

> He was also a colonel in the Union Army—but I have some hesitancy in mentioning him in connection with the two gallant old warriors of whom I have been writing. He was a typical "damnyankee," and I apply the term with all the opprobrium that it can convey. Sober he was crabbed and unsociable. Drunk he was quarrelsome and offensive. Col. Culbreath always carried a heavy gnarled oak walking stick—like an Irish shillalah—and he used it on the cranium of Horace Greeley Thomas a number of times to my knowledge.
>
> George Bell recently told me of a near-duel in which Col. Thomas and Capt. W. E. Sweat, a Confederate veteran were involved. Capt. Sweat was not more than five feet tall, but no man was big enough to bluff him. The men met in Dominic Ghira's saloon at the northeast corner of Jackson and Franklin Sts. As the result of a quarrel—about the war—challenge for a duel with shotguns was issued and accepted. Both men left the place to secure guns. Thomas was first to return, but Sweat came in soon after with a single-barrel gun over his shoulder. As he lowered the weapon to get ready to shoot, the entire load of buckshot rolled out of the barrel—in his excitement he had neglected to place a wadding over the shot charge. Bystanders interfered to disarm Thomas, who tried to shoot his defenseless opponent, and the duel was called off.[35]

84. Col. H. C. Culbreath. (Grismer, *Tampa*)

That any spirit of bipartisan cooperation could survive the community stresses that followed the municipal election of August 1876 and led to the general election in November amazes from the distance of time, while the possibility that duels might have ensued seems perfectly plausible. Perhaps the event most symbolic of the likelihood that regional, racial, political, and personal animosities might shackle Tampans to future political and social strife came at a moment close to election day. On November 11, 1876, James McKay, Sr., died. More than any other individual, he had attempted over the past sixteen years to keep the community together and to direct it toward advances in society, economy, and attitude. During the Civil War's darkest days, he had succeeded against all odds. His voice had continued to speak in a moderate tone in Reconstruction days. Tampans sorely would miss that voice in the years ahead.[36]

As it was, McKay's final decline coincided with an onslaught that brought the full fury of Reconstruction-era politics home to Tampa. Many details sadly are lacking, although as moderate a man as H. R. Benjamin acknowledged, "We have lived here through one of the hottest campaigns, perhaps, ever known to this country." Sheriff William F. White later alleged that Democrats openly intimidated many Republicans. "Several parties said to me that they would vote the republican ticket if they dared to," he related to a congressional investigative committee. "One gentleman that we expected would vote the republican ticket, in fact told us so repeatedly," White stated, "told me after the election, that he went to the polls and intended to vote a republican ticket." The sheriff concluded: "But, says he—he stopped there—'I just didn't dare to do it.' Says he, 'You northern republicans can vote as you please, but a southern republican cannot.'" D. B. McKay remembered that "there was open and general talk of renewing the Civil War."[37]

Before anyone realized it was happening, election day saw Tampans trying to kill each other as ballots were counted. W. Hester Brown, a Democrat, presided as county judge. After Sheriff White discovered the ballot boxes unattended by Brown, he and the judge clashed over how the votes should be tallied. Their quarrel, as White recalled, lasted long enough for a crowd to gather outside the courthouse. He noted, "We could not agree at all for some time."[38] As the officials disputed the matter, young D. B. McKay happened near on the way to seeing his ailing grandfather. He picked up the story at the point when Brown and White had begun to count returns:

> I was visiting my Grandfather McKay's at the corner of Washington and Franklin Strs. I heard a great noise, loud shouting and

> many gunshots nearby and to the east and with childish curiosity and no thought of the danger I ran in that direction. From the corner of the fence I saw 35 or 40 . . . men grouped at the corner of Col. W. G. Ferris' store and about as many Negroes at the Postoffice corner diagonally across the street. Both groups appeared fully armed and they were exchanging fire. Finally the Negroes broke and ran.
>
> Old Tom Clarke, the leader of the Negroes, took refuge in the Courthouse. He was badly wounded, and was taken to his home on Harrison St., a little east of the old cemetery. He recovered, and until his death was considered a great hero by many of his people. A number were wounded on each side in the battle, but none were killed.[39]

Under the circumstances, Hillsborough County's votes weighed heavily in favor of Democratic "redemption" of the state, although the issue statewide and in the presidential race remained in question for months. In January 1877, the Supreme Court of Florida allowed Democrat George F. Drew to take the oath of office as governor. Those Republican Hillsborough County officials who did not resign by month's end were fired by the state's new executive. Nationally, Republican Rutherford B. Hayes ultimately received Florida's electoral votes, by which margin he gained the presidency in March. Before that month had expired, a small delegation of African Americans from Florida had visited with Hayes at the White House. Among those who sought the new president's protection and reassurances stood Tampa's Peter W. Bryant.[40]

The most common sensation felt at Tampa in January 1877 must have been relief that the elections were over, although anxieties about the future probably came in a close second. Still, the citrus boom promised prosperity beyond dreams, as more settlers took up lands and the Democrats tried their hand at bringing to town the iron ribbons of a railroad. Interestingly, on December 12, 1876, it had snowed, and a "cold north wind" had dropped temperatures close to freezing. The extremes of weather in the town's past were unknown to most newcomers, so little thought was given to the event. As time would prove, a serious mistake had been made.[41]

85. This photograph of Franklin Street businesses looks forward in time, showing the Tampa Bay Hotel (opened in 1891) in the background. The newfound prosperity of Tampa, evident in the foreground buildings, had its roots in the turnaround of the mid-1870s. (TBHC)

Abbreviations

FHQ	*Florida Historical Quarterly*
FP	Tampa *Florida Peninsular*
FSA	Florida State Archives, Tallahassee
FT-U&C	Jacksonville *Florida Times-Union and Citizen*
LC	Library of Congress, Washington, DC
NA	National Archives, Washington, DC
ORA	*War of the Rebellion: A Compilation of the Officials Records of the Union and Confederate Armies*
ORN	*Officials Records of the Union and Confederate Navies in the War of the Rebellion*
PKY	P. K. Yonge Library of Florida History, University of Florida, Gainesville
RG	Record Group
SLF	State Library of Florida, Tallahassee
SMN	*Savannah Morning News*
ST	Tampa *Sunland Tribune*
TBH	*Tampa Bay History*
TBHC	Tampa Bay History Center
TDT	*Tampa Daily Times*
TG	*Tampa Guardian*
TH	*Tampa Herald*
TMT	*Tampa Morning Tribune*
TPL	Tampa-Hillsborough County Public Library
TST	*Tampa Sunday Tribune*
USFSC	University of South Florida Special Collections, Tampa
WF	Tallahassee *Weekly Floridian*
WPA	Work Projects Administration

CHAPTER I

[1] *ST*, October 5, 1878.

[2] Chamberlin, "Fort Brooke," 130; *FP*, March 12, 1859.

[3] Brown, "Politics, Greed, Regulator Violence, and Race," 25-26.

[4] Brown, *Tampa Before the Civil War*, 148-150; Sherrill, *Call to Greatness*, 14.

[5] Sherrill, *Call to Greatness*, 14-16; Frazier, "Circuit Riding Preachers," 39-40; *TST*, October 4, 1954; Hillsborough County Deed Records, Book C, 80; McNally, *Catholic Parish Life*, 22-23.

[6] Brown, "Tampa and the Coming of the Railroad," 13; Charleston (SC) *Southern Christian Advocate*, February 13, 1862.

[7] Brown, "Tampa and the Coming of the Railroad," 13-14; idem, *Jewish Pioneers of the Tampa Bay Frontier*, 11-13; Knetsch, "Madison Starke Perry," 13-33; *FP*, February 16, April 5, 1860.

[8] McPherson, *Battle Cry of Freedom*, 170-233; Craven, *Coming of the Civil War*, 409.

[9] Brown, *Tampa Before the Civil War*, 126-29; Oliver O. Howard to Lizzie Howard, March 29, 1857, Howard Papers.

[10] Brown, *Ossian Bingley Hart*, 105-106; idem, "Politics, Greed, Regulator Violence, and Race in Tampa," 27.

[11] *FP*, January 28, 1860.

[12] *TST*, July 24, 1955; Brown, *Tampa Before the Civil War*, 98-99, 130-31; *TDT*, October 11, 1924.

[13] Brown, *Tampa Before the Civil War*, 89-102; *FP*, February 15, 1868.

[14] *TMT*, August 24, 1920; *TST*, July 24, 1955.

[15] *TMT*, August 24, 1920; Harrison, *Reminiscences of Judge Charles E. Harrison*, 12, 14; *TST*, July 24, 1955.

[16] *FP*, March 24, 1860; Kennedy, *Population of the United States in 1860*, 54; Brown, *Tampa Before the Civil War*, 126; McKay, "History of Tampa of the Olden Days," 79.

[17] 1861 Hillsborough County tax roll; *TST*, June 17, 1951.

[18] 1860 United States census returns, Hillsborough County, Florida (slave schedule); Welch, *Tampa's Elected Officials*, 9.

[19] VanLandingham, "Captain William B. Hooker," 9.

[20] *TST*, April 4, 1948; Knetsch, "John Darling," 6-17; Brown, *Tampa Before the Civil War*, 65-66; Sherrill, *Call to Greatness*, 21-25.

[21] Brown, *Tampa Before the Civil War*, 98-99, 114-15, 117-18; McKay, *Pioneer Florida*, II, 25; Baxley, Gordon and Rodriguez, *Sleeping Around*, 87; *TDT*, December 20, 1921; "Reminiscences of Old Aunt Sarah, A Former Slave of Grandmother's" in Florida Negro Papers.

[22] Brown, *Tampa Before the Civil War*, 117-118; idem, *Genealogical Records*, 24, 29; *TST*, July 14, 1946, March 26, 1950, March 22, 1953, May 3, 1959; Pizzo, *Tampa Town*, 76.

[23] Orrick and Crumpacker, *Tampa Tribune*, 16-17; Grismer, *Tampa*, 318, 323.

[24] Brown, *Florida's Peace River Frontier*, 123-26; idem, *Fort Meade*, 36-39; idem, "As Far As Our Eyes Will Let Us See," 43-73.

[25] Grismer, *Tampa*, 118, 133-34; *FP*, January 14, March 24, 1860, March 16, 1861; *TST*, April 4, 1948.

[26] Brown, "Tampa's James McKay," 411-14; idem, *Florida's Peace River Frontier*, 146-47.

[27] *FP*, April 14, 1860; James McKay to Lorenzo Thomas, October 20, 1861, Letters Received by the Office of the Adjutant General (Main Series), 1861-1870, M-619, roll 22, NA; McKay, "History of Tampa of the Olden Days," 83; Chamberlin, "Fort Brooke," 130.

[28] *FP*, March 3, 1860.

[29] Ibid., July 7, 28, August 4, 1860; McKay, "History of Tampa of the Olden Days," 83; VanLandingham, "Tampa is the Place of Places," 93.

[30] *TDT*, December 20, 1921; Brown, "Tampa's James McKay," 414.

[31] *FP*, February 18, 25, March 24, July 7, August 11, 1860.

[32] Ibid., March 24, 1860; 1860 United States Census, Hillsborough County, Florida (population schedule).

[33] VanLandingham, "Tampa is the Place of Places," 95, 97.

[34] Orrick and Crumpacker, *Tampa Tribune*, 16; *FP*, March 17, 24, 1860.

[35] *FP*, September 15, 1860; Minutes of the Mayor's Court, City of Tampa (August 21, 1857-May 1882), 70-72.

[36] *FP*, October 6, 20, 27, 1860; VanLandingham, "James T. Magbee," 9-11; Knetsch, "Forging the Florida Frontier," 33; Brown, *Florida's Peace River Frontier*, 134-35.

[37] *FP*, October 20, 1860; Brown, "Very Much Attached to Tampa," 67.

[38] *FP*, August 26, December 1, 1860.

[39] Ibid., December 1, 1860.

[40] Ibid., December 1, 1860; Brown, *Ossian Bingley Hart*, 113.

[41] *Tallahassee Sentinel*, August 24, 1872; Brown, "Tampa's James McKay," 415.

[42] VanLandingham, "James Gettis," 38; Menton, *Grove*, 34; Brown, *Ossian Bingley Hart*, 110-15.

CHAPTER 2

[1] Grismer, *Tampa*, 137-38; Waters, "Tampa's Forgotten Defenders," 3.

[2] Ibid.; *FP*, January 19, 1861.

[3] John Darling to Andrew Johnson, August 19, 1865, Case Files of Applications From Former Confederates for Presidential Pardons, 1865-1867 ("Amnesty Papers"), Office of the Adjutant General, M-1003, roll 15, NA; *FP*, February 2, 1861.

[4] *FP*, January 26, May 11, 1861; *TST*, December 6, 1959; Waters, "Tampa's Forgotten Defenders," 4-5.

[5] *FP*, January 26, 1861; Brown, *Ossian Bingley Hart*, 115-16; "Composition Book," n.p., Lesley Papers; Farr, *Sketch*, 16; Matthew P. Lyons to Richard Comba (with enclosure), September 4, 1867, Letters Received, box 5, Dept. and Dist. of Florida, 1865-1869, RG 393, Part One, NA; Jacksonville *Florida Union*, November 30, 1867.

[6] Brown, "Civil War," 231-34; Robinson, "Memoirs," 4; *TS*, August 24, 1872.

[7] *FP*, March 23, April 20, May 4, 1861; McKay, "History of Tampa of the Olden Days," 83; Waters, "Tampa's Forgotten Defenders," 3.

[8] *FP*, March 23, May 11, 1861.

[9] Ibid., May 18, 1861.

[10] Brown, "Tampa's James McKay," 414-16; *FP*, May 11, 1861.

[11] Brown, "Tampa's James McKay," 416-17; Sherrill, *Call to Greatness*, 17-18; Van-Landingham, "James Gettis," 38.

[12] Brown, "Tampa's James McKay," 416.

[13] James McKay to William H. Seward, February 11, 1862, Correspondence Regarding Prisoners of War, 1861-62, box 7, General Records of the Department of State, Civil War Papers, RG 59, entry 491, NA; John Darling [to the governor], June 27, 1861, Incoming Correspondence of Governor Madison Starke Perry, RG 101, Series 577, FSA.

[14] *New Orleans Bee*, July 10, 1861; *FP*, July 6, 1861; McKay to Seward, February 11, 1862.

[15] Brown, "Tampa's James McKay," 417-18; James McKay to Lorenzo Thomas, December 7, 1861, in *ORA*, Series 2, II, 967.

[16] Brown, "Tampa's James McKay," 418-19; Petition of Citizens of Clear Water Harbor, August 15, 1861, Incoming Correspondence of Governor Madison Starke Perry, RG 101, series 577, box 1, FSA.

[17] Waters, "Tampa's Forgotten Defenders," 5-6.

[18] *New York Herald*, September 15, 1861.

[19] W. L. L. Bowen to Edward Hopkins, November 24, 1861, in W. L. L. Bowen Confederate Military Records, Fourth Florida Infantry, RG 109, NA.

[20] Prouty, "War Comes to Tampa Bay," 37, 38, 48, 61; *New York Herald*, January 30, 1862.

[21] *Savannah Republican*, December 23, 1861; Waters, "Tampa's Forgotten Defenders," 6-7; Prouty, "War Comes to Tampa Bay," 39; Charleston (SC) *Southern Christian Advocate*, February 13, 1862.

[22] Johns, *Florida During the Civil War*, 71; *ORN*, I, vol. 17, p. 68; Charleston (SC) *Southern Christian Advocate*, February 13, 1862; *New York Herald*, March 2, 1862.

[23] Long, *Civil War Day by Day*, 156-72.

[24] Prouty, "War Comes to Tampa Bay," 41-47.

[25] *Boston Daily Journal*, March 21, 1862; Welch, *Tampa's Elected Officials*, 11.

[26] *TMT*, January 26, 1901; R. B. Thomas to Andrew Johnson, August 21, 1865, Case Files of Applications from Former Confederates for Presidential Pardons, 1865-1867 ("Amnesty Papers"), M-1003, roll 15, NA.

[27] Waters, "Tampa's Forgotten Defenders," 7; Prouty, "War Comes to Tampa Bay," 52-59.

[28] Prouty, "War Comes to Tampa Bay," 59; *Boston Daily Journal*, April 18, 30, 1862.

[29] Falero, "Naval Engagements in Tampa Bay, 1862," 135-37; Prouty, "When War

Came to Tampa Bay," 54; Maria Louisa Daegenhardt reminiscences, 3-4.

[30] Johns, *Florida During the Civil War*, 60-68; Long, *Civil War Day by Day*, 194-205.

[31] *FP*, January 26, 1861.

[32] Ibid., February 2, 1861; Welch, *Tampa's Elected Officials*, 10; Tampa *Sunny South*, February 19, 1861, quoted in *Tampa Tribune*, October 29, 1891.

[33] Stone, "Capt. Leroy G. Lesley," 28; McKay, "Tampa of the Olden Days," 79-80; VanLandingham, "Captain William B. Hooker," 11; C. L. Friebele Account Book, 1860-1863, pp. 386-87; Gordon, "Missions of Tampa," 59.

[34] *New Orleans Bee*, August 6, 1861; *Boston Daily Journal*, March 21, 1862; Stafford, "Egmont Key," 22.

[35] Hillsborough County Commission Minutes, Book A (1846-1863), 118-22, 129-33.

[36] See Weatherford, *History of Women in Tampa*, 25-26, and Brown, *Women on the Tampa Bay Frontier*, 49-52.

[37] Farr, *Sketch*, 16.

[38] Maria Louisa Daegenhardt reminiscences, 2-3; *TST*, May 4, 1952.

[39] Hartman and Coles, *Biographical Rosters*, II, 694-704, IV, 1376-77; McKay, "Tampa of the Olden Days," 84; *TST*, December 6, 1959; Coulter, *Confederate States of America*, 314.

[40] VanLandingham, "Tampa is the Place of Places," 97; *New York Herald*, March 24, 1862.

[41] Prouty, "War Comes to Tampa Bay," 58.

CHAPTER 3

[1] Brown, "Tampa's James McKay," 421-23.

[2] Brown, *Florida's Peace River Frontier*, 146-50, 197; Taylor, *Rebel Storehouse*, 92-94. See also, Taylor, "Rebel Beef."

[3] Brown, "Tampa's James McKay," 420-21; James McKay to Lorenzo Thomas, October 20, 1861, Letters Received by the Office of the Adjutant General (Main Series), 1861-1870, M-619, roll 22, NA.

[4] Brown, "Tampa's James McKay," 421-23.

[5] Ibid., 422-23; Johns, *Florida During the Civil War*, 60; James McKay to Lorenzo Thomas, April 24, 1862, in *ORA*, series 2, II, 981-82.

[6] Hillsborough County Commission Minutes, Book A (1846-1863), 133; McDuffee, *Lures of Manatee*, 129; *New York Herald*, July 24, 1862.

[7] Waters, "Florida's Confederate Guerrillas," 133-39; idem, "Tampa's Forgotten Defenders," 8.

[8] *ORA*, series 1, XIV, 111; Waters, "Florida's Confederate Guerrillas," 139-40.

[9] Schellings, "On Blockade Duty," 62.

[10] Augusta (GA) *Southern Christian Recorder*, August 14, 1862.

[11] *Baltimore Sun*, July 26, 1862; *New York Herald*, July 24, 1862; *TST*, April 23, 1939.

[12] VanLandingham, "James Gettis," 38.

[13] Du Bois, *Black Reconstruction*, 80.

[14] Maria Louisa Daegenhardt reminiscences, 6-7.

[15] The words "in 1865" have been omitted from the end of the Sarah Hanes Brown quotation, since they clearly are erroneous as Tampa suffered no bombardment in

1865. Theodore Lesley, "Reminiscences of Old Aunt Sarah, A Former Slave of Grandmother's," 5, in box 7, folder 3, Florida Negro Papers; Hawes, "One-time slave sheds light on life in Tampa."

[16] McPherson, *Battle Cry of Freedom*, 502-504, 538-44, 545, 557-58; Jacksonville *Florida Union*, June 1, 1867; Brown, *Ossian Bingley Hart*, 115.

[17] Dick Robles interview in "Composition Book," n.p., Lesley Papers.

[18] Lesley, "Reminiscences of Old Aunt Sarah," 3.

[19] Rivers, *Slavery in Florida*, 247-48; H. H. Hunter, *History of Mt. Sinai Church*, quoted in Muse, "Negro History, Tampa, Florida," 5; Mitchell, *African American Religious History in Tampa Bay*, 6.

[20] Wynn, "History of Mt. Sinai A.M.E. Zion Church," n.p.; Mitchell, "African American Religious History in Tampa Bay," 6-7; Carlton, Moore, and Capitano, *History of the First Methodist Church, Tampa, Florida*, 23-24.

[21] Waters, "Florida's Confederate Guerrillas," 141; Dick Robles interview in "Composition Book," n.p., Lesley Papers.

[22] Columbus (GA) *Daily Inquirer*, November 13, 1862, quoting the Tallahassee *Floridian*, November 8, 1862, quoting the Ocala *Home Journal*.

[23] *Macon Daily Telegraph* quoted in Hartman and Coles, *Biographical Rosters*, III, 890-91; Coles and Ferry, "Hot, Cold, Whiskey Punch," 59; Taylor, "Civil War Incident," 77-79.

[24] Coles and Ferry, "Hot, Cold, Whiskey Punch," 60; *New York Tribune*, April 29, 1863.

[25] Coles and Ferry, "Hot, Cold, Whiskey Punch," 60; *TST*, April 23, 1939, June 17, 1951; John Darling to Hugh A. Corley, April 4, 1863, Incoming Correspondence of the Internal Improvement Trust Fund, RG 593, series 914, box 11, FSA.

[26] Sherrill, *Call to Greatness*, 20; McNally, *Catholic Parish Life*, 23, 27; VanLandingham, "Union Occupation of Tampa," 11.

[27] Brown, *Florida's Peace River Frontier*, 153; Hartman and Coles, *Biographical Rosters*, I, 450-58.

[28] Ivey, "John T. Lesley," 5, 7.

[29] Coulter, *Confederate States of America*, 314.

[30] *ORN*, I, vol. 17, p. 309; Boggess, *Veteran of Four Wars*, 67; Paterson (NJ) *Daily Press*, September 13, 1866.

[31] Coulter, *Confederate States of America*, 315; Brown, *Florida's Peace River Frontier*, 152-53; VanLandingham, "My National Troubles," 60.

[32] Waters, "Florida's Confederate Guerrillas," 142-43.

[33] Edwards, "College Girl in Wartime," 201; Orrick and Crumpacker, *Tampa Tribune*, 16-17; Ossian B. Hart to Duval County probate judge, April 3, 1863, Mary E. Hart guardianship papers, file no. 899, Duval County probate records.

[34] McNally, *Catholic Parish Life*, 23, 27-28; Sherrill, *Call to Greatness*, 20-21.

[35] Edwards, "College Girl in Wartime," 200-201.

[36] Jacksonville *Florida Republican*, January 31, 1856, January 7, 1857; Ley, *Fifty-Two Years in Florida*, 96; Charleston (SC) *Southern Christian Advocate*, February 13, 1862; Augusta (GA) *Southern Christian Advocate*, August 14, 1862, December 10, 1863; Macon (GA) *Southern Christian Advocate*, December 14, 1865.

[37] Hartman and Coles, *Biographical Rosters*, II, 694; VanLandingham, "James Gettis," 38; Sherrill, *Call to Greatness*, 23; John A. Henderson to Andrew Johnson, August 21, 1865, and Erasmus M. Thompson to Johnson, July 10, 1865, Case Files of Applications from Former Confederates for Presidential Pardons, 1865-1867 ("Amnesty Papers"), M-1003, roll 15, NA.

[38] Grismer, *Tampa*, 143; Brown, *Florida's Peace River Frontier*, 147-51, 156-57; Taylor, *Rebel Storehouse*, 96; Coles and Waters, "Indian Fighter, Confederate Soldier, Blockade Runner, and Scout," 47-49.

[39] Brown, "Tampa's James McKay," 424.

[40] Buker, *Blockaders, Refugees, & Contrabands*, 65-68; Waters, "Tampa's Forgotten Defenders," 9-10; *New York Herald*, November 9, 1863; Hawes, "Civil War account tells of ship burning."

[41] Tallahassee *Weekly Floridian*, July 1, 1873. Also see *New York Herald*, November 9, 1863; *ORN*, I, vol. 17, pp. 570-77; *ORA*, series 1, XXVIII, pt. 2, p. 735; Buker, *Blockaders, Refugees, & Contrabands*, 65-68.

[42] *ORN*, I, vol. 17, p. 571; *TST*, April 23, 1939; Maria Louisa Daegenhardt reminiscences, 6; Buker, *Blockaders, Refugees, & Contrabands*, 66.

[43] Brown, "Tampa's James McKay," 424-25.

[44] Ibid., 425-26; Taylor, *Rebel Storehouse*, 100-102.

[45] Brown, "Tampa's James McKay," 426-27; James McKay to P. W. White, September 27, 1863, White Papers; Akerman, *Florida Cowman*, 87-90; Taylor, *Rebel Storehouse*, 101-104.

[46] Coulter, *Confederate States of America*, 314, 322; Brown, "Tampa's James McKay," 427-28.

CHAPTER 4

[1] Boggess, *Veteran of Four Wars*, 70.

[2] Buker, *Blockaders, Refugees, & Contrabands*, 60-61; *ORN*, I, vol. 17, p. 309; Hawes, "Father's dying wish sent sons into Navy"; entry of August 21, 1865, John A. Wilder notebook (1865), Wilder Papers.

[3] Buker, *Blockaders, Refugees, & Contrabands*, 121-24; Brown, *Florida's Peace River Frontier*, 159-60. See also, Coles, "Farm From Fields of Glory," 258-60, and Dillon, "Civil War in South Florida."

[4] *ORA*, series 1, XXVIII, pt. 2, 751; *TST*, June 20, 1948.

[5] Waters, "Tampa's Forgotten Defenders," 11; *ORA*, series 1, XXXV, pt. 1, pp. 484-87; Henry A. Crane to "Genl.," February 24, 1864, Department and District of Key West, 1861-1868, Letters Received, 1861-1865, RG 393, entry 2269, box 1, NA.

[6] Pleasants W. White to L. B. Northrop, March 17, 1864, P. W. White Letterbook (July 15, 1863-April 12, 1864), White Papers.

[7] Stone, "James Dopson Green"; Brown, *Florida's Peace River Frontier*, 161-63; James McKay to Pleasants W. White, March 25, 1864, White Papers.

[8] Brown, "Tampa's James McKay," 428; McKay to White, March 25, 1864; Taylor, *Rebel Storehouse*, 116-19. See also Taylor, "Cow Cavalry."

[9] Lesley, "Organization of the Confederate Cattle Battalion of Florida," 9 (copy in Peeples Collection).

[10] Brown, *Florida's Peace River Frontier*, 160-67; Wilder, "Wedding at the Parker House," 165.

[11] Taylor, "Cow Cavalry," 202; Harris, "When War Came to Polk County," 4-5.

[12] Taylor, "Cow Cavalry," 201-205; Lesley, "Organization of the Confederate Cattle Battalion of Florida," 11-12; Hartman and Coles, *Biographical Rosters*, V, 2019-34.

[13] Henry A. Crane to Daniel Woodbury, June 18, 1864, Letters Received, 1861-

1865, Dept. and Dist. of Key West, RG 393, entry 2269, NA; Stone, *Lineage of John Carlton*, 17-21, 36.

[14] Brown, *Fort Meade*, 46-47; Livingston, "Willoughby Tillis," 10.

[15] James McKay to Pleasants W. White, May 3, 1864, White Papers; John Darling to E. M. L'Engle, May 10, 1864, E. M. L'Engle Papers; McKay, "History of Tampa of the Olden Days," 84; *ORA*, series 1, XXXV, pt. 1, p. 389-91; *ORN*, series 1, XVII, 694; Brown, "Tampa's James McKay," 428-29; Pizzo, *Tampa Town*, 70.

[16] For more details on the May 1864 occupation of Tampa, see Grismer, *Tampa*, 147-48; Pizzo, *Tampa Town*, 70-71; VanLandingham, "Union Occupation of Tampa," 9-16; Hawes, "How Masonic tolls were returned to Tampa lodge"; Brown, *Ossian Bingley Hart*, 132-35.

[17] Chapin, *By-Gone Days*, 87; *ORA*, series 1, XXXV, pt. 1, 390-91; VanLandingham, "Union Occupation of Tampa," 11.

18 TMT, August 24, 1920, and Mrs. Anne Givens Harrison interview in *Hillsborough County Personalities* (both quoted in VanLandingham, "Union Occupation of Tampa," 13-14).

[19] *TMT*, August 24, 1920.

[20] *New York Herald*, May 20, 1864.

[21] Maria Louisa Daegenhardt reminiscences, 8.

[22] Coles, "Unpretending Service," 53; *ORN*, series 1, XVII, 694; Augusta *Daily Chronicle & Sentinel*, May 19, 1864.

[23] Coles, "Unpretending Service," 53; Chapin, *By-Gone Days*, 87, 89.

[24] *ORA*, series 1, XXXV, pt. 1, p. 390.

[25] Pizzo, *Tampa Town*, 70; VanLandingham, "Union Occupation of Tampa," 14; Darling to L'Engle, May 10, 1864.

[26] *Hillsborough Lodge No. 25, F. & A. M., 1850-1976*, 14; *History of Royal Arch Masonry*, 786-87; *TDT*, June 4, 1955. On the return of the jewels and other property of the masonic lodges, see Hawes, "How Masonic tools were returned to Tampa lodge."

[27] *TDT*, December 20, 1921.

[28] Mrs. Anne Givens Harrison interview in *Hillsborough County Personalities*.

[29] *ORA*, series 1, XXXV, pt. 1, pp. 389-91; Maria Louisa Daegenhardt reminiscences, 8-9.

[30] Chapin, *By-Gone Days*, 89-90.

[31] *New York Herald*, May 20, 1864; Darling to Johnson, August 19, 1865.

[32] McKay, "History of Tampa of the Olden Days," 84-85.

[33] *ORA*, series 1, XXXV, pt. 1, pp. 389-91; McKay, "History of Tampa of the Olden Days," 85.

[34] Brown, *Fort Meade*, 47; idem, *Jewish Pioneers of the Tampa Bay Frontier*, 15; Ivey, "John T. Lesley," 7-8; VanLandingham, "My National Troubles," 63-64; Hartman and Coles, *Biographical Rosters*, V, 1994, 1996; Landers, "Last Wildcat," 18-21; E. G. Wilder, "Attack on Salt Works, Tampa, Fla., 1864" (typescript in Waters Collection); Coles, "Unpretending Service," 53; Matthews, *Edge of Wilderness*, 260.

[35] Taylor, "Cow Cavalry," 198-213; Brown, *Florida's Peace River Frontier*, 172-174; Boggess, *Veteran of Four Wars*, 69-70.

[36] Maria Louisa Daegenhardt reminiscences, 10.

[37] Ibid., 11-13.

[38] Farr, *Sketch*, 15.

[39] Maria Louisa Daegenhardt reminiscences, 7; Mrs. Anne Givens Harrison interview, 3; *TMT*, August 24, 1920.

[40] VanLandingham, "Tampa is the Place of Places," 98.

[41] Charleston (SC) *Southern Christian Advocate*, February 13, 1862; Pleasants W. White to S. B. French, March 22, 1864, P. W. White Letterbook (July 15, 1863-April 12, 1864), White Papers; Brown, "Very much attached to Tampa," 68.

[42] *ORA*, series 1, XXXV, pt. 1, p. 390; William S. Spencer to state comptroller, September 11, 1864, Incoming Correspondence of the Comptroller, RG 350, series 554, box 3, FSA; Augusta (GA) *Southern Christian Advocate*, November 3, 1864.

[43] Catharine Hart to My dear Mother, Sisters & Brothers, January 5, 1865, Snodgrass Papers (this letter is published in Brown, "Very much attached to Tampa," 68); Boggess, *Veteran of Four Ways*, 74.

CHAPTER 5

[1] Coles, "Terrible and Sad Result," 153-59.

[2] *ORA*, series 1, XLIX, pt. 2, p. 984; Hartman and Coles, *Biographical Rosters*, V, 1783-96.

[3] McKay, "History of Tampa of the Olden Days," 86; *FP*, July 21, 1866; Hillsborough County Commission Minutes, Book B, 37.

[4] John Darling to Andrew Johnson, August 19, 1865, Case Files of Applications from Former Confederates for Presidential Pardons ("Amnesty Papers"), M-1003, roll 15, NA; Jacksonville *Florida Union*, September 16, 1865.

[5] John T. Sprague to R. C. Drum, February 28, 1868, Letters Sent by the Department of Florida and Successor Commands, April 18, 1861-January 1869, M-1096, roll 2, NA.

[6] Hillsborough County Commission Minutes, Book B, 19; *ORA*, series 1, XLIX, pt. 2, p. 984; Taylor, "Cow Cavalry," 214; Kite-Powell, "Escape of Judah P. Benjamin," 64-65; McKay, "History of Tampa of the Olden Days," 86; Brown, *Jewish Pioneers of the Tampa Bay Frontier*, 16-21.

[7] *New York Times*, October 1, 1865.

[8] *New York Herald*, August 20, 1865.

[9] Hartman and Coles, *Biographical Rosters*, II, 698, V, 1994, 1996, 1998.

[10] Grismer, *Tampa*, 150; Hillsborough County Deed Records, Book C, 234-38; Littrell, *Riley County, Kansas, Officials and Their Families*, 14-16; Manhattan (KS) *Independent*, February 23, 1867.

[11] 1860 United States census, Hillsborough County, Florida (population schedule); *FP*, March 8, April 5, 26, 1856; Boggess, *Veteran of Four Wars*, 75; VanLandingham, "James Alderman," 15-16; Hillsborough County Deed Records, Book C, 479; *FP*, December 15, 1866; Tallahassee *Semi-Weekly Floridian*, April 23, 1867; *TST*, June 17, 1951.

[12] *TST*, July 14, 1946, October 29, 1950; Brown, *Genealogical Records 18-23, 24-25, 49-50, 71-72*; *TDT*, July 27, 1923; Hawes, "One-time slave sheds light on life in Tampa."

[13] Muse, "Negro History, Tampa, Florida," 4; *FP*, February 15, 1868.

[14] "Looking Backward Through the Long Vista of Years When Tampa Was But a Settlement" from an unidentified Tampa newspaper, c. 1913, clipping in clippings scrapbook, "Tampa/Syracuse, New York," Tampa Historical Society.

[15] John A. Wilder to Eben Jenks Loomis, August 28, 1865, Wilder Papers; Work

Projects Administration Statewide Rare Books Project, "Military Dispatches, Head Quarters, District of Middle Florida, August 10, 1865-September 25, 1865," 46-47; *FP*, July 28, 1866.

[16] Capt. Tyler to Lt. E. Anderson, July 17, 1865, Letters Sent by the Dept. of Florida and Successor Commands, April 18, 1861-January 1869, M-1096, roll 2.

[17] Maria Louisa Daegenhardt reminiscences, 15.

[18] Entry of August 21, 1865, John A. Wilder notebook (1865), Wilder Papers; Hartman and Coles, *Biographical Rosters*, II, 868.

[19] McKay, "History of Tampa of the Olden Days," 86; *TDT*, December 18, 1923.

[20] *New York Times*, October 1, 1865; Tallahassee *Semi-Weekly Floridian*, April 23, 1867.

[21] George F. Thompson to Thomas W. Osborn, December 17, 1865, Letters Received by the Dept. and Dist. of Florida, 1865-1869, RG 393, Part One, box 1, NA.; James D. Green to Osborn, June 5, 1866, Letters Received by the Assistant Commissioner for Florida, 1865-1869, box 1, Records of the Bureau of Freedmen, Refugees, and Abandoned Lands, RG 105, NA; *Fort Meade Leader*, June 12, 1913.

[22] Brown, "Tampa's James McKay," 432-33; McKay, "History of Tampa of the Olden Days," 86.

[23] Brown, *Florida's Peace River Frontier*, 198-99; Brown, "Tampa's James McKay," 432-33; *FP*, August 25, September 29, October 15, 1866.

[24] Hawes, "Former rebels saw error of their ways"; entry of December 1, 1865, George F. Thompson Journal (December 1865-January 1866), PKY.

[25] *FP*, May 26, June 23, July 21, August 4, September 1, 1866; Grismer, *Tampa*, 151, 321; *TST*, July 14, 1946, May 26, 1950, May 3, 1959; Orrick and Crumpacker, *Tampa Tribune*, 19.

[26] *FP*, May 26, 1866, January 26, August 24, 1867.

[27] Brown, *Florida's Peace River Frontier*, 196-97; *FP*, March 2, 1867; *TST*, July 24, 1955.

[28] Mitchell, *African American Religious History in Tampa Bay*, 6-7; Brown, *Genealogical Records, 62-63*; "Mt. Sinai African Methodist Episcopal Zion Church" and "Beulah Baptist Institutional Church" in Work Projects Administration Church Questionnaires, Florida Collection, State Library of Florida.

[29] *Tallahassee Sentinel*, April 30, 1867; Gordon, "Missions of Tampa," 59-60; McNally, *Catholic Parish Life*, 26-28; Sherrill, *Call to Greatness*, 21; Tallahassee *Floridian & Journal*, January 14, 1860; Macon (GA) *Southern Christian Advocate*, December 14, 1865, December 21, 1866; *Savannah Daily Republican*, March 18, 1867.

[30] *Tallahassee Sentinel*, April 30, 1867; Brown, *Teachers and Schools on the Tampa Bay Frontier*, 45-47.

[31] Orrick and Crumpacker, *Tampa Tribune*, 19; *FP*, July 7, 1866.

[32] Foner, *Reconstruction*, 177-83; Shofner, *Nor Is It Over Yet*, 34-36.

[33] Brown, *Ossian Bingley Hart*, 159-61; Paterson (NJ) *Daily Press*, September 13, 1866; *Tallahassee Sentinel*, September 7, 1872.

[34] Brown, *Ossian Bingley Hart*, 160-62; Shofner, *Nor Is It Over Yet*, 43; Jacksonville *Florida Times*, January 11, 1866; Tallahassee *Semi-Weekly Floridian*, December 19, 1865; *New York Times*, December 25, 1865; Ivey, "John T. Lesley," 8; Sherrill, *Call to Greatness*, 23; VanLandingham, "James Gettis," 39.

[35] VanLandingham, "James Gettis," 39; *FP*, May 26, June 23, August 18, 1866.

[36] C. R. Mobley to Assistant Commissioner, June 25, 1867, Letters Received by the Assistant Commissioner for Florida, Bureau of Freedmen, Refugees, and Abandoned

Lands, RG 105, box 4, NA; Luther Smith to J. H. Lyman, November 1, 1866, *House Executive Documents*, 40th Cong., 2d sess., No. 57, p. 93; Richard Comba to Lyman, December 17, 1866, Letters Received by the Dept. and Dist. of Florida, 1865-1869, RG 393, Part One, box 1, NA; Boggess, *Veteran of Four Wars*, 75.

[37] *FP*, March 30, 1867; Smith to Lyman, November 1, 1866.

[38] Welch, *Tampa's Elected Officials*, 12-13; *FP*, May 26, August 18, September 1, 15, October 27, 1866.

[39] Minutes of the Mayor's Court, City of Tampa (August 21, 1857-May 1882), 83-107; *FP*, October 30, November 10, 17, 24, 1866.

[40] Pizzo, *Tampa Town*, 72; *FP*, February 7, 1867.

[41] *FP*, September 25, 1866; Maria Louisa Daegenhardt reminiscences, 16-17.

[42] VanLandingham, "Captain William B. Hooker," 13-14.

CHAPTER 6

[1] Foner, *Reconstruction*, 176-280; Du Bois, *Black Reconstruction*, 325-79; Trefousse, *Andrew Johnson*, 193-310; Mencken, *New Dictionary of Quotations*, 1010.

[2] Brown, *Ossian Bingley Hart*, 175-76, 181-82.

[3] Ibid., 181-85; Foner, *Reconstruction*, 261-71; Paterson (NJ) *Daily Press*, September 13, 1866.

[4] Brown, *Ossian Bingley Hart*, 195-96; idem, *Florida's Black Public Officials*, 5-9, 113; O. B. Hart to James F. Meline, September 5, 1867, and "Consolidated Election Returns, Florida, Up to 12 O'clock M., Nov. 20, 1867" in Records of the Third Military District, 1867-1868, Bureau of Civil Affairs, RG 393, Part One, NA.

[5] Brown, *Ossian Bingley Hart*, 188-89; Richard Comba to E. C. Woodruff, May 31, 1867, Letters Received by Dept. and Dist. of Florida, 1865-1869, RG 393, Part One, box 4, NA.

[6] Minutes of the Mayor's Court, City of Tampa (August 21, 1857-May 1882), 90; *FP*, July 6, 1867; Jacksonville *Florida Union*, July 27, 1867.

[7] Matthew P. Lyons to Comba, September 4, 1867, and Petition of Qualified Voters of the County of Hillsborough to Major Richard Comba, August 30, 1867, Letters Received by the Dept. and Dist. of Florida, 1865-1869, box 5.

[8] Seventeenth Electoral District Election Results, 1867 District Recapitulation, Territorial and Statehood Election Returns (1824-1870), RG 156, series 21, box 10, FSA; Orrick and Crumpacker, *Tampa Tribune*, 19-20.

[9] C. R. Mobley to O. B. Hart, November 16, 1867, Third Military District, 1867-1868, Bureau of Civil Affairs, RG 393, Part One, box 5, NA; Richard Comba to Charles F. Larrabee, December 31, 1867, Letters Received (1867-1869), Dept. and Dist. of Florida, 1865-1869, box 5; Jacksonville *Florida Union*, December 7, 1867; *FP*, May 9, July 4, September 19, 1868; Brown, *Florida's Peace River Frontier*, 189.

[10] Harrison, *Reminiscences*, 12.

[11] Ibid., 20.

[12] Jacksonville *Florida Daily Times*, February 15, 1882; Brown, "Tampa's James McKay," 433; idem, *Florida's Peace River Frontier*, 198; McDuffee, *Lures of Manatee*, 191; Harrison, *Reminiscences*, 8.

[13] Hillsborough County Deed Records, Book C, 234, 480, 696, 707; *FP*, July 20, 1867, February 22, 1868.

[14] *FP*, February 23, March 2, 1867, February 29, 1868.

[15] Foner, *Reconstruction*, 246; Davis, *Civil War and Reconstruction*, 451; Shofner,

Nor Is It Over Yet, 64, 70, 134; *FP*, June 29, July 27, 1867.

[16] Comba to Allan H. Jackson, June 30, 1867, Unentered Letters and Reports, 1865-1868, Asst. Comm. for Florida, Bureau of Freedmen, Refugees, and Abandoned Lands, RG 105, NA.

[17] *FP*, June 29, July 31, 1867; General U. S. Land Office Papers, Vol. 3: Ledgers, Gainesville, Vol. 8, Registers of Florida Homestead Certificates 1873:June-1884:August, n.p., Florida Dept. of Environmental Protection.

[18] *FP*, April 6, 1867.

[19] Ibid., May 11, June 5, 1867; Jacksonville *Florida Union*, July 27, 1867.

[20] Comba to Larrabee, June 30, August 31, 1867, Letters Received, Dept. and Dist. of Florida, 1865-1869, box 5.

[21] Comba to Larrabee, August 31, 1867; *St. Augustine Examiner*, September 7, 1867; King, *History of the Practice of Medicine in Manatee County*, 51-52; Grismer, *Tampa*, 153, 324; VanLandingham, "Tampa is the Place of Places," 100.

[22] *Ocala Banner*, quoted in Jacksonville *Florida Union*, October 19, 1867; *FP*, June 27, 1868; Brown, *Florida's Peace River Frontier*, 405.

[23] Comba to Larrabee, October 31, 1866, Letters Received, Dept. and Dist. of Florida, 1865-1869, box 5; Littrell, *Riley County, Kansas, Officials and Their Families*, 34.

[24] *FP*, June 6, 1868; Bethell, *History of Point Pinellas*, 25.

[25] Langley, *America in the Age of Revolution*, 272; *FP*, February 22, 1868.

[26] Brown, *Florida's Peace River Frontier*, 198; *FP*, October 24, 1868.

[27] Williams, "This is the Story of My Life," 52; John A. Henderson to E. M. L'Engle, October 25, 1868, Edward M. L'Engle Papers; *FP*, February 15, 1868.

[28] *FP*, February 15, May 30, July 18, 1868; Comba to Larrabee, April 30, 1868, Letters Received, Dept. and Dist. of Florida, 1865-1869, box 5.

[29] John T. Sprague to R. C. Drum, February 28, 1868, Old Book 251, Dept. of the South, 117-19, in Letters Sent by the Dept. of Florida and Successor Commands, April 18, 1861-January 1869, M-1096, roll 2, NA; Comba to Larrabee, May 31, 1868, Letters Received, Dept. and Dist. of Florida, 1865-1869, box 5.

[30] Davis, *Civil War and Reconstruction*, 491-516; Shofner, *Nor Is It Over Yet*, 177-88; Brown, *Ossian Bingley Hart*, 206-214.

[31] Shofner, *Nor Is It Over Yet*, 187; Henderson to L'Engle, March 25, 1868, Edward M. L'Engle Papers.

[32] *FP*, April 17, May 9, 1868; Brown, *Florida's Black Public Officials*, 83, 92, 115; Henderson to L'Engle, April 19, 1868, Edward M. L'Engle Papers.

[33] Comba to Larrabee, April 30, 1868.

[34] Ibid., May 31, 1868; *FP*, May 9, 1868; Shofner, *Nor Is It Over Yet*, 192-93.

[35] *FP*, May 16, June 6, 1868; Jacksonville *Florida Union*, June 1, 1868.

[36] *FP*, August 1, December 2, 1868; Ivey, "John T. Lesley," 8-9; idem, *Life and Times of John Thomas Lesley*, 20-21; *TDT*, July 14, 1913.

[37] Commissions of Hillsborough County officers, 1868, in vol. 28, Commissions of Office Books, RG 156, series 259, FSA.

[38] VanLandingham, "James T. Magbee," 12-13; *FP*, August 22, 1868.

[39] Orrick and Crumpacker, *Tampa Tribune*, 20; VanLandingham, "James T. Magbee," 13-15; *FP*, October 24, 1868.

[40] *TST*, October 20, 1946, August 3, 1958; Hillsborough County Deed Records, Book D, 523.

[41] *FP*, May 30, October 24, 1868, January 9, 1869.

[42] Ibid., January 9, 1869.

[43] *Laws of Florida* (1869), 22; Welch, *Tampa's Elected Officials*, 13-14.

[44] Welch, *Tampa's Elected Officials*, 14-15; Ivey, "John T. Lesley," 8; *TST*, June 20, 1948.

CHAPTER 7

[1] *FP*, February 20, April 21, 28, 1868; Chamberlin, "Fort Brooke," 137.

[2] *FP*, June 2, 1869; Jacksonville *Florida Union*, June 17, 1869.

[3] Hillsborough County Commission Minutes Book, Book B, 104.

[4] Brown, *Florida's Peace River Frontier*, 204-205; *FP*, August 11, October 27, 1869, August 24, 1870; *Tallahassee Sentinel* quoted in *Savannah Daily Advertiser*, August 26, 1869.

[5] Hall and Rise, *From Local Courts to National Tribunals*, 179; *FP*, September 29, 1869, May 4, December 14, 1870; *TST*, June 17, 1951.

[6] Brown, *Genealogical Records*, 22-23, 49-50, 54-56, 61; *TST*, October 29, 1950.

[7] Ferrell, "History of St. Paul A.M.E. Church," 179-80; Wynn, "History of Mt. Sinai A.M.E. Zion Church," n.p.; *FP*, December 15, 1869.

[8] *FP*, April 28, August 18, 1869 May 11, 1870; William G. Vance to Allen H. Jackson, June 30, July 31, 1867, Unentered Letters and Reports, 1865-1868, Asst. Comm. for Florida, Bureau of Freedmen, Refugees, and Abandoned Lands, RG 105, NA; Weatherford, *History of Women in Tampa*, 29; Hillsborough County Deed Records, Book D, 909.

[9] *FP*, March 7, August 8, 1868, June 16, 1869.

[10] Shofner, *Nor Is It Over Yet*, 209; Brown, "Tampa and the Coming of the Railroad," 14; *Laws of Florida* (1869, extra sess.), 38.

[11] *FP*, June 16, July 28, 1869.

[12] Commissions of Hillsborough County officers, 1869-1870, in Vol. 28, Commissions of Office Books, RG 156, series 259, FSA; *FP*, May 11, 1870; VanLandingham, "To Faithfully Discharge My Duty," 6.

[13] *FP*, October 13, November 3, 10, 1869.

[14] Brown, *Jewish Pioneers of the Tampa Bay Frontier*, 27-31; *FP*, August 4, 1869.

[15] Hillsborough County Deed Records, Book C, 599, 709; Brown, *Jewish Pioneers of the Tampa Bay Frontier*, 28-29.

[16] *FP*, December 15, 1869.

[17] Brown, *Jewish Pioneers of the Tampa Bay Frontier*, 30-31; *FP*, March 9, 1870.

[18] *FP*, September 29, November 3, 1869.

[19] Ibid., January 5, June 8, 1870; Brown, *Genealogical Records*, 24-25, 42-43; idem, *Florida's Black Public Officials*, 162.

[20] *FP*, January 12, 1870; *Laws of Florida* (1870), 54, 79.

[21] Foster and Foster, *Beechers, Stowes, and Yankee Strangers*, 64-65, 88-89; Sanford *South Florida Argus*, February 17, 1887.

[22] *FP*, May 23, July 6, 1870; Brown, *Jewish Pioneers of the Tampa Bay Frontier*, 38.

[23] Nolan, *Fifty Feet in Paradise*, 1-3.

[24] Brown, *Jewish Pioneers of the Tampa Bay Frontier*, 38-39.

[25] Ibid.; *FP*, October 5, 1870, January 4, 1871.

[26] Brown, *Florida's Peace River Frontier*, 219-20; idem, *Jewish Pioneers of the Tampa Bay Frontier*, 34-36; *FP*, November 9, 1870.

[27] Shofner, *Nor Is It Over Yet*, 214-16; Klingman, *Josiah Walls*, 35-38; idem, *Neither Dies Nor Surrenders*, 35-39; *FP*, October 26, November 16, 1870, March 8, 1871.

[28] Brown, *Ossian Bingley Hart*, 245-46, 248, 259, 291, 300.

[29] *FP*, October 12, 1870, April 5, July 22, September 23, 1871; *Savannah Daily Republican*, January 28, 1871; VanLandingham, "James T. Magbee," 14-15; Hammond, *Medical Profession*, 225-26.

[30] Brown, *Jewish Pioneers of the Tampa Bay Frontier*, 40-41; *FP*, March 15, 1871.

[31] *FP*, February 18, 1871; *WF*, May 9, 1871; Brown, *Florida's Black Public Officials*, 80, 97, 100, 131, 162.

[32] *FP*, January 4, June 3, 1871; Brown, *Florida's Peace River Frontier*, 205.

[33] *FP*, June 24, July 8, 1871.

[34] Turner, *Faith of Our Fathers*, n.p.

[35] *FP*, September 30, 1871; *FP*, August 19, 1871, quoted in *WF*, September 5, 1871.

[36] *FP*, September 16, 23, 30, October 7, November 25, 1871; Hammond, *Medical Profession*, 652; Harrison, *Reminiscences*, 27; Rivers, "They . . . Exalt Humbug," 10.

[37] Welch, "Tampa's Election Officials," 17; Harrison, *Reminiscences*, 24-25; VanLandingham, "James T. Magbee," 15; *FP*, October 21, 1871; *WF*, October 31, 1871.

[38] *FP*, December 23, 1871; Brown, *Teachers and Schools on the Tampa Bay Frontier*, 50-54; *Narrative Reports of County Superintendents, 1869-70 to 1879-80*, 27; Hillsborough County Commission Minutes, Book C, 3-38.

[39] *Savannah Daily Republican*, March 20, 1872; *TDT*, October 17, 1930.

[40] *Savannah Daily Republican*, January 27, February 10, March 20, 1872; *WF*, February 20, 1872; *SMN*, May 23, 1872; *TDT*, October 19, 1927, October 17, 1930; Sherrill, *Call to Greatness*, 25; *TST*, September 13, 1953.

[41] Williams, "This is the Story of My Life," 54; *TMT*, August 24, 1920; Hillsborough County Commission Minutes, Book C, 49.

[42] Brown, *Florida's Peace River Frontier*, 198-99; Akerman, *Florida Cowman*, 104-117; *TDT*, October 17, 1930.

[43] Akerman, *Florida Cowman*, 110-112; Robinson, *History of Hillsborough County*, 271-73; *TDT*, December 20, 1921; Ivey, "John T. Lesley," 8-10; VanLandingham, "To Faithfully Discharge My Duty," 9-10.

[44] Brown, *Florida's Peace River Frontier*, 219-22; idem, *Fort Meade*, 56-61.

[45] Brown, *Jewish Pioneers of the Tampa Bay Frontier*, 33-34; *FP*, August 19, 1871.

[46] Brown, *Ossian Bingley Hart*, 277-78; Akerman, *Florida Cowman*, 124.

[47] See, generally, Brown, *Ossian Bingley Hart.*

CHAPTER 8

[1] Brown, *Ossian Bingley Hart*, 262, 266-68; "The Florida Election—Official State Canvass" in Election Returns (1862-1887), vol. 1, p. 70, RG 156, series 1258, FSA.

[2] Brown, *Ossian Bingley Hart*, 275-79; idem, *Jewish Pioneers of the Tampa Bay Frontier*, 52-54.

[3] Brown, *Ossian Bingley Hart*, 275-81.

[4] Appointments, vol. 30, n.p., and vol. 2, 108-113, RG 156, series 1284, FSA; Senate Reports, 44th Congress, 2d sess., No. 611, 309; *Savannah Daily Republican*, May 27, 1873.

[5] Appointments, vol. 30, n.p., and vol. 2, 108-113, RG 156, series 1284, FSA; Sherrill, *Call to Greatness*, 23-24; *Hillsborough Lodge No. 25, F. & A. M., 1850-1976*, 11.

[6] Minutes of the Mayor's Court, City of Tampa (August 21, 1857-May 1882), 148-49; Harrison, *Reminiscences*, 36; *SMN*, March 4, 1873.

[7] Brown, *Florida's Peace River Frontier*, 240-41; idem, *Jewish Pioneers of the Tampa Bay Frontier*, 43-44.

[8] *SMN*, December 12, 1873, September 1, 1874; Savannah *Advertiser-Republican*, December 10, 1873.

[9] Brown, *Florida's Peace River Frontier*, 246-48; *TST*, October 28, 1951, February 22, March 15, December 22, 1953, September 18, 1955.

[10] *TST*, February 1, 1953.

[11] Ibid.; *TG* quoted in *WF*, November 25, 1873.

[12] Hillsborough County Commission Minutes, Book C, 36-106.

[13] Hillsborough County Deed Records, Book D, 58, 263-66, 938; Tract Book, vol. 16, pp. 8-14, Land Records and Title Section, Division of State Lands, Florida Dept. of Environmental Protection; Brown, *Tampa Before the Civil War*, 64, 70, 93-94.

[14] Hillsborough County Deed Records, Book D, 82, 222, 264; Ferrell, "History of St. Paul A.M.E. Church," 179. See also Baxley, Gordon, and Rodriguez, *History of Oaklawn Cemetery and St. Louis Catholic Cemetery*.

[15] Hillsborough County Deed Records, Book D, 109, 204, 264.

[16] Hawks, *Florida Gazetteer*, 47; Walker, *Statistics*, 98.

[17] Hawks, *Florida Gazetteer*, 47; Ivey, "Accidental Pioneer," 33; Harrison, *Reminiscences*, 44, 58-59; Brown, *Fort Meade*, 66, 70.

[18] DeFoor, *Odet Philippe*, 44-45; Coles and Ferry, "Hot, Cold, Whiskey Punch," 56; Brown, *Fort Meade*, 37-38; *FP*, February 29, 1868.

[19] Cyrus Charles, Benjamin Taylor, and Mills Holloman homestead application files, Florida Land Entry Files, Records of the Bureau of Land Management, RG 49, NA.

[20] *FP*, August 21, 1879; Hillsborough County Deed Records, Book D, 498, 584, 620, 627, 631, 634, 675, 736, 829-31, E, 110-16; 1870 Hillsborough County census; *TG*, January 10, 1880.

[21] *SMN*, August 12, October 4, 1873; Savannah *Advertiser-Republican*, September 10, 1873.

[22] Tract Book, Vol. 16, pp. 8-18, 218-30; *ST*, March 31, 1877; Hillsborough County Deed Records, Book C, 619, 734, D, 423, 661; Register of Entries Made Under the Homestead Act, Gainesville, Florida, Land Office, April 1873-April 1878, Florida Dept. of Environmental Protection.

[23] Hillsborough County Deed Records, Book D, 59-62; *Laws of Florida* (1877), 118-19.

[24] Brown, *Ossian Bingley Hart*, 286-88; idem, *Jewish Pioneers of the Tampa Bay Frontier*, 47-50; Savannah *Advertiser-Republican*, September 10, 1873.

[25] Hillsborough County Deed Records, Book D, 156-57; Welch, *Tampa's Elected Officials*, 18; Grismer, *Tampa*, 334; *TST*, June 20, 1948; *ST*, April 13, 1882; Harrison, *Reminiscences*, 30.

[26] Minutes of the Mayor's Court, City of Tampa (August 21, 1857-May 1882), 111-21.

[27] Hillsborough County Commission Minutes, Book C, 61; *SMN*, October 4, 1873; Harrison, *Reminiscences*, 38-41; Attaway, *Hurricanes*, 27.

[28] *Frank Leslie's Illustrated Newspaper*, October 4, 1873, pp. 67-68, November 22, 1873, p. 183; Foner, *Reconstruction*, 512-69.

[29] Savannah *Advertiser-Republican*, September 10, 18, 1873; *TDT*, October 18, 1927, October 17, 1930; *TST*, November 7, 1954.

[30] Brown, *Jewish Pioneers of the Tampa Bay Frontier*, 43-44; *WF*, November 25, 1873; *SMN*, December 12, 1873, Savannah *Advertiser-Republican*, December 10, 1873, January 6, 1874; Jacksonville *Tri-Weekly Union*, January 6, 1874.

[31] Harrison, *Reminiscences*, 52-54; Savannah *Advertiser-Republican*, April 17, 1874; *SMN*, April 9, 1874; VanLandingham, "James T. Magbee," 17.

[32] Brown, *Ossian Bingley Hart*, 294-96; *SMN*, April 9, 1874; Savannah *Advertiser-Republican*, April 17, 1874; Harrison, *Reminiscences*, 54-56; VanLandingham, "James T. Magbee," 17.

[33] *SMN*, April 9, 1874; Savannah *Advertiser-Republican*, April 17, 1874; Harrison, *Reminiscences*, 56.

[34] *SMN*, June 30, 1874; Savannah *Advertiser-Republican*, June 9, 1874; Jacksonville *Tri-Weekly Florida Union*, September 12, 1874; *Savannah Daily Advertiser*, December 4, 1874; New York *South*, October 21, 1874; *WF*, April 27, 1875.

[35] Eagan, *Sixth Annual Report*, 189; Brown, *Fort Meade*, 61-62; *TG*, April 25, 1874, quoted in *SMN*, May 5, 1874; Ivey, "Accidental Pioneer," 34-35.

[36] Minutes of the Mayor's Court, City of Tampa (August 21, 1857-May 1882), 126-27, 136-37; Hillsborough County Commission Minutes, Book C, 100.

[37] Brown, *Florida's Black Public Officials*, 78, 95, 97; Jacksonville *Tri-Weekly Florida Union*, August 18, 1874; Jacksonville *New South*, August 19, 1874; Savannah *Advertiser-Republican*, September 10, 1873; Chamberlin, "Fort Brooke," 138.

[38] Savannah *Advertiser-Republican*, September 10, 1873; Grismer, *Tampa*, 306, 334; Elliott, *The Best of Its Kind*, 146-47; *TDT*, August 8, 1924.

[39] *TG* quoted in *SMN*, May 12, 1874.

[40] Hillsborough County Deed Records, Book D, 214-37; Grismer, *Tampa*, 321; *Clear Water Times*, March 14, 1874; *ST*, June 15, 1878; *FT-U&C*, April 2, 1899; Hillsborough County Commission Minutes, Book C, 60, 64.

[41] Mueller, *Lykes Family History*, 14, 34; Grismer, *Tampa*, 343-44.

[42] Sherrill, *Call to Greatness*, 24; VanLandingham, "James T. Magbee," 17.

CHAPTER 9

[1] See Brown, *Tampa Before the Civil War*, 123-55.

[2] Sherrill, *Call to Greatness*, 20; Turner, *Faith of Our Fathers*, n.p.; *SMN*, October 4, 1875, December 7, 1875; Lanier, *Letters*, 35.

[3] *ST*, March 31, June 2, 16, 1877; *TST*, April 4, 1948.

[4] *TST*, January 12, 1947; *TMT*, October 4, 1912; 1870 Hillsborough County census (population schedule); Hillsborough County Deed Records, Book D, 766; Grismer, *Tampa*, 327-28.

[5] General U. S. Land Office Papers, Vol. 3: Ledgers, Gainesville, Vol. 8: Registers of Final Homestead Certificates 1873: June 1884: August, n.p., Land Records and Title Section, Division of State Lands, Fla. Dept. of Environmental Protection; Hillsborough County Deed Records, Book D, 355, 387, 419, 438-39, 584, 658, 680, 777, 781, 938, E, 67.

[6] Hillsborough County Deed Records, Book D, 264-66, 323, 345, 348, 350, 390, 400, 419, 423, 462; Mormino and Pizzo, *Tampa: The Treasure City*, 134.

[7] Hillsborough County Deed Records, Book D, 353, E, 15.

[8] Ibid., Book D, 498, 620, E, 220.

[9] Hillsborough County Commission Minutes, Book C, 107-115, 124, 143, 161; Hillsborough County Deed Records, Book D, 498, 672.

[10] Bethell, *Bethell's History of Point Pinellas*, 34; *Tallahassee Sentinel*, September 18, 1875.

[11] *SMN*, December 23, 1875; Hurner, "Robert Mugge," 18-19.

[12] Benjamin, "Climate and Society of Tampa," 393; *TG*, November 6, 1875, quoted in *Semi-Tropical 1* (November 1875), 190; Grismer, *Tampa*, 335; *ST*, December 4, 1879.

[13] Hillsborough County Commission Minutes, Book C, 148-50.

[14] Ibid., 148.

[15] Ibid.

[16] Brown, *Genealogical Records*, 51-56; Hillsborough County Deed Records, Book D, 591.

[17] *TG*, September 4, November 13, December 11, 1875, quoted in *Semi-Tropical 1* (October 1875), 117, (November 1875), 183, (December 1875), 244.

[18] *WF*, April 27, May 18, 1875; *SMN*, April 28, 1875, February 23, 1876; *Semi-Tropical*, Vol. 1 (October 1875), 117, (November 1875), 183, 190, (December 1875), 244, Vol. 2 (August 1876), 490-91.

[19] *TG* quoted in *WF*, March 21, 1876.

[20] Lanier, *Florida*, 36, 88, 101-102, 143, 203, 205; idem, *Letters*, 35-36; Jackson, "Sidney Lanier," 121-24; VanLandingham, "Orange Grove Hotel," 93-95.

[21] Jackson, "Sidney Lanier," 122-23.

[22] *Semi-Tropical* 3 (July 1877), 213.

[23] Wells, *Facts for Immigrants*, 6.

[24] Hillsborough County Commission Minutes, Book C, 209-211, 216-18.

[25] "From Jacksonville to Tampa," *Semi-Tropical* 2 (August 1876), 454-55; Foster and Foster, *Beechers, Stowes, and Yankee Strangers*, 102-106.

[26] *Bay City Tribune* quoted in *ST*, May 12, 1877; *ST*, May 12, June 2, September 22, 1877; Benjamin, "Climate and Society of Tampa," 395.

[27] *ST*, July 20, 27, August 3, 10, December 21, 1878, November 6, December 4, 1879; Welch, *Tampa's Elected Officials*, 18.

[28] Orrick and Crumpacker, *Tampa Tribune*, 21; *SMN*, March 14, 1876.

[29] *Jacksonville Daily Florida Union*, August 14, 1876; *Tallahassee Sentinel*, August 19, 1876.

[30] *ST*, May 12, June 2, 1877; Shofner, *Nor Is It Over Yet*, 300-307.

[31] *ST*, April 7, 1877; Welch, *Tampa's Elected Officials*, 19.

[32] Minutes of the Mayor's Court, City of Tampa (August 21, 1857-May 1882), 143-49; Hillsborough County Commission Minutes, Book C, 153; *ST*, April 7, 1877.

[33] Benjamin, "Climate and Society of Tampa," 395; Mormino and Pizzo, *Tampa: The Treasure City*, 134.

[34] *Bay City Tribune* quoted in *ST*, May 12, 1877.

[35] *TST*, January 12, 1947.

[36] Grismer, *Tampa*, 319.

[37] Senate Reports, 44th Congress, 2d sess., No. 611, 308; *TST*, August 11, 1946; Benjamin, "Climate and Society of Tampa," 395.

[38] Senate Reports, 44th Congress, 2d sess., No. 611, 307.
[39] *TST*, August 11, 1946.
[40] Manley and Brown, *Supreme Court of Florida*, 251-56; *ST*, March 31, 1877.
[41] *Jacksonville Florida Union*, December 13, 1876.

86. The *Tahoma* was so frequently seen in Tampa Bay waters during the Civil War that it almost could be considered a character in Tampa's story. A wooden-hulled, 4th rate screw propeller gunboat built in 1861 at Wilmington, Delaware, it was among a group of "ninety-day gunboats" produced at breakneck speed to equip the Union's naval blockading force. As its description suggests, it was completed within ninety days of beginning construction. The *Tahoma* engaged in actions in and around Tampa Bay, including encounters off the Pinellas peninsula, Gadsden's Point, Anclote Keys, and the Peace River.

Bibliography

Manuscripts

Church Records. Questionnaires of the Florida Writers' Program, Work Projects Administration. Florida Collection, SLF.

Daegenhardt, Maria Louisa. Reminiscences. Historical Association of Southern Florida, Miami.

Florida Negro Papers. University of South Florida Library Special Collections.

Friebele, C. L. Account Book, 1860-1863. Tampa Historical Society.

Gordon, Julius J. Historical notes and files. Tampa.

Howard, Oliver O. Papers. Bowdoin College Library Special Collections. Brunswick, ME.

L'Engle, Edward M. Papers. Southern Historical Collection, University of North Carolina, Chapel Hill.

Lesley, Theodore. Papers. University of South Florida Library Special Collections.

Miscellaneous manuscripts collection. LC.

Miscellaneous newspaper scrapbooks. Tampa Historical Society, Tampa.

Noyes, Alonzo B. Papers. PKY.

Peeples, Vernon. Historical Collection. Punta Gorda.

Pizzo, Anthony P. Papers. USFSC.

Snodgrass, Dena E. Collection. PKY.

Thompson, George F. Journal. PKY.

Waters, Zack C. Historical Collection. Rome, Georgia.

Webb, Alexander Stewart. Papers. Yale University Library, New Haven, CT.

White, Pleasants W. Papers. Florida Historical Society Library, Cocoa.

Wilder, John A. Papers. Yale University Library, New Haven.

Public Documents, Public Records, and Maps

Adjutant General, Office of the. Case Files of Applications from Former Confederates for Presidential Pardons, 1865-1867 ("Amnesty Papers"). M-1003. NA.

_________. Letters Received (Main Series), 1861-1870. M-619. NA.

Bureau of Freedmen, Refugees, and Abandoned Lands. Letters Received by the Assistant Commissioner for Florida, 1865-1866. RG 105, NA.

__________. Unentered Letters and Reports, 1865-1868, Assistant Commissioner for Florida. RG 105, NA.

Bureau of Land Management. Florida Land Entry Files. RG 49. NA.

Confederate Military Records. RG 109. NA.

Duval County. Probate Records. Duval County Courthouse, Jacksonville.

Eagan, Dennis. *Sixth Annual Report of the Commissioner of Lands and Immigration of the State of Florida, for the year ending December 31, 1874.* Tallahassee: State of Florida, 1874.

Florida. Appointments. RG 156, series 1284. FSA.

__________. Commissions, 1827-1978. RG 156, series 259 and 259A. FSA.

__________. Comptroller, Office of the. Incoming Correspondence, 1845-1906. RG 350, series 554. FSA.

__________. Department of Environmental Protection, Division of State Lands, Land Records and Title Section. Correspondence files.

__________. __________. Papers of the U. S. Land Office, Gainesville, Florida.

__________. __________. Registers of Entries Made Under the Homestead Act.

__________. __________. Tract Books.

__________. Election Returns (1862-1887). RG 156, series 1258. FSA.

__________. Governor, Office of the. Governors' Correspondence, 1849-1871. RG 101, series 577. FSA.

__________. House of Representatives, Office of the Clerk. *People of Lawmaking in Florida, 1822-1991.* Tallahassee: Florida House of Representatives, 1991.

__________. Internal Improvement Trust Fund. Incoming Correspondence. RG 593, series 914. FSA.

__________. *Laws of Florida.*

__________. State and Territorial Election Returns. RG 156, series 21. FSA.

Hillsborough County. County Commission Minute Books.

__________. Deed Records.

__________. Marriage Records.

__________. School Board Minute Books.

__________. Tax rolls, 1861-1878.

Kennedy, Joseph C. G. *Population of the United States in 1860; Compiled from the Original Returns of the Eighth Census.* Washington, DC: Government Printing Office, 1864.

Narrative Reports of County Superintendents, 1869-70 to 1879-80. Tallahassee: Thomas D. Bailey, State Superintendent of Public Instruction, 1962.

Tampa. Minutes of the Mayor's Court (August 21, 1857-May 1882). City of Tampa Archives.

United States Congress Serial Set. Washington, DC.

U. S. Decennial Censuses, 1860-1880. Manuscript returns. Available at FSA and TPL.

U. S. Department of State. Civil War Papers. Correspondence Regarding Prisoners of War, 1861-1862. RG 59. NA.

U. S. Department of Veterans Affairs. Military pension records. Washington, DC.

U. S. Department of War. Letters Received by the Dept. and Dist. of Florida, 1865-1869. RG 393, Part One. NA.

_________. Letters Received by the Dept. and Dist. of Key West, 1861-1865. RG 393, Part One. NA.

_________. Letters Sent by the Dept. of Florida and Successor Commands, April 18, 1861-January 1869. M-1096. NA.

_________. Third Military District, 1867-1868, Bureau of Civil Affairs. RG 393, Part One. NA.

Walker, Francis A. *The Statistics of the Population of the United States . . . Compiled from the Original Returns of the Ninth Census*. Washington: Government Printing Office, 1872.

Welch, W. Curtis. *Tampa's Elected Officials: A Narrative Chronology of Municipal Elections and Tampa's Elected Officials From 1849 to 1886*. Tampa: City of Tampa Archives, 1997.

Work Projects Administration, Statewide Rare Books Project. "Military Dispatches, Head Quarters, District of Middle Florida, August 10, 1865-September 25, 1865." Typescript, Tallahassee, 1940.

Work Projects Administration, Writers' Program. *Hillsborough County Personalities*. Jacksonville: WPA Writers' Program, n.d.

_________. *Negro History in Florida*. Jacksonville: WPA Writers' Program, 1936.

Newspapers and Periodicals

Augusta (GA) *Daily Chronicle & Sentinel*, 1864.

Augusta (GA) *Southern Christian Advocate*, 1862-1864.

Baltimore Sun, 1862.

Boston Daily Journal, 1862.

Brooksville *Hernando Today*, 1999.

Charleston (SC) *Southern Christian Advocate*, 1862.

Clear Water Times, 1874.

Columbus (GA) *Daily Inquirer*, 1862.

Fort Meade Leader, 1913.
Frank Leslie's Illustrated Newspaper, 1873.
Jacksonville *Daily Florida Union*, 1876.
Jacksonville *Florida Daily Times*, 1882.
Jacksonville *Florida Republican*, 1856-1857.
Jacksonville *Florida Times*, 1866.
Jacksonville *Florida Times-Union and Citizen*, 1899.
Jacksonville *Florida Union*, 1865-1869, 1876.
Jacksonville *New South*, 1874.
Jacksonville *Tri-Weekly Florida Union*, 1874.
Macon (GA) *Southern Christian Advocate*, 1865-1866.
Manhattan (KS) *Independent*, 1867.
New Orleans Bee, 1861.
New York Herald, 1861-1865.
New York *South*, 1874.
New York Times, 1865.
Paterson (NJ) *Daily Press*, 1866.
Putnam's Magazine, 1868.
St. Augustine Examiner, 1867.
Sanford *South Florida Argus*, 1887.
Savannah *Advertiser-Republican*, 1873-1874.
Savannah Daily Advertiser, 1869, 1874.
Savannah Daily Repubican, 1867, 1871-1873.
Savannah Morning News, 1872-1876.
Savannah Republican, 1861.
The Semi-Tropical, 1875-1878.
Tallahassee *Floridian & Journal*, 1860.
Tallahassee *Semi-Weekly Floridian*, 1865-1867.
Tallahassee Sentinel, 1867-1876.
Tallahassee *Weekly Floridian*, 1871-1877.
Tampa Daily Times, 1912-1923.
Tampa *Florida Peninsular*, 1860-1861, 1866-1871.
Tampa Guardian, 1877-1880, 1886.
Tampa Morning Tribune, 1904-2000.
Tampa Sunday Tribune, 1939-2000.
Tampa *Sunland Tribune*, 1877-1883.

Secondary Sources

Akerman, Joe A., Jr. *Florida Cowman: A History of Florida Cattle Raising.*

Kissimmee: Florida Cattlemen's Association, 1976.

Anthony, Otis, and Marilyn T. Wade. *A Collection of Historical Facts about Black Tampa*. Tampa: Tampa Electric Company, n.d.

Attaway, John A. *Hurricanes and Florida Agriculture*. Lake Alfred: Florida Science Source, 1999.

Baxley, John H., Julius J. Gordon, and Diane Rodriguez. *The History of Oaklawn Cemetery and St. Louis Catholic Cemetery*. 2 vols. Tampa: Baxley, Gordon, and Rodriguez, 1991.

_________. *Sleeping Around: A Study of Hotels of Tampa, Florida, From 1830 to 1925*. Tampa: Baxley, Gordon, and Rodriguez, 1995.

Benjamin, Henry R. "The Climate and Society of Tampa." *Semi-Tropical* 3 (July 1877): 393-96.

Bethell, John A. *Bethell's History of Point Pinellas*. Reprint ed. St. Petersburg: Great Outdoors Publishing Co., 1962.

Boggess, Francis C. M. *A Veteran of Four Wars: The Autobiography of F. C. M. Boggess*. Arcadia: Champion Job Rooms, 1900.

Brady, Rowena Ferrell. *Things Remembered: An Album of African Americans in Tampa*. Tampa: University of Tampa Press, 1997.

Brown, Canter, Jr. *African Americans on the Tampa Bay Frontier*. Tampa: Tampa Bay History Center, 1997.

_________. *Children on the Tampa Bay Frontier*. Second Edition. Tampa: Tampa Bay History Center, 1997.

_________. "The Civil War, 1861-1865." In *The New History of Florida*, ed. by Michael Gannon. Gainesville: University Presses of Florida, 1996.

_________. "The East Florida Coffee Land Expedition of 1821: Plantations or a Bonapartist Kingdom of the Indies?" *Tequesta* 51 (1991): 7-28.

_________. "The Florida Crisis of 1826-1827 and the Second Seminole War." *Florida Historical Quarterly* 73 (April 1995): 419-442.

_________. *Florida's Black Public Officials, 1867-1924*. Tuscaloosa: University of Alabama Press, 1998.

_________. *Florida's Peace River Frontier*. Orlando: University of Central Florida Press, 1991.

_________. *Fort Meade, 1849-1900*. Tuscaloosa: University of Alabama Press, 1995.

_________. *Genealogical Records of the African American Pioneers of Tampa and Hillsborough County*. Tampa: Tampa Bay History Center, 2000.

_________. *Jewish Pioneers of the Tampa Bay Frontier*. Tampa: Tampa Bay History Center, 1999.

_________. *Ossian Bingley Hart, Florida's Loyalist Reconstruction Governor*.

Baton Rouge: Louisana State University Press, 1997.

__________. "Politics, Greed, Regulator Violence, and Race in Tampa, 1858-1859." *Sunland Tribune* 20 (November 1994): 25-30.

__________. "Tampa and the Coming of the Railroad, 1853-1884." *Sunland Tribune* 17 (November 1991): 13-18.

__________. *Tampa Before the Civil War*. Tampa: University of Tampa Press, 1999.

__________. "Tampa's James McKay and the Frustration of Confederate Cattle-Supply Operations in South Florida." *Florida Historical Quarterly* 70 (April 1992): 409-33.

__________. *Teachers and Schools on the Tampa Bay Frontier*. Tampa: Tampa Bay History Center, 1997.

__________. *Women on the Tampa Bay Frontier*. Tampa: Tampa Bay History Center, 1997.

Brown, Canter, Jr., ed. "'As Far As Our Eyes Will Let Us See': The 'Peas Creek Expedition' of 1860." *Tampa Bay History* 12 (Spring/Summer 1990): 43-79.

__________. "'Very much attached to Tampa': The Civil War-Era Letters of Catharine Campbell Hart, 1860-1865." *Sunland Tribune* 23 (November 1997): 63-69.

Bruton, Quintilla Geer. *Plant City: Its Origins and History*. Winston-Salem, NC: Hunter Publishing Company, 1984.

Buker, George E. *Blockaders, Refugees, & Contrabands: Civil War on Florida's Gulf Coast, 1861-1865*. Tuscaloosa: University of Alabama Press, 1993.

Canova, Andrew P. *Life and Adventures in South Florida*. Palatka: Southern Sun Publishing House, 1883.

Carlton, Lynn, Caroline Moore, and Mary Capitano, eds. *History of the First Methodist Church, Tampa*. Tampa: First United Methodist Church, 1996.

Chamberlin, Donald L. "Fort Brooke: A History." MA thesis: Florida State University, 1968.

Church, George B., Jr. *The Life of Henry Laurens Mitchell, Florida's 16th Governor*. New York: Vantage Press, 1978.

Coles, David James. "Cattle Wars: The Civil War in South Florida, 1864-1865." In *Proceedings of the Florida Cattle Frontier Symposium*. Kissimmee: Florida Cattlemen's Association, 1995.

__________. "Far From Fields of Glory: Military Operations in Florida During the Civil War." Ph.D. diss., Florida State University, 1996.

__________. "'A Terrible and Sad Result': The End of the Civil War in Florida, March-June 1865." In *Proceedings of the 90th Annual Meeting of the Florida Historical Society at St. Augustine, May 1992*. Tampa: Florida Historical Society, 1992.

_________. "Unpretending Service: The *James L. Davis*, the *Tahoma*, and the East Gulf Blockading Squadron." *Florida Historical Quarterly* 71 (July 1992): 41-62.

Coles, David J., and Richard J. Ferry. "'Hot, Cold, Whiskey Punch': The Civil War Letters of Charles H. Tillinghast, U.S.N." *Sunland Tribune* 49-64.

Coles, David J., and Zack C. Waters. "Indian Fighter, Confederate Soldier, Blockade Runner, and Scout: The Life and Letters of Jacob E. Mickler." *El Escribano* 34 (1997): 35-69.

Coulter, E. Merton. *The Confederate States of America 1861-1865*. Baton Rouge: Louisiana State University Press, 1950.

Covington, James W. "The Hackley Grant, the Fort Brooke Military Reservation and Tampa." *Sunland Tribune* 6 (November 1980): 4-9.

_________. "Some Observations Concerning the History of Fort Brooke and Tampa." *Sunland Tribune* 22 (November 1996): 41-43.

_________. *The Story of Southwestern Florida*. 2 vols. New York: Lewis Historical Publishing Company, Inc., 1957.

Craven, Avery. *The Coming of the Civil War*. Chicago: University of Chicago Press, 1942.

Crofts, Daniel W. *Reluctant Confederates: Upper South Unionists in the Secession Crisis*. Chapel Hill: University of North Carolina Press, 1989.

Davis, William Watson. *The Civil War and Reconstruction in Florida*. New York: Columbia University, 1913; reprint ed., Gainesville: University of Florida Press, 1964.

DeFoor, J. Allison, II. *Odet Philippe: Peninsular Pioneer*. Safety Harbor: Safety Harbor Museum, 1997.

Denham, James M. *"A Rogue's Paradise": Crime and Punishment in Antebellum Florida, 1821-1861*. Tuscaloosa: University of Alabama Press, 1997.

Denham, James M., and Canter Brown, Jr., eds. *Cracker Times and Pioneer Lives: The Florida Reminiscences of George Gillett Keen and Sarah Pamela Williams*. Columbia: University of South Carolina Press, 2000.

Dillon, Rodney E. "The Civil War in South Florida." Master's thesis, University of Florida, 1980.

Du Bois, W. E. B. *Black Reconstruction in America, 1860-1880*. New York: Atheneum, 1992.

Edwards, Kate F. "A College Girl in Wartime." *Georgia Review* 1 (Summer 1947): 198-206.

Elliott, Brenda J. *The Best of Its Kind: The Incredible American Heritage of the Dixon Ticonderoga Company*. Kissimmee: The Dixon Ticonderoga Company, 1996.

Falero, Frank, Jr. "Naval Engagements in Tampa Bay, 1862." *Florida Historical Quarterly* 46 (October 1967): 134-40.

Farr, Cynthia K. *A Sketch from the Life of Mrs. Nancy Jackson*. Tampa: n.p., 1900.

Ferrell, Andrew J., Sr. "The History of St. Paul A.M.E. Church." In *Things Remembered: An Album of African Americans in Tampa*, by Rowena Ferrell Brady. Tampa: University of Tampa Press, 1997.

Fishburne, Charles Carroll, Jr. *The Cedar Keys in the 19th Century*. Quincy: Sea Hawk Publications, 1993.

Foner, Eric. *Reconstruction, 1863-1877: America's Unfinished Revolution*. New York: Harper & Row, 1988.

Foster, John T., Jr., and Sarah Whitmer Foster. *Beechers, Stowes, and Yankee Strangers: The Transformation of Florida*. Gainesville: University Press of Florida, 1999.

Frazier, Norma Goolsby. "Circuit Riding Preachers: They Sowed the Seed." *Sunland Tribune* 21 (November 1995): 35-42.

__________. "Education: From its Beginnings in the Territory to Present." *Sunland Tribune* 19 (November 1993): 35-41.

Gannon, Michael, ed. *The New History of Florida*. Gainesville: University Presses of Florida, 1996.

Gordon, Julius J. *Biographical Census of Hillsborough County, Florida, 1850*. Tampa: Julius J. Gordon, 1989.

__________. *Census, Hillsborough County, Florida, 1841-1883, Volume II*. Tampa, Julius J. Gordon, 1991.

__________. *German-American Influence in Tampa, Florida 1840-1900*. Tampa: Julius J. Gordon, 1991.

Gordon, Julius J., ed. "The Missions of Tampa": Excerpts From the Diary of Father Clavreul, 1863-1877." *Tampa Bay History* 13 (Fall/Winter 1991): 57-68.

Greenberg, Mark I., William Warren Rogers, and Canter Brown, Jr., eds. *Florida's Heritage of Diversity: Essays in Honor of Samuel Proctor*. Tallahassee: Sentry Press, 1997.

Grismer, Karl H. *Tampa: A History of the City of Tampa and the Tampa Bay Region of Florida*. St. Petersburg: St. Petersburg Printing Co., 1950.

Hall, Kermit L., and Eric W. Rise. *From Local Courts to National Tribunals: The Federal District Courts of Florida, 1821-1990*. Brooklyn, NY: Carlson Publishing, Inc., 1991.

Hammond, E. Ashby. *The Medical Profession in 19th Century Florida: A Biographical Register*. Gainesville: George A. Smathers Libraries of the University of Florida, 1996.

Harris, William Lloyd. "When War Came to Polk County: Battle at Bowlegs Creek 20 February, 1864." *Polk County Historical Quarterly* 11 (March 1985): 4-5.

Harrison, Charles E. *Genealogical Records of the Pioneers of Tampa and of Some*

Who Came After Them. Tampa: E. W. B. Willey, 1915.

_________. *Reminiscences of Judge Charles E. Harrison*. Ed. by Canter Brown, Jr. Tampa: Tampa Bay History Center, 1997.

Hartman, David W., and David J. Coles, comps. *Biographical Rosters of Florida's Confederate and Union Soldiers, 1861-1865*. 6 vols. Wilmington, NC: Broadfoot Publishing Company, 1995.

Hawes, Leland. "Church marks 150th year." *Tampa Sunday Tribune*, July 28, 1996.

_________. "Civil War account tells of ship burning." *Tampa Sunday Tribune*, July 8, 1990.

_________. "Father's dying wish sent sons into Navy." *Tampa Sunday Tribune*, May 5, 1991.

_________. "Former Rebels saw error of their ways." *Tampa Sunday Tribune*, June 3, 1990.

_________. "How Masonic tools were returned to Tampa lodge." *Tampa Sunday Tribune*, April 10, 1988.

_________. "One-time slave sheds light on life in Tampa." *Tampa Sunday Tribune*, June 5, 1988.

_________. "Tampa-born sheriff." *Tampa Sunday Tribune*, July 23, 1995.

_________. "Yellow fever link to mosquito credited to Tampa doctor." *Tampa Sunday Tribune*, December 12, 1999.

Hawks, J. M. *The Florida Gazetteer*. New Orleans: Bronze Pen Steam Book and Job Office, 1871.

Hillsborough County Personalities. Jacksonville: Federal Writers' Project, 1937.

Hillsborough County Sheriff's Office, 1845-1995. Tampa: Hillsborough County Sheriff's Office, 1995.

Hillsborough Lodge No. 25, F. & A.M., 1850-1976. Tampa: Hillsborough Lodge No. 25, n.d.

Howe, Kathleen S. "Stepping into Freedom: African Americans in Hillsborough County, Florida, During the Reconstruction Era." *Tampa Bay History* 20 (Fall/Winter 1998): 4-30.

_________. "Stepping into Freedom: An Analysis of the African-American Community in Hillsborough County, Florida, During the Reconstruction Era." Master's thesis, University of South Florida, 1997.

Hurner, Margaret Regener. "Robert Mugge—Pioneer Tampan." *Sunland Tribune* 15 (November 1989): 18-23.

Ingalls, Robert P. *Urban Vigilantes in the New South: Tampa, 1882-1936*. Knoxville: University of Tennessee Press, 1988.

Ivey, Donald J. "The Accidental Pioneer: Capt. Jim McMullen and the Taming of the Pinellas Peninsula." *Sunland Tribune* 22 (November 1996): 22-40.

__________. "John T. Lesley: Tampa's Pioneer Renaissance Man." *Sunland Tribune* 21 (NOvember 1995): 3-20.

__________. *The Life and Times of John Thomas Lesley (A.D. 1835-1913), A Chronological Biography*. Largo: priv. pub., n.d.

Jackson, Lena E. "Sidney Lanier in Florida." *Florida Historical Quarterly* 15 (October 1936): 118-24.

Johns, John E. *Florida During the Civil War*. Gainesville: University of Florida Press, 1963.

King, Robert E. *A History of the Practice of Medicine in Manatee County, Florida*. Bradenton: Manatee Memorial Hospital, 1985.

Klingman, Peter D. *Josiah Walls: Florida's Black Congressman of Reconstruction*. Gainesville: University of Florida Press, 1976.

__________. *Neither Dies Nor Surrenders: A History of the Republican Party in Florida, 1867-1970*. Gainesville: University of Florida Press, 1984.

Kite-Powell, Rodney H., II. "The Escape of Judah P. Benjamin." *Sunland Tribune* 22 (November 1996): 63-74.

Knetsch, Joe. "Forging the Florida Frontier: The Life and Career of Captain Samuel E. Hope." *Sunland Tribune* 20 (November 1994): 31-42.

__________. "John Darling, Indian Removal, and Internal Improvements in South Florida, 1848-1856." *Tampa Bay History* 17 (Fall/Winter 1995): 6-19.

__________. "Madison Starke Perry vs. David Levy Yulee: The Fight for the Tampa Bay Route." *Sunland Tribune* 23 (November 1997): 13-23.

Landers, Roger Rice. "Freedmen's Bureau becomes a force in Hernando." *Hernando Today*, August 4, 1999.

Landers, Roger Rice, ed. *"The Last Wildcat": The Short Record of T. B. Ellis, Sr.* Brooksville: Genealogical Society of Hernando County, 1998.

Langley, Lester D. *The Americas in the Age of Revolution, 1750-1850*. New Haven: Yale University Press, 1996.

Lanier, Sidney. *Florida: Its Scenery, Climate, and History*. Phildelphia: J. P. Lippincott & Co., 1875. Reprint ed., Gainesville: University of Florida Press, 1973.

__________. *Letters of Sidney Lanier: Selections From His Correspondence, 1866-1881*. New York: Charles Scribner's Sons, 1899.

Lesley, Theodore. "The Organization of the Confederate Cattle Battalion of Florida." Unpublished paper read before the Florida Historical Society Regional Meeting, Mountain Lake, Florida, February 8, 1940.

Ley, John C. *Fifty-Two Years in Florida*. Nashville: Publishing House of the M. E. Church, South, 1899.

Littrell, J. Harvey. *Riley County, Kansas, Officials and Their Families, 1855-1900*. Manhattan, KS: Riley County Historical Society, 1996.

Livingston, Richard M. "Willoughby Tillis, 1808-1895." *South Florida Pioneers* 39/40 (January-April 1984): 4-11.

Long, E. B. *The Civil War Day by Day: An Almanac, 1861-1865*. Garden City, NY: Doubleday & Company, 1971.

Manley, Walter W., II, and Canter Brown, Jr., eds. *The Supreme Court of Florida and Its Predecessor Courts, 1821-1917*. Gainesville: University Presses of Florida, 1997.

Marks, Henry S. *Who Was Who in Florida*. Huntsville, AL: Strode Publishers, 1973.

Matthews, Janet Snyder. *Edge of Wilderness: A Settlement History of Manatee River and Sarasota Bay*. Tulsa, OK: Caprine Press, 1983.

McDonogh, Gary W. *The Florida Negro: A Federal Writers' Project Legacy*. Jackson: University Press of Mississippi, 1993.

McDuffee, Lillie B. *The Lures of Manatee, A True Story of South Florida's Glamorous Past*. Manatee: Lillie B. McDuffee, 1933.

McKay, Donald B. *Pioneer Florida*. 3 vols. Tampa: Southern, 1959.

McKay, James, Jr. "History of Tampa of the Olden Days." *Sunland Tribune* 17 (November 1991): 78-87.

McNally, Michael J. *Catholic Parish Life on Florida's West Coast, 1860-1968*. N.p.: Catholic Media Ministries, 1996.

McPherson, James M. *Battle Cry of Freedom: The Civil War Era*. New York: Oxford University Press, 1988.

Mencken, H. L. *A New Dictionary of Quoations on Historical Principles from Ancient and Modern Sources*. New York: Alfred A. Knopf, 1942.

Menton, Jane Aurell. *The Grove: A Florida Home Through Seven Generations*. Tallahassee: Sentry Press, 1998.

Mitchell, Mozella G. *African American Religious History in Tampa Bay*. Tampa: National Conference of Christians and Jews, 1992.

Mohlman, Geoffrey. "Anclote Keys Lighthouse: Guiding Light to Safe Anchorage." *Florida Historical Quarterly* 78 (Fall 1999): 159-88.

__________. "Bibliography of Resources Concerning the African American Presence in Tampa: 1513-1995." Master's thesis, University of South Florida, 1995.

Mormino, Gary R., and Anthony P. Pizzo. *Tampa: The Treasure City*. Tulsa, OK: Continental Heritage Press, 1983.

Muse, Violet. "Negro History, Tampa, Florida." In *Negro History in Florida*. Ed. by Work Projects Administration Writers' Project. Jacksonville: Federal Writers' Project, 1936.

Nolan, David. *Fifty Feet in Paradise: The Booming of Florida*. San Diego: Harcourt Brace Jovanovich, 1984.

Olson, Yetive Brooks. *History of the DeSoto Chapter, Daughters of the American*

Revolution and Old School House, Tampa, Florida. Tampa: DeSoto Chapter, Daughters of the American Revolution, 1996.

Orrick, Bentley, and Harry L. Crumpacker. *The Tampa Tribune, A Century of Florida Journalism.* Tampa: University of Tampa Press, 1998.

Pizzo, Anthony P. *Tampa Town, 1824-1886: Cracker Village with a Latin Accent.* Miami: Hurricane House, 1969.

Prouty, Ronald N., ed. "War Comes to Tampa Bay: The Civil War Diary of Robert Watson." *Tampa Bay History* 10 (Fall/Winter 1988): 36-65.

Reiger, John Franklin. "Anti-war and Pro-Union Sentiment in Confederate Florida." Master's thesis, University of Florida, 1966.

Rerick, Rowland H. *Memoirs of Florida.* 2 vols. Atlanta: Southern Historical Association, 1902.

Rivers, Larry E. "'He Treats His Fellow Man Properly': Building Community in a Multi-Cultural Florida." In *Amid Political, Cultural, and Civic Diversity: Building A Sense of Statewide Community in Florida*, ed. by Lance deHaven-Smith and David Colburn. Dubuque, Iowa: Kendall/Hunt Publishing Company, 1998.

__________. *Slavery in Florida, From Territorial Days To Emancipation.* Gainesville: University Presses of Florida, 2000.

Rivers, Larry E., and Canter Brown, Jr. "African Americans in South Florida: A Home and a Haven for Reconstruction-Era Leaders." *Tequesta* 56 (1996): 5-23.

__________. *"Laborers in the vineyard of the Lord": The Beginnings of the AME Church in Florida, 1865-1895.* Gainesville: University Presses of Florida, publication in press.

Rivers, Larry O. "'They . . . Exalt Humbug at the Expense of Science and Truth': Dr. John P. Wall and the Fight Against Yellow Fever in Late-Nineteenth Century Florida." *Sunland Tribune* 25 (November 1999), 9-18.

Robinson, Calvin. "The Memoirs of Calvin L. Robinson: Concerning the Experiences of the Robinson Family in Jacksonville During the Civil War." Typescript, Jacksonville, n.d.

Robinson, Ernest Lauren. *History of Hillsborough County, Florida.* St. Augustine: Record Co., 1928.

Rogers, William Warren, and Canter Brown, Jr. *Florida's Clerks of the Circuit Court: Their History and Experiences.* Tallahassee: Sentry Press, 1996.

Schellings, William J. "On Blockade Duty in Florida Waters: Excerpts From a Union Officer's Diary." *Tequesta* 15 (1955): 55-72.

Sherrill, William W. *A Call to Greatness, A History of the First Baptist Church, Tampa, Florida, 1859-1984.* Orlando: Golden Rule Press, Inc., n.d.

Shofner, Jerrell. *Nor Is It Over Yet: Florida in the Era of Reconstruction, 1863-1877.* Gainesville: University of Florida Press, 1974.

Stafford, John W. "Egmont Key: Sentinel of Tampa Bay." *Tampa Bay History* 2 (Spring/Summer 1980): 15-29.

Stone, Spessard. "James D. Green, 1823-1886." *South Florida Pioneers* 45/46 (July/Oct. 1985): 2-6.

_________. "The Know-Nothings of Hillsborough County." *Sunland Tribune* 19 (November 1993): 3-8.

_________. *Lineage of John Carlton.* Wauchula: priv. pub., 1998.

_________. "Rev. Capt. Leroy G. Lesley: Tampa's Fighting Parson." *Sunland Tribune* 23 (November 1997): 25-33.

Sturtevant, William C., ed. "R. H. Pratt's Report on the Seminole in 1879." *Florida Anthropologist* 9 (March 1956): 1-24.

Taylor, Robert A. "A Civil War Incident on Tampa Bay: Two Contemporary Views." *Tampa Bay History* 13 (Spring/Summer 1991): 77-79.

_________. "Cow Cavalry: Munnerlyn's Battalion in Florida." *Florida Historical Quarterly* 64 (October 1986): 196-214.

_________. "Rebel Beef: Florida Cattle and the Confederacy, 1861-1865." Master's thesis, University of South Florida, 1985.

_________. "Rebel Beef: Florida Cattle and the Confederate Army, 1862-1864." *Florida Historical Quarterly* 67 (July 1988): 15-31.

_________. *Rebel Storehouse: Florida in the Confederate Economy.* Tuscaloosa: University of Alabama Press, 1995.

Thompson, Arthur W. "David Yulee: A Study of Nineteenth Century American Thought and Enterprise." Ph.D. diss., Columbia University, 1954.

Trefousse, Hans L. *Andrew Johnson: A Biography.* New York: W. W. Norton & Co., 1989.

Turner, Nancy. *Faith of Our Fathers: A History of St. Andrew's Episcopal Church.* Tampa: St. Andrew's Episcopal Church, n.d.

VanLandingham, Kyle S. "Captain William B. Hooker: Florida Cattle King." *Sunland Tribune* 22 (November 1996): 3-18.

_________. *In Pursuit of Justice: Law & Lawyers in Hillsborough County, 1846-1996.* Tampa: Hillsborough County Bar Association, 1996.

_________. "James Alderman, 1801-1880." *South Florida Pioneers* 14 (October 1977): 15-16.

_________. "James Gettis: Tampa Pioneer Lawyer." *Sunland Tribune* 23 (November 1997): 35-42.

_________. "James T. Magbee: "'Union Man, Undoubted Secessionist, and High Priest in the Radical Synagogue.'" *Sunland Tribune* 20 (November 1994): 7-23.

_________. "'To Faithfully Discharge My Duty': The Life and Career of Perry Green Wall." *Sunland Tribune* 23 (November 1997): 3-12.

VanLandingham, Kyle S., ed. "'My National Troubles': The Civil War Papers of William McCullough." *Sunland Tribune* 20 (November 1994): 59-86.

__________. "Orange Grove Hotel." *Sunland Tribune* 18 (November 1992): 93-95.

__________. "'Tampa is the Place of Places': The William G. Ferris Family Collection." *Sunland Tribune* 22 (November 1996): 93-104.

__________. "The Union Occupation of Tampa, May 6-7, 1864." *Sunland Tribune* 19 (November 1993): 9-16.

Waters, Zack C. "Florida's Confederate Guerillas: John W. Pearson and the Oklawaha Rangers." *Florida Historical Quarterly* 70 (October 1991): 133-49.

__________. "Tampa's Forgotten Defenders: The Confederate Commanders of Fort Brooke." *Sunland Tribune* 17 (November 1991): 3-12.

Weatherford, Doris. *A History of Women in Tampa*. Tampa: The Athena Society, 1991.

Wells, George W. *Facts For Immigrants, Comprising a Truthful Description of the Five Following Counties of South Florida, To-Wit: Hernando, Hillsboro, Polk, Manatee and Monroe*. Jacksonville: Press Book and Job Office, 1877.

Westergard, Virginia W., and Kyle S. VanLandingham. *Parker & Blount in Florida*. Okeechobee: priv. pub., 1983.

Wilder, John A. "The Wedding at the Parker House." *Putnam's Magazine* (August 1868): 163-78.

Williams, Kate Barnwell. "This is the Story of My Life." *Tampa Bay History* 9 (Spring/Summer 1987): 49-65.

Wynn, Sarah. "History of Mt. Sinai A.M.E. Zion Church." In *Mt. Sinai African Methodist Episcopal Zion Church: One Hundred and Twenty-Fifth Anniversary, Sunday, February 28, 1988*. Tampa: Mt. Sinai AME Zion Church, 1988.

Index

C

D

G

H

I

J

K

L

M

N

O

P

Q

R

S

T

U

V

W

Y

Z